Schedule

82nd Period ③	83rd Period ⑬	84th Period ㉓	85th Period ㉝
86th Period 55	87th Period 65	88th Period 75	89th Period 85
90th Period 95	91st Period 117	92nd Period 127	93rd Period 137
94th Period 147	Bonus ① 157	Bonus ② 159	

My Neighbor Seki

7

* THIS IS A WORK OF FICTION. NAMES, CHARACTERS, PLACES AND INCIDENTS ARE PRODUCTS OF THE AUTHOR'S IMAGINATION OR USED FICTITIOUSLY. ANY RESEMBLANCE TO ACTUAL EVENTS OR LOCALES OR PERSONS, LIVING OR DEAD, IS ENTIRELY COINCIDENTAL.

My Neighbor Seki

Tonari no Seki-kun

7

Takuma Morishige

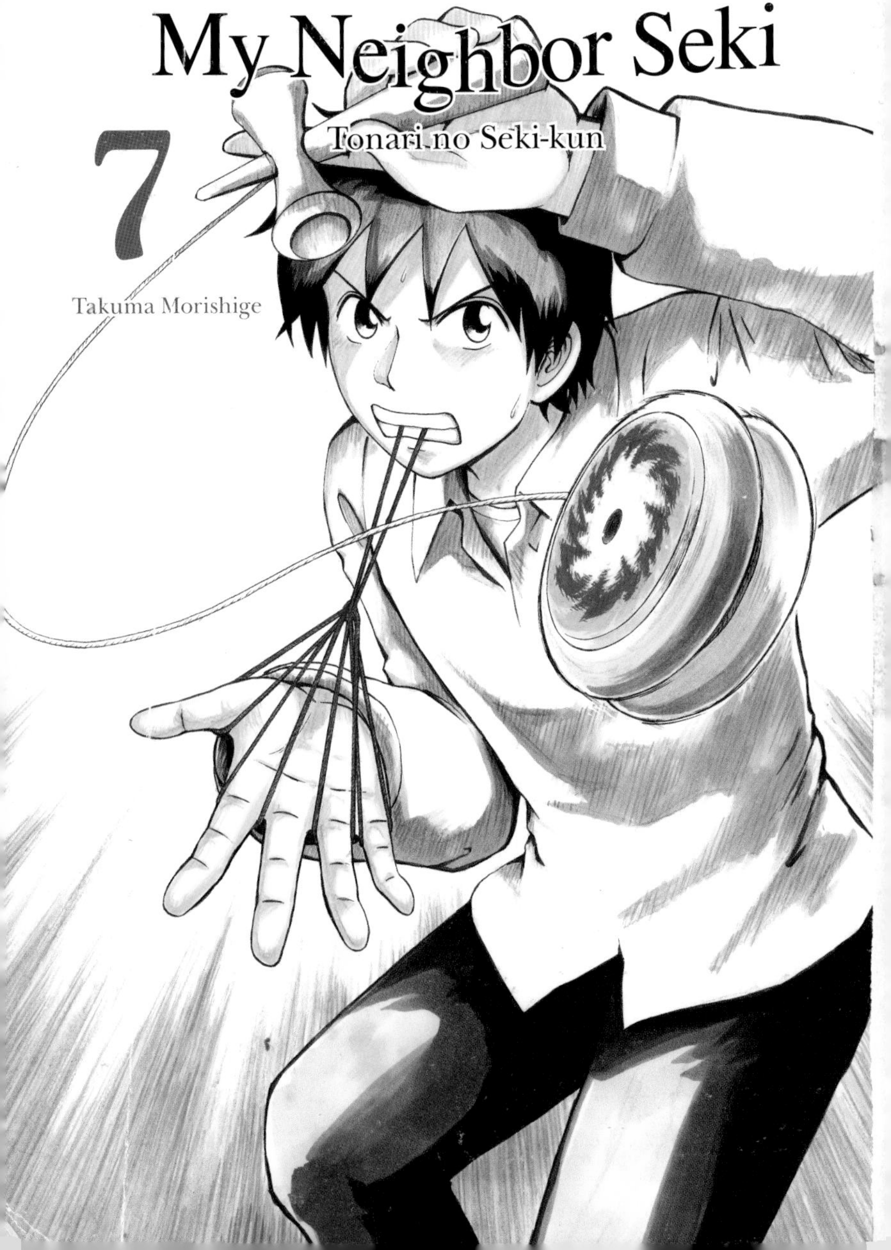

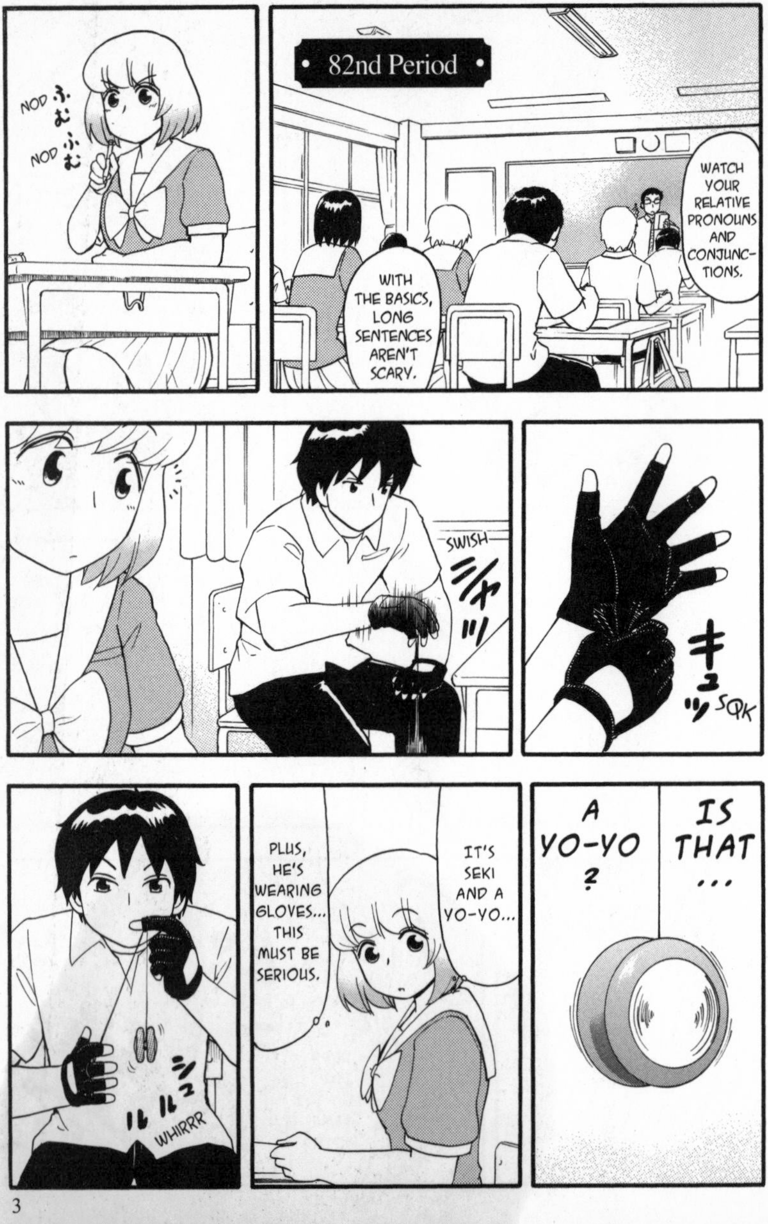
• 82nd Period •
WATCH YOUR RELATIVE PRONOUNS AND CONJUNCTIONS.
WITH THE BASICS, LONG SENTENCES AREN'T SCARY.
NOD ふむ
NOD ふむ
キュッ SQK
SWISH シャッ
IS THAT...
A YO-YO?
IT'S SEKI AND A YO-YO...
PLUS, HE'S WEARING GLOVES... THIS MUST BE SERIOUS.
シュルル WHIRRR

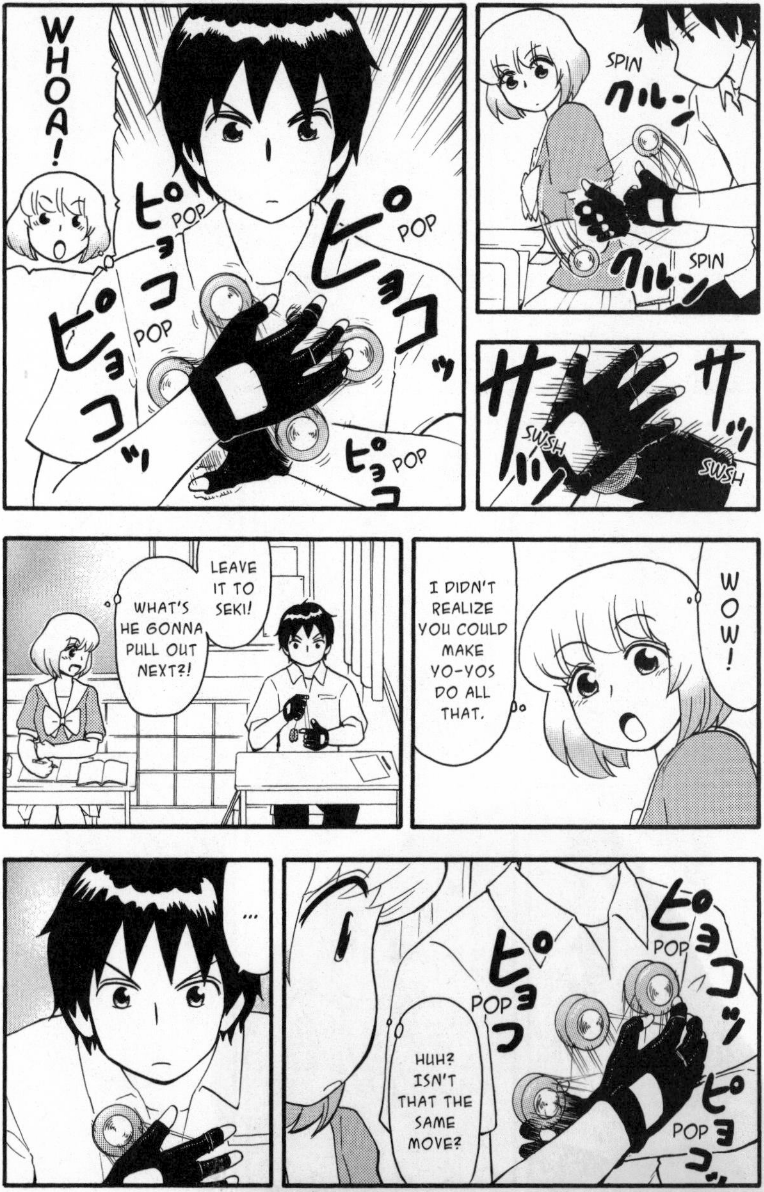
SPIN
クルン
SPIN
クルン
サッ
SWSH
サッ
SWSH
WHOA!
ピョコ
POP
ピョコッ
POP
ピョコ
POP
ピョコッ
POP
ピョコ
POP
WOW!
I DIDN'T REALIZE YOU COULD MAKE YO-YOS DO ALL THAT.
LEAVE IT TO SEKI!
WHAT'S HE GONNA PULL OUT NEXT?!
ピョコッ
POP
ピョコ
POP
ピョコッ
POP
HUH? ISN'T THAT THE SAME MOVE?
...

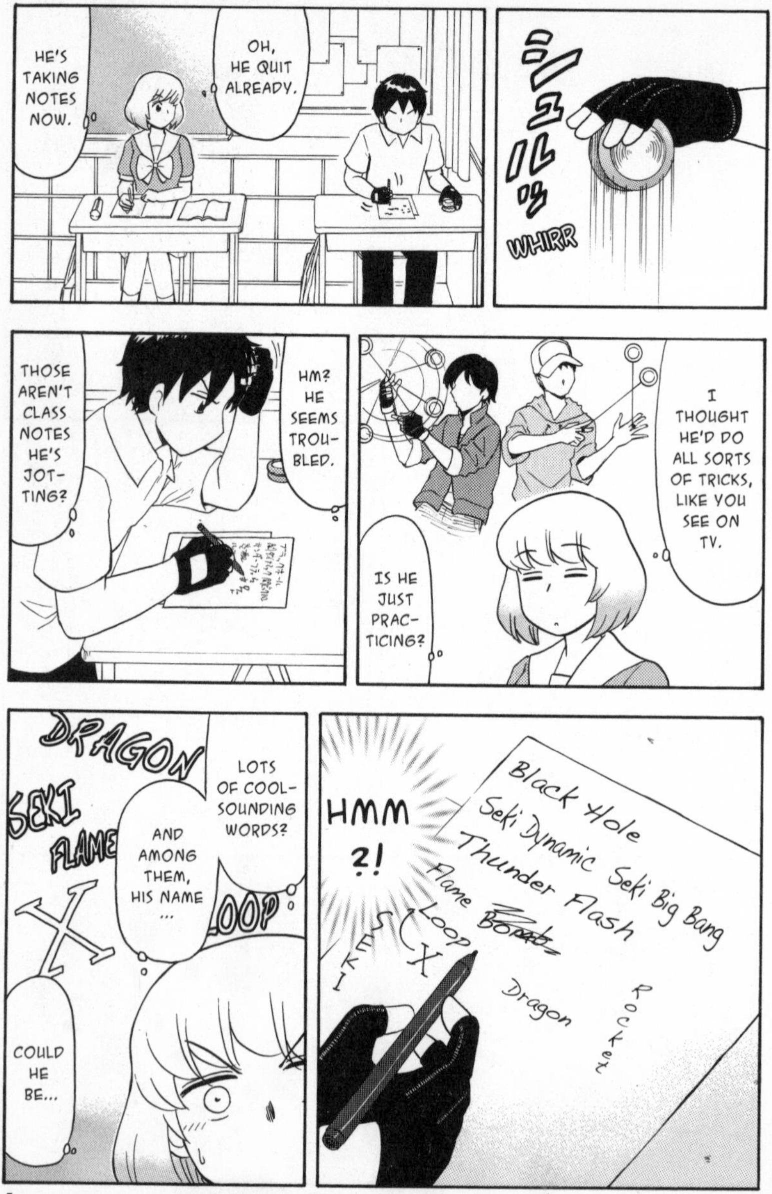

シュルルッ
WHIRR
OH, HE QUIT ALREADY.
HE'S TAKING NOTES NOW.
I THOUGHT HE'D DO ALL SORTS OF TRICKS, LIKE YOU SEE ON TV.
IS HE JUST PRACTICING?
HM? HE SEEMS TROUBLED.
THOSE AREN'T CLASS NOTES HE'S JOTTING?
HMM ?!
Black Hole
Seki Dynamic Seki Big Bang
Thunder Flash
Flame Bomb
Loop
X
SEKI
Dragon
Rocket
DRAGON
SEKI
FLAME
X
LOOP
LOTS OF COOL-SOUNDING WORDS?
AND AMONG THEM, HIS NAME ...
COULD HE BE...

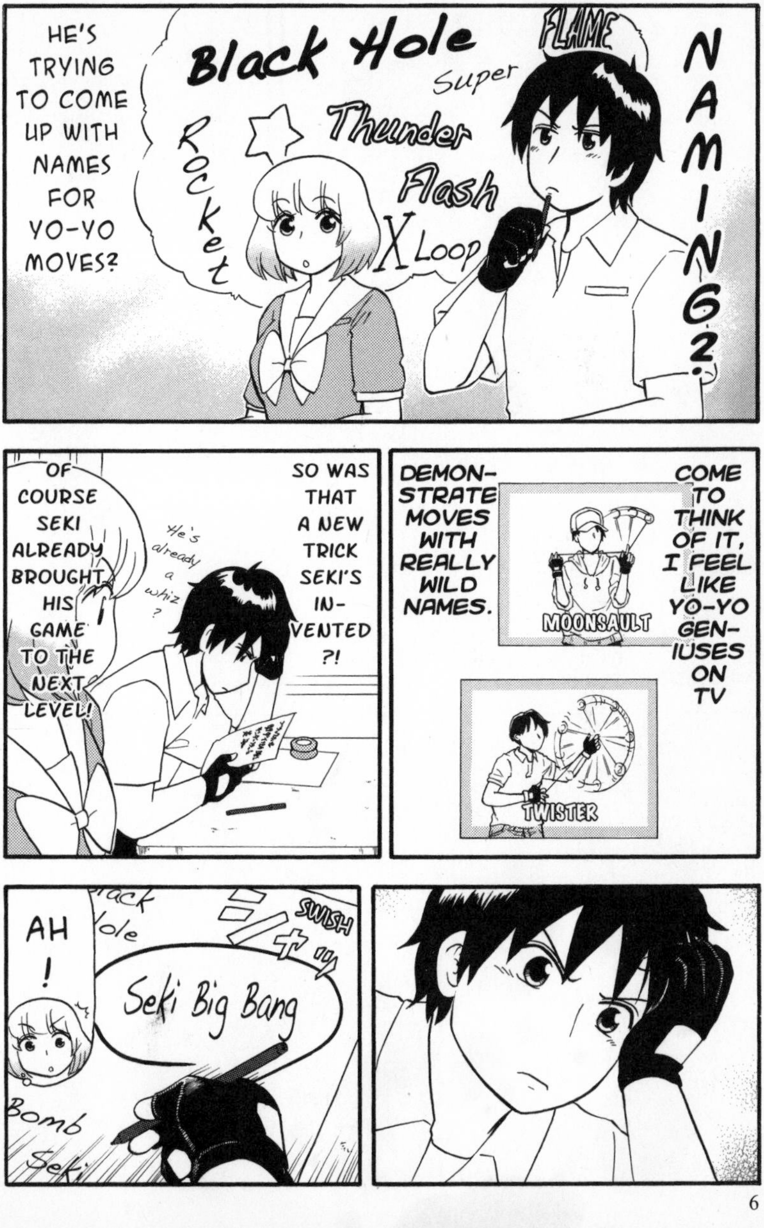
NAMING 2?
FLAME
Black Hole
Super
Thunder
Flash
Rocket
X Loop
HE'S TRYING TO COME UP WITH NAMES FOR YO-YO MOVES?
COME TO THINK OF IT, I FEEL LIKE YO-YO GEN-IUSES ON TV
DEMON-STRATE MOVES WITH REALLY WILD NAMES.
MOONSAULT
TWISTER
SO WAS THAT A NEW TRICK SEKI'S IN-VENTED ?!
He's already a whiz ?
OF COURSE SEKI ALREADY BROUGHT HIS GAME TO THE NEXT LEVEL!
SWISH
Seki Big Bang
AH !
Bomb
Seki

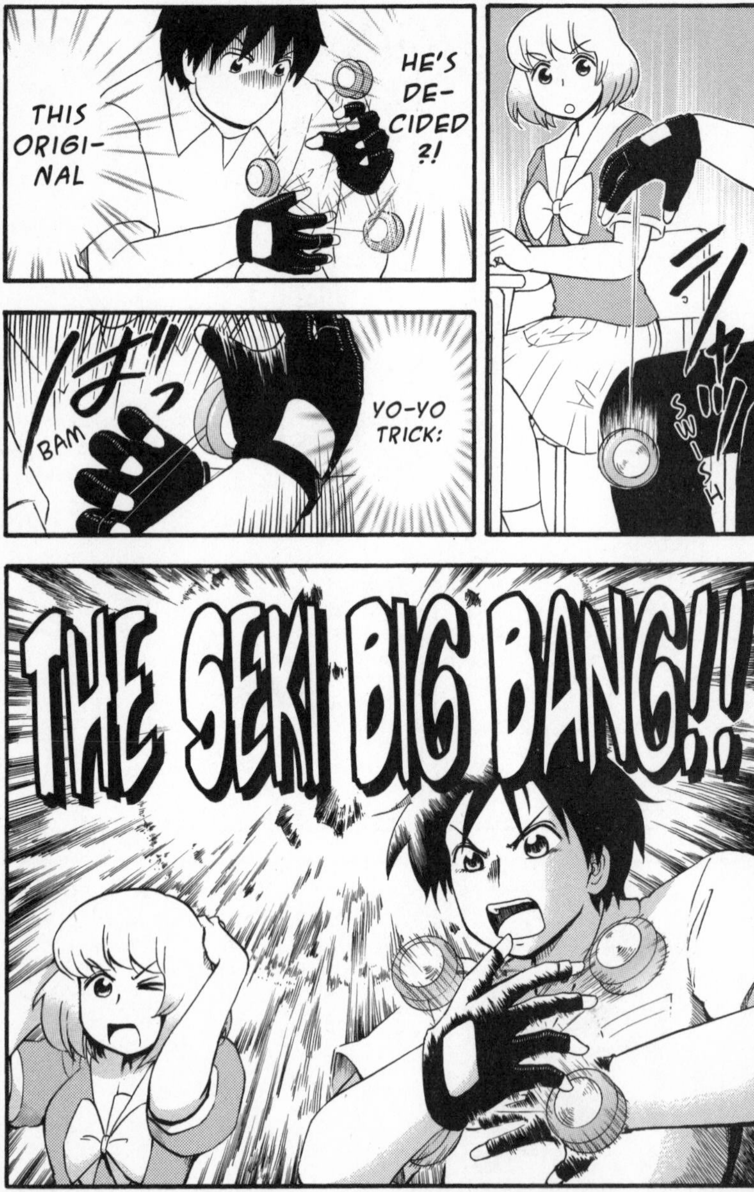
SWISH
HE'S DE-CIDED?!
THIS ORIGI-NAL
YO-YO TRICK:
ばっ
BAM
THE SEKI BIG BANG!!

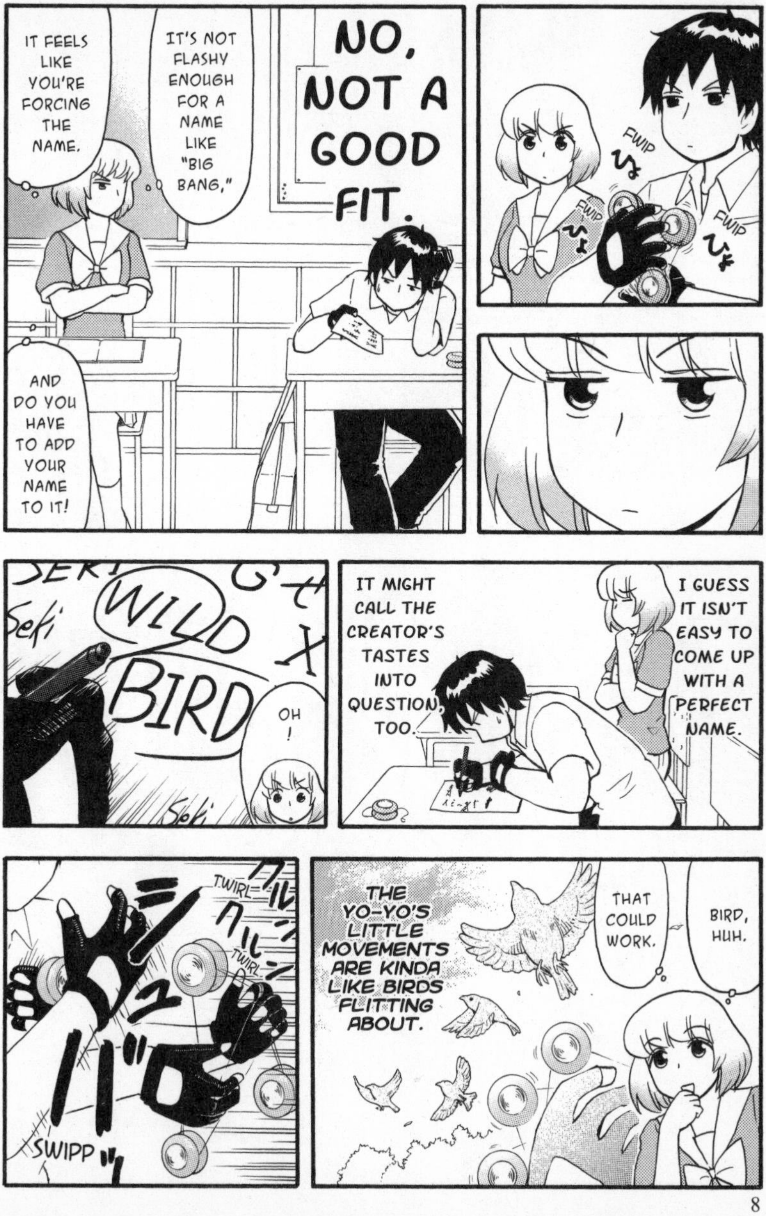
FWIP ひょ
FWIP ひょ
FWIP ひょ
NO, NOT A GOOD FIT.
IT'S NOT FLASHY ENOUGH FOR A NAME LIKE "BIG BANG,"
IT FEELS LIKE YOU'RE FORCING THE NAME.
AND DO YOU HAVE TO ADD YOUR NAME TO IT!
I GUESS IT ISN'T EASY TO COME UP WITH A PERFECT NAME.
IT MIGHT CALL THE CREATOR'S TASTES INTO QUESTION, TOO.
WILD X BIRD
Seki
OH!
Seki
BIRD, HUH.
THAT COULD WORK.
THE YO-YO'S LITTLE MOVEMENTS ARE KINDA LIKE BIRDS FLITTING ABOUT.
TWIRL
TWIRL
SWIPP

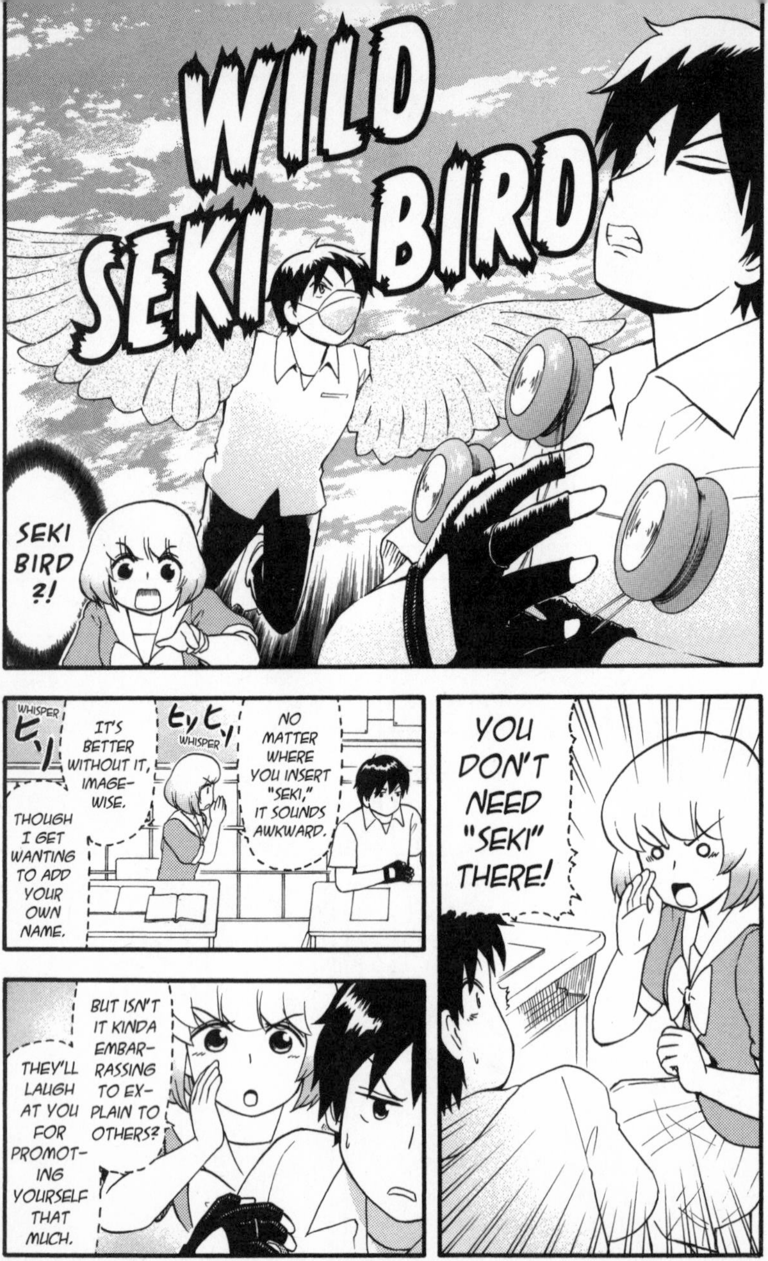

WILD SEKI BIRD
SEKI BIRD?!
YOU DON'T NEED "SEKI" THERE!
WHISPER ヒソヒソ
NO MATTER WHERE YOU INSERT "SEKI," IT SOUNDS AWKWARD.
IT'S BETTER WITHOUT IT, IMAGE-WISE.
WHISPER ヒソ
THOUGH I GET WANTING TO ADD YOUR OWN NAME.
BUT ISN'T IT KINDA EMBAR-RASSING TO EX-PLAIN TO OTHERS?
THEY'LL LAUGH AT YOU FOR PROMOT-ING YOURSELF THAT MUCH.

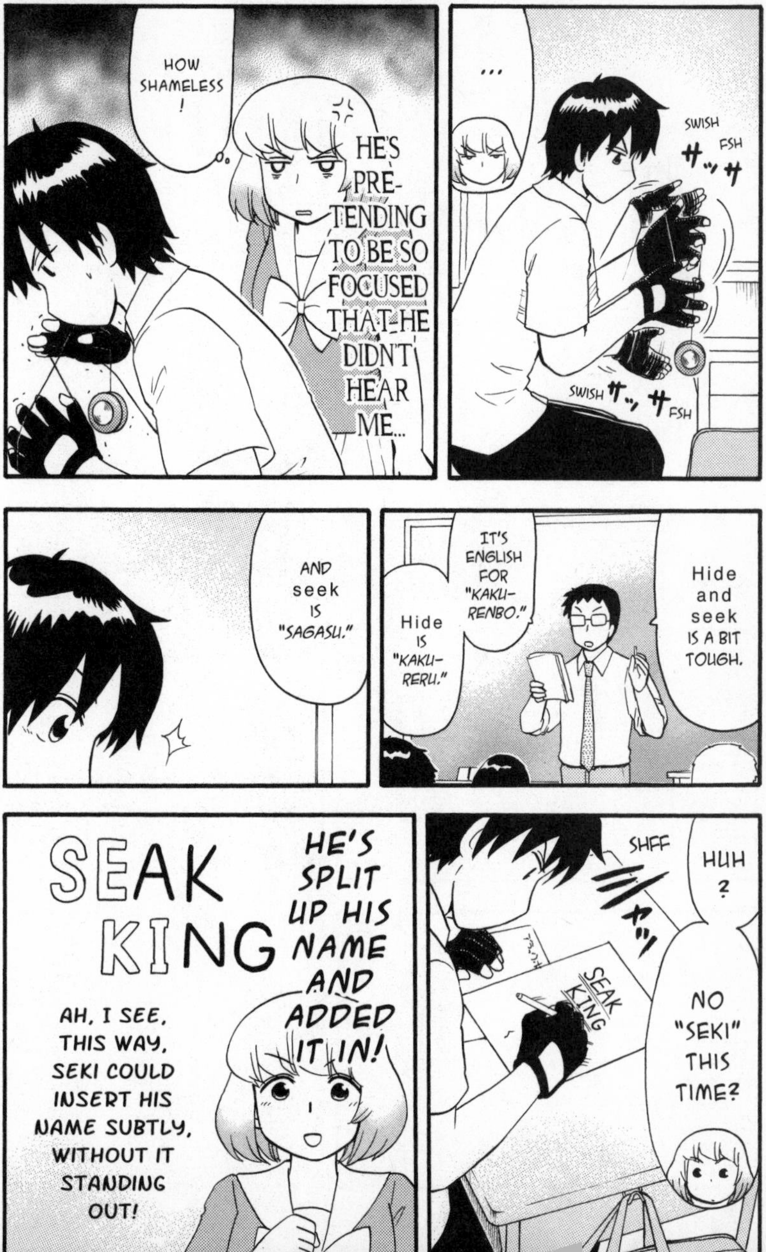
...
SWISH
FSH
サッサ
SWISH サッ サ FSH
HOW SHAMELESS!
HE'S PRE-TENDING TO BE SO FOCUSED THAT HE DIDN'T HEAR ME...
Hide and seek IS A BIT TOUGH.
IT'S ENGLISH FOR "KAKU-RENBO."
Hide IS "KAKU-RERU."
AND seek IS "SAGASU."
SHFF
シャッ
HUH?
NO "SEKI" THIS TIME?
SEAK KING
SEAK KING
HE'S SPLIT UP HIS NAME AND ADDED IT IN!
AH, I SEE. THIS WAY, SEKI COULD INSERT HIS NAME SUBTLY, WITHOUT IT STANDING OUT!

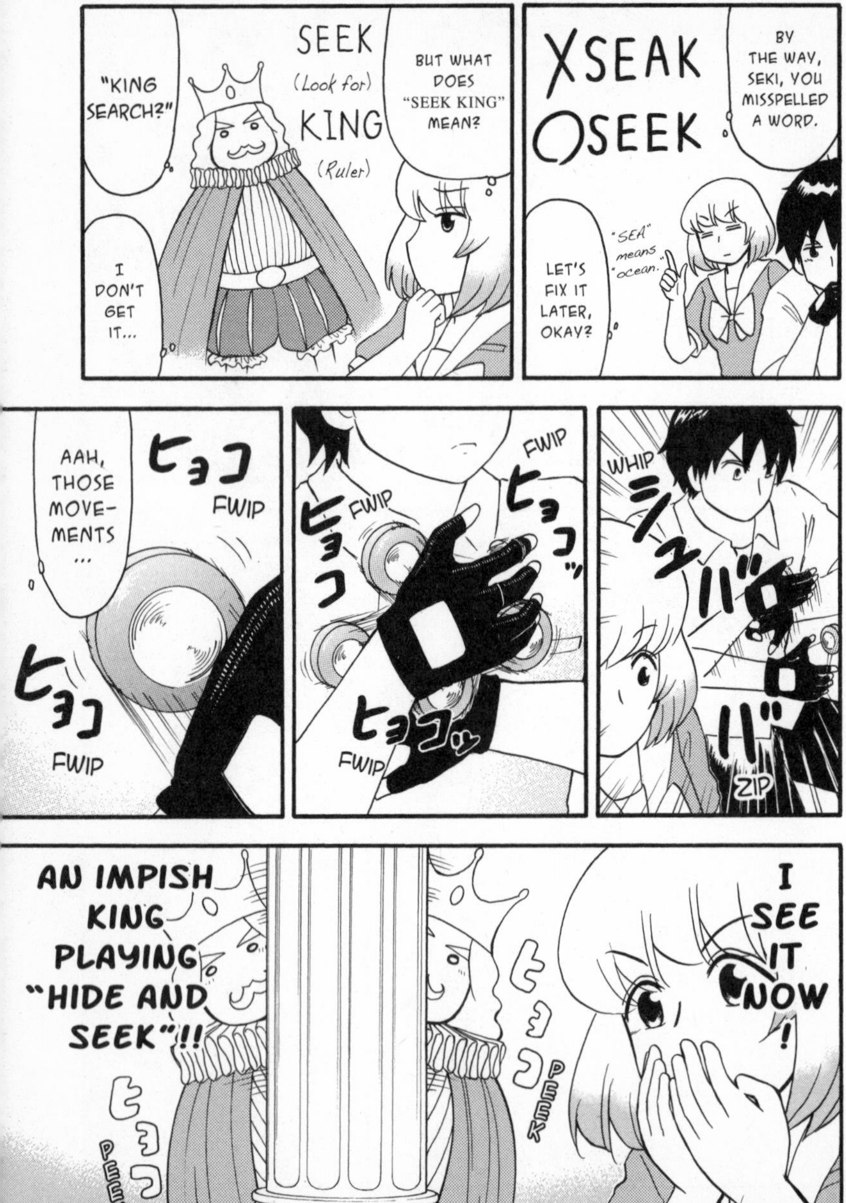
BY THE WAY, SEKI, YOU MISSPELLED A WORD.
XSEAK
○SEEK
"SEA" means "ocean."
LET'S FIX IT LATER, OKAY?
BUT WHAT DOES "SEEK KING" MEAN?
SEEK (Look for)
KING (Ruler)
"KING SEARCH?"
I DON'T GET IT...
WHIP
シュ
バタバタ
ZIP
FWIP
ヒョコッ
ヒョコ
FWIP
ヒョコッ
FWIP
ヒョコ
FWIP
AAH, THOSE MOVEMENTS...
ヒョコ
FWIP
I SEE IT NOW!
AN IMPISH KING PLAYING "HIDE AND SEEK"!!
ヒョコ
PEEK
ヒョコ
PEEK

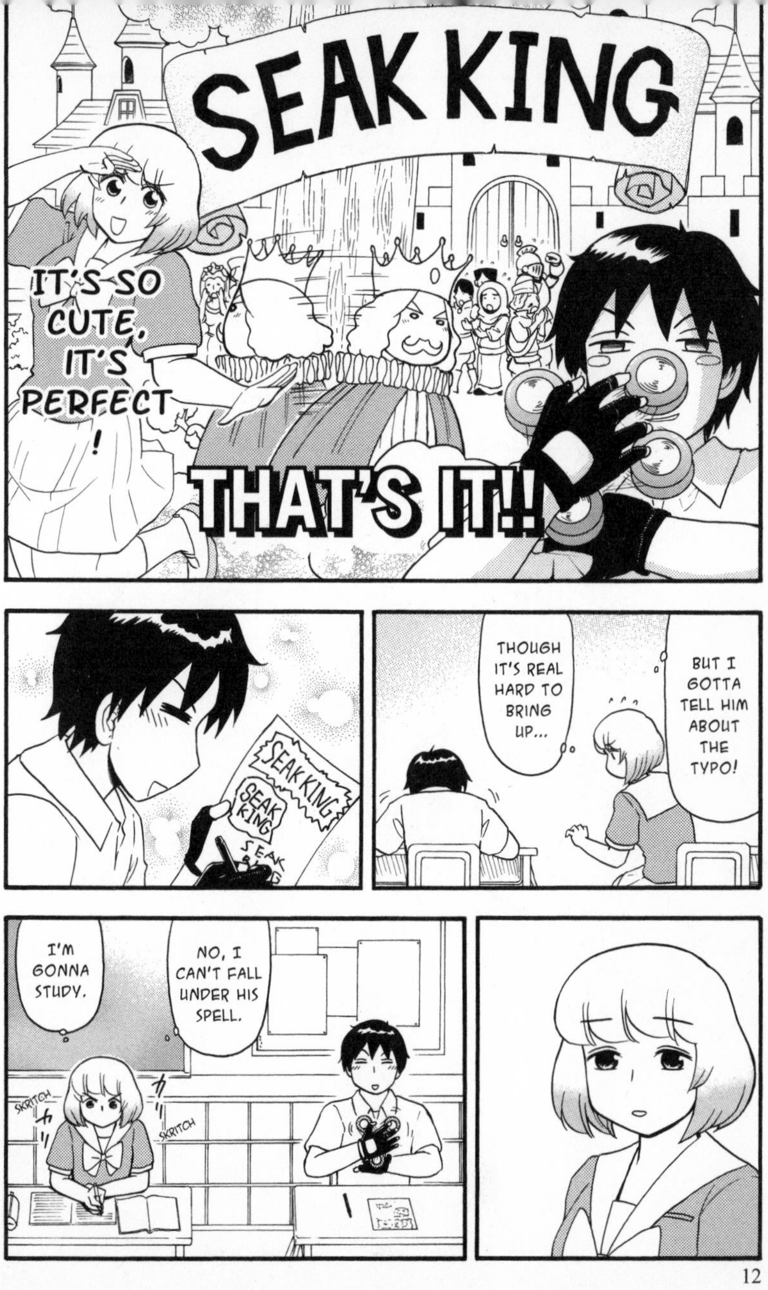
SEAK KING
IT'S SO CUTE, IT'S PERFECT!
THAT'S IT!!
THOUGH IT'S REAL HARD TO BRING UP...
BUT I GOTTA TELL HIM ABOUT THE TYPO!
SEAK KING
SEAK KING
NO, I CAN'T FALL UNDER HIS SPELL.
I'M GONNA STUDY.
SKRITCH
SKRITCH

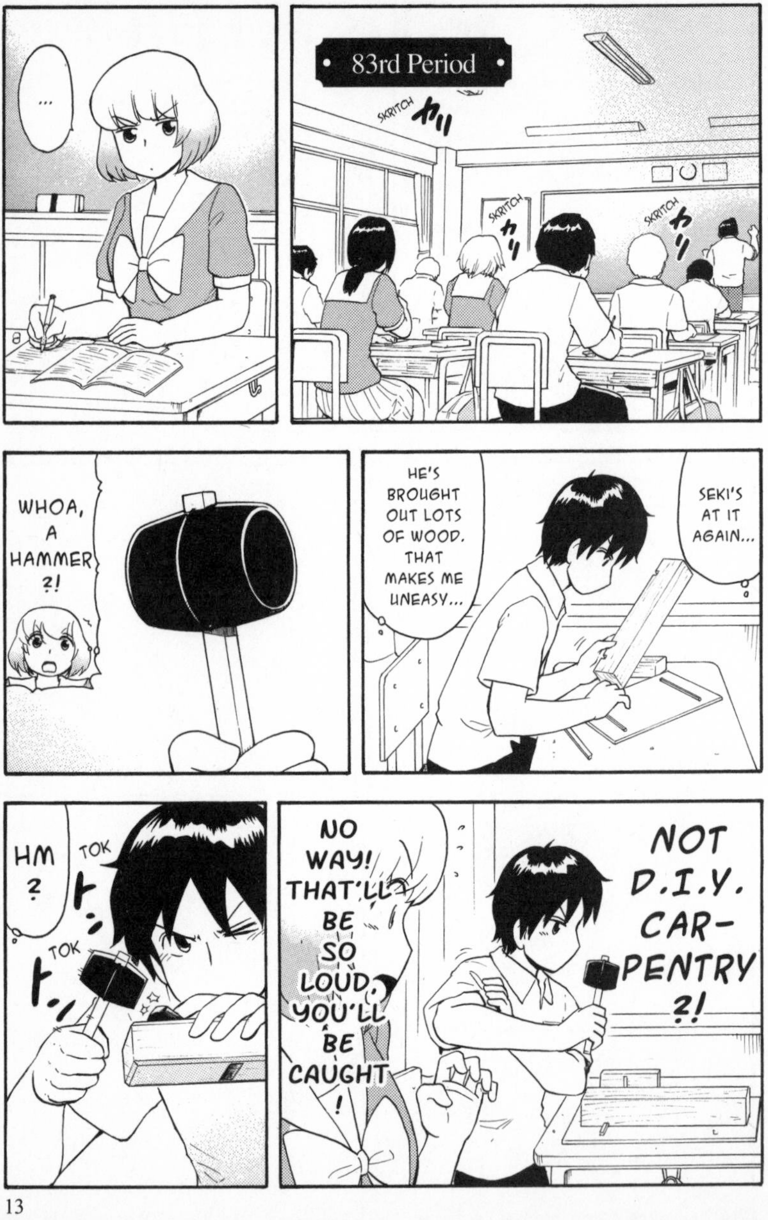
83rd Period
SKRITCH
SKRITCH
SKRITCH
...
SEKI'S AT IT AGAIN...
HE'S BROUGHT OUT LOTS OF WOOD. THAT MAKES ME UNEASY...
WHOA, A HAMMER?!
NOT D.I.Y. CAR-PENTRY?!
NO WAY! THAT'LL BE SO LOUD, YOU'LL BE CAUGHT!
HM?
TOK
TOK

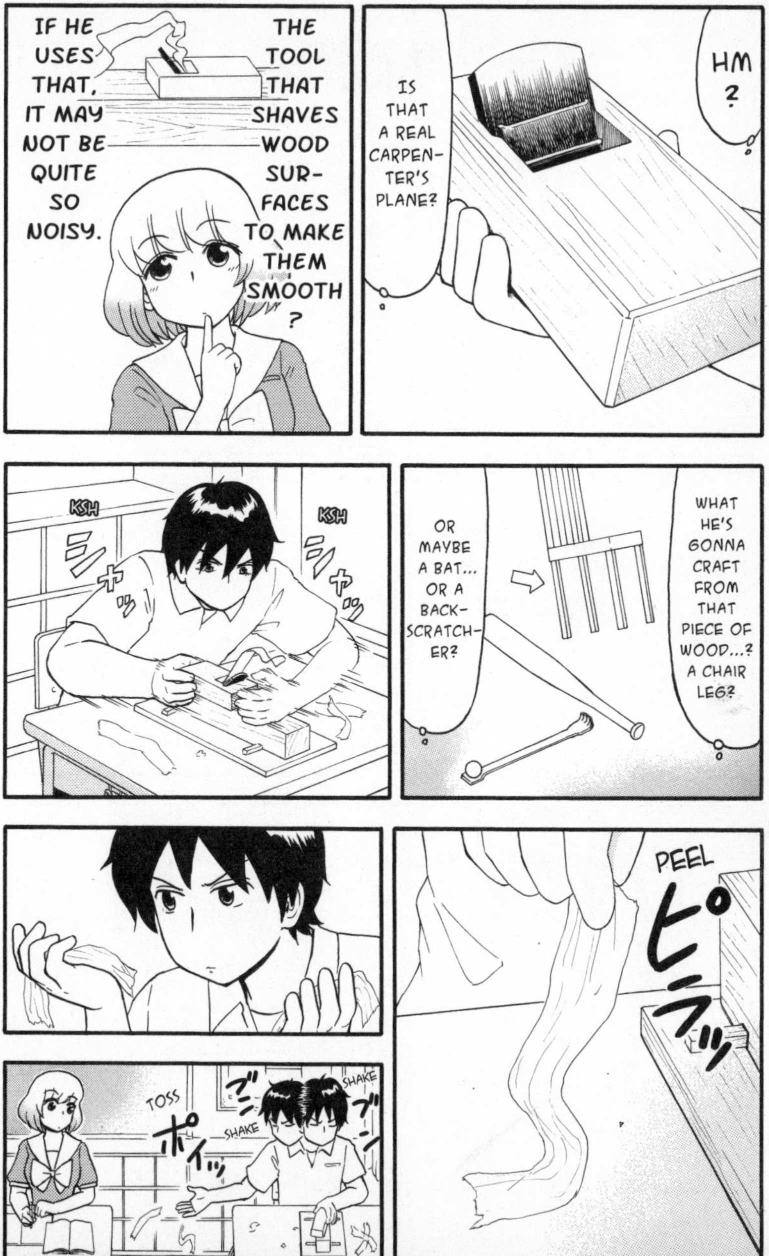
HM?
IS THAT A REAL CARPEN-TER'S PLANE?
THE TOOL THAT SHAVES WOOD SUR-FACES TO MAKE THEM SMOOTH?
IF HE USES THAT, IT MAY NOT BE QUITE SO NOISY.
WHAT HE'S GONNA CRAFT FROM THAT PIECE OF WOOD...? A CHAIR LEG?
OR MAYBE A BAT... OR A BACK-SCRATCH-ER?
KSH
KSH
PEEL
SHAKE
TOSS
ポイッ
SHAKE

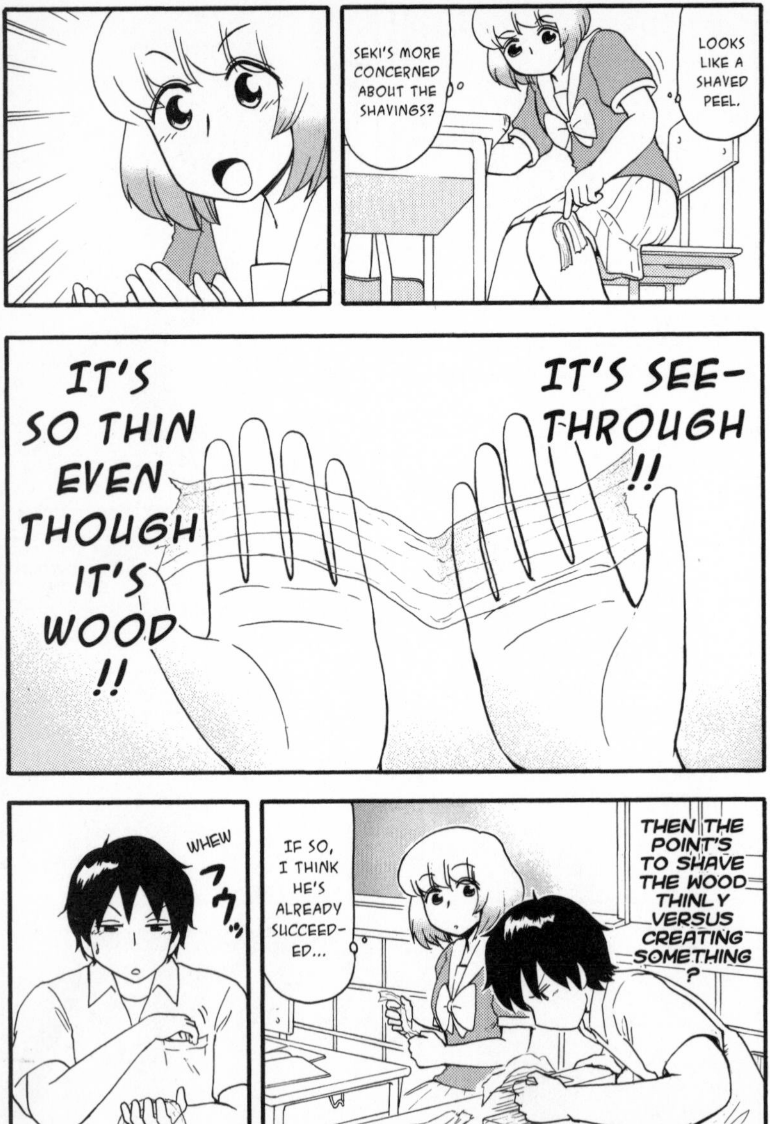
LOOKS LIKE A SHAVED PEEL.
SEKI'S MORE CONCERNED ABOUT THE SHAVINGS?
IT'S SEE-THROUGH!!
IT'S SO THIN EVEN THOUGH IT'S WOOD!!
THEN THE POINT'S TO SHAVE THE WOOD THINLY VERSUS CREATING SOMETHING?
IF SO, I THINK HE'S ALREADY SUCCEED-ED...
WHEW
フウッ

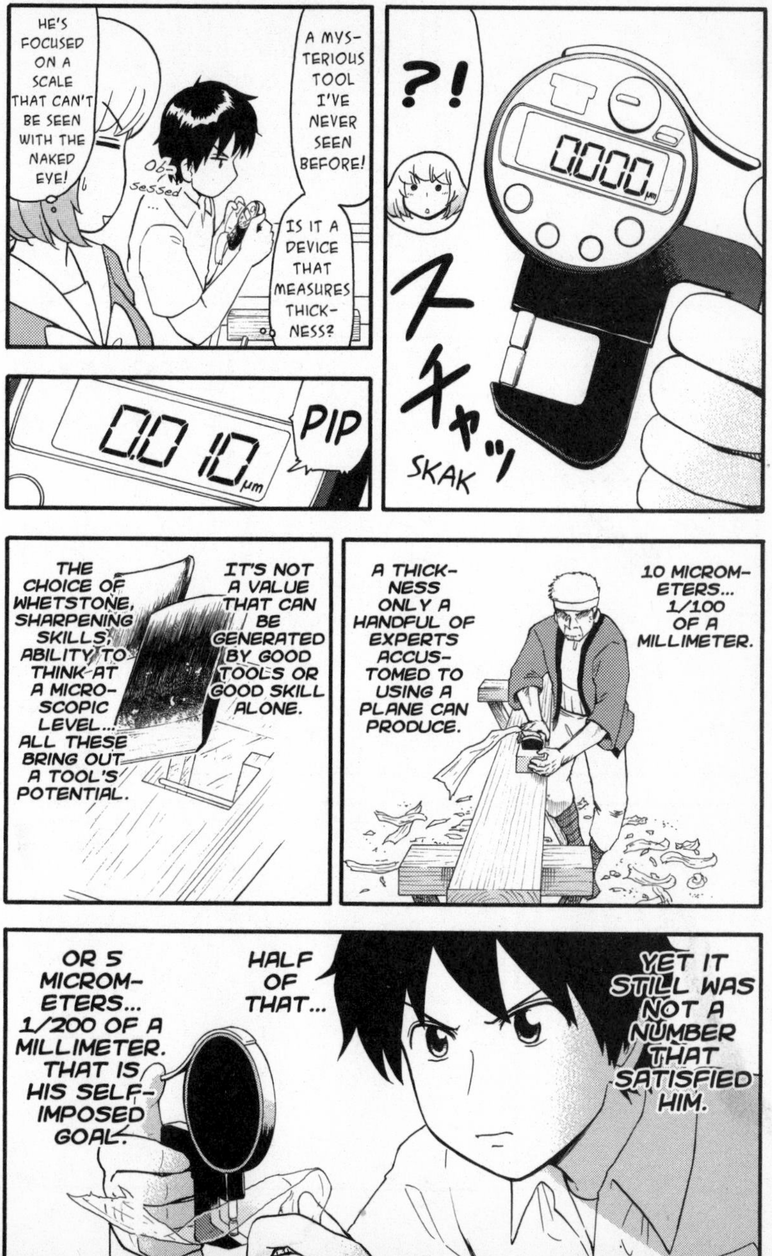
?!
0.000 μm
SKAK
A MYSTERIOUS TOOL I'VE NEVER SEEN BEFORE!
IS IT A DEVICE THAT MEASURES THICKNESS?
HE'S FOCUSED ON A SCALE THAT CAN'T BE SEEN WITH THE NAKED EYE!
Obsessed
...
0.010 μm
PIP
10 MICROMETERS... 1/100 OF A MILLIMETER.
A THICKNESS ONLY A HANDFUL OF EXPERTS ACCUSTOMED TO USING A PLANE CAN PRODUCE.
IT'S NOT A VALUE THAT CAN BE GENERATED BY GOOD TOOLS OR GOOD SKILL ALONE.
THE CHOICE OF WHETSTONE, SHARPENING SKILLS, ABILITY TO THINK AT A MICROSCOPIC LEVEL... ALL THESE BRING OUT A TOOL'S POTENTIAL.
YET IT STILL WAS NOT A NUMBER THAT SATISFIED HIM.
HALF OF THAT...
OR 5 MICROMETERS... 1/200 OF A MILLIMETER. THAT IS HIS SELF-IMPOSED GOAL.

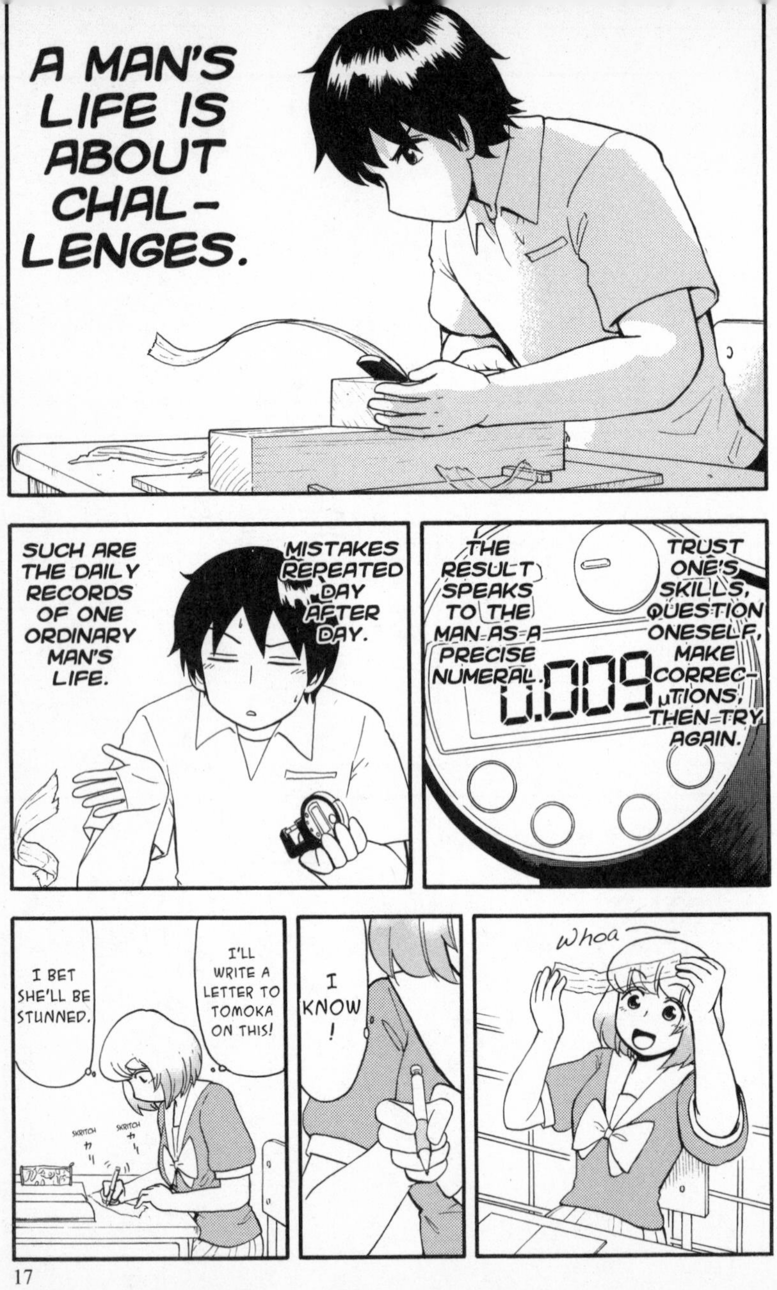
A MAN'S LIFE IS ABOUT CHAL-LENGES.
TRUST ONE'S SKILLS, QUESTION ONESELF, MAKE CORREC-TIONS, THEN TRY AGAIN.
THE RESULT SPEAKS TO THE MAN AS A PRECISE NUMERAL.
0.009
MISTAKES REPEATED DAY AFTER DAY.
SUCH ARE THE DAILY RECORDS OF ONE ORDINARY MAN'S LIFE.
Whoa—
I KNOW!
I'LL WRITE A LETTER TO TOMOKA ON THIS!
I BET SHE'LL BE STUNNED.
SKRITCH
SKRITCH

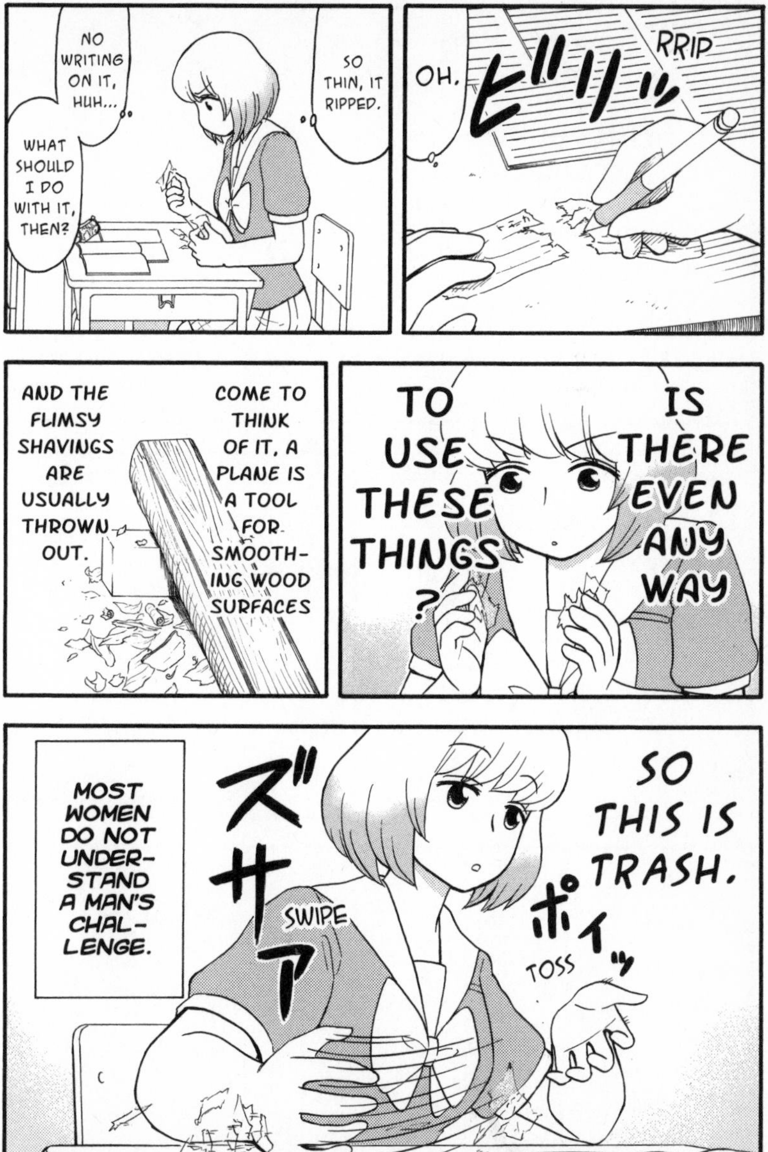
RRIP
ビリッ
OH.
SO THIN, IT RIPPED.
NO WRITING ON IT, HUH...
WHAT SHOULD I DO WITH IT, THEN?
IS THERE EVEN ANY WAY
TO USE THESE THINGS?
COME TO THINK OF IT, A PLANE IS A TOOL FOR SMOOTHING WOOD SURFACES
AND THE FLIMSY SHAVINGS ARE USUALLY THROWN OUT.
SO THIS IS TRASH.
ポイッ
TOSS
ズサァ
SWIPE
MOST WOMEN DO NOT UNDERSTAND A MAN'S CHALLENGE.

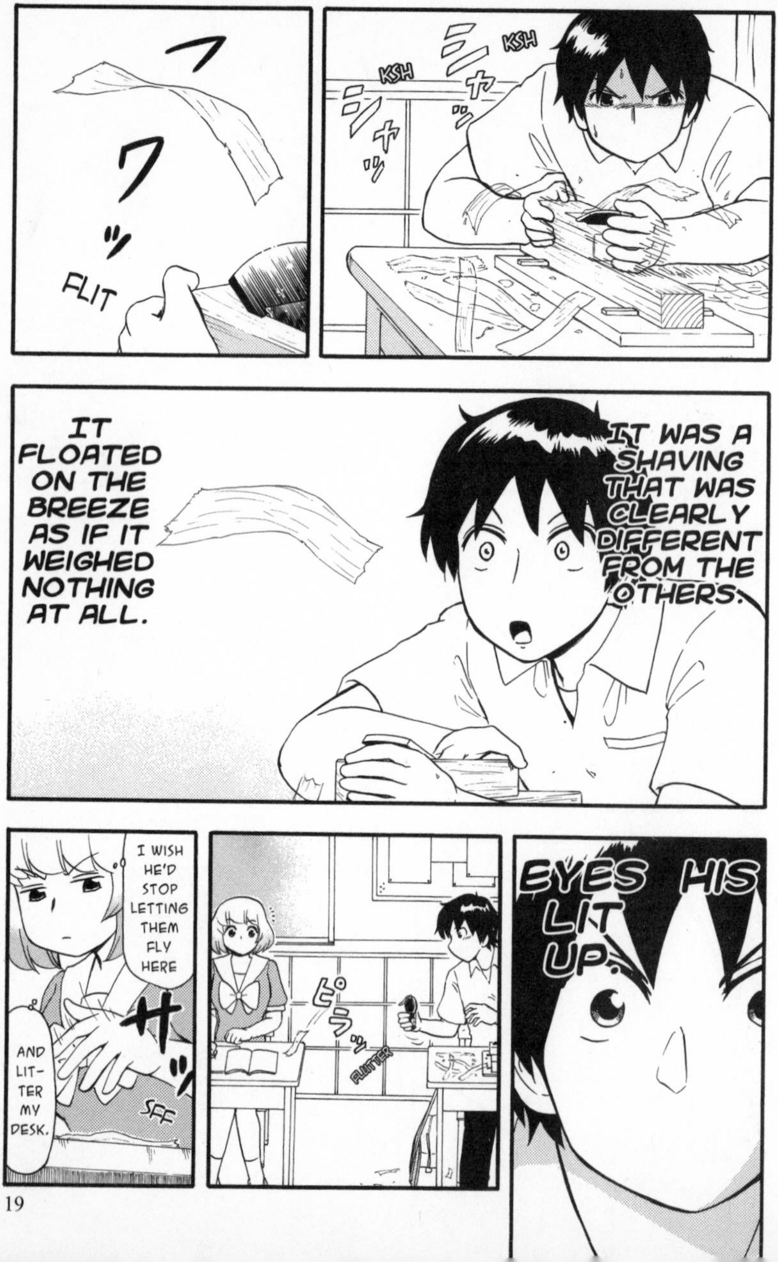
KSH
KSH
シャッ
シャッ
フワッ
FLIT
IT WAS A SHAVING THAT WAS CLEARLY DIFFERENT FROM THE OTHERS.
IT FLOATED ON THE BREEZE AS IF IT WEIGHED NOTHING AT ALL.
EYES HIS
LIT
UP.
ピラッ
FLUTTER
I WISH HE'D STOP LETTING THEM FLY HERE
AND LIT-TER MY DESK.
サッ
SFF

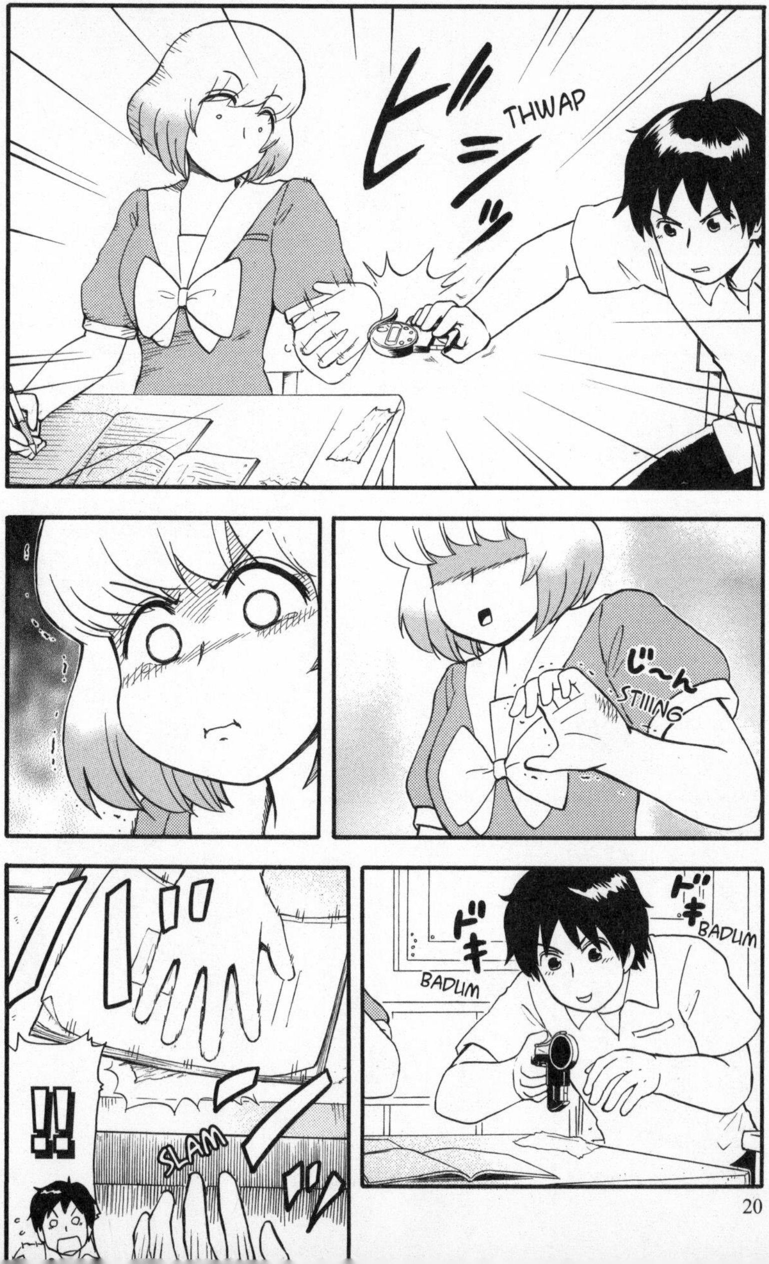
ビシッ
THWAP
じ〜ん
STIIING
ドキ
BADUM
ドキ
BADUM
!!
SLAM

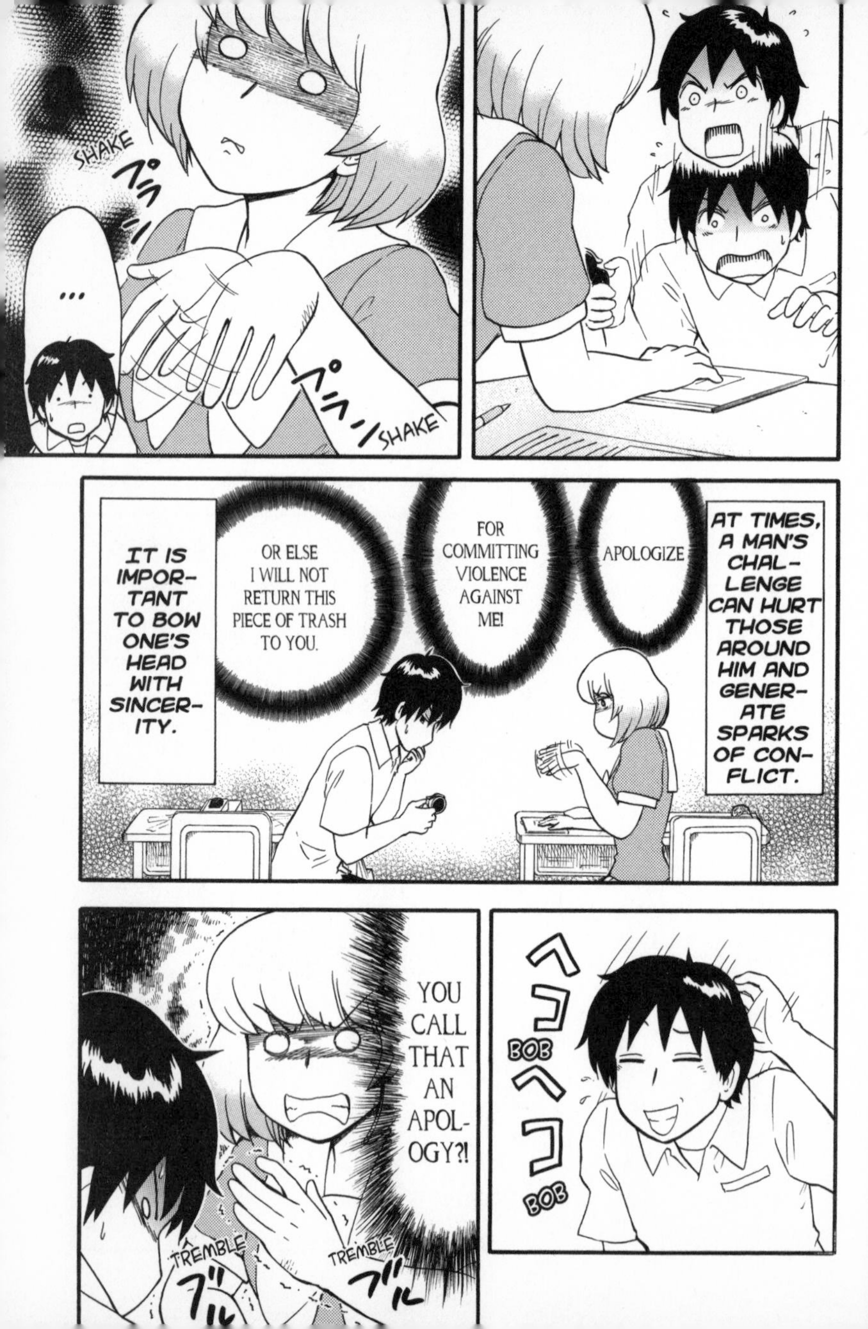
SHAKE
...
SHAKE
AT TIMES, A MAN'S CHAL-LENGE CAN HURT THOSE AROUND HIM AND GENER-ATE SPARKS OF CON-FLICT.
APOLOGIZE
FOR COMMITTING VIOLENCE AGAINST ME!
OR ELSE I WILL NOT RETURN THIS PIECE OF TRASH TO YOU.
IT IS IMPOR-TANT TO BOW ONE'S HEAD WITH SINCER-ITY.
BOB
BOB
YOU CALL THAT AN APOL-OGY?!
TREMBLE
TREMBLE

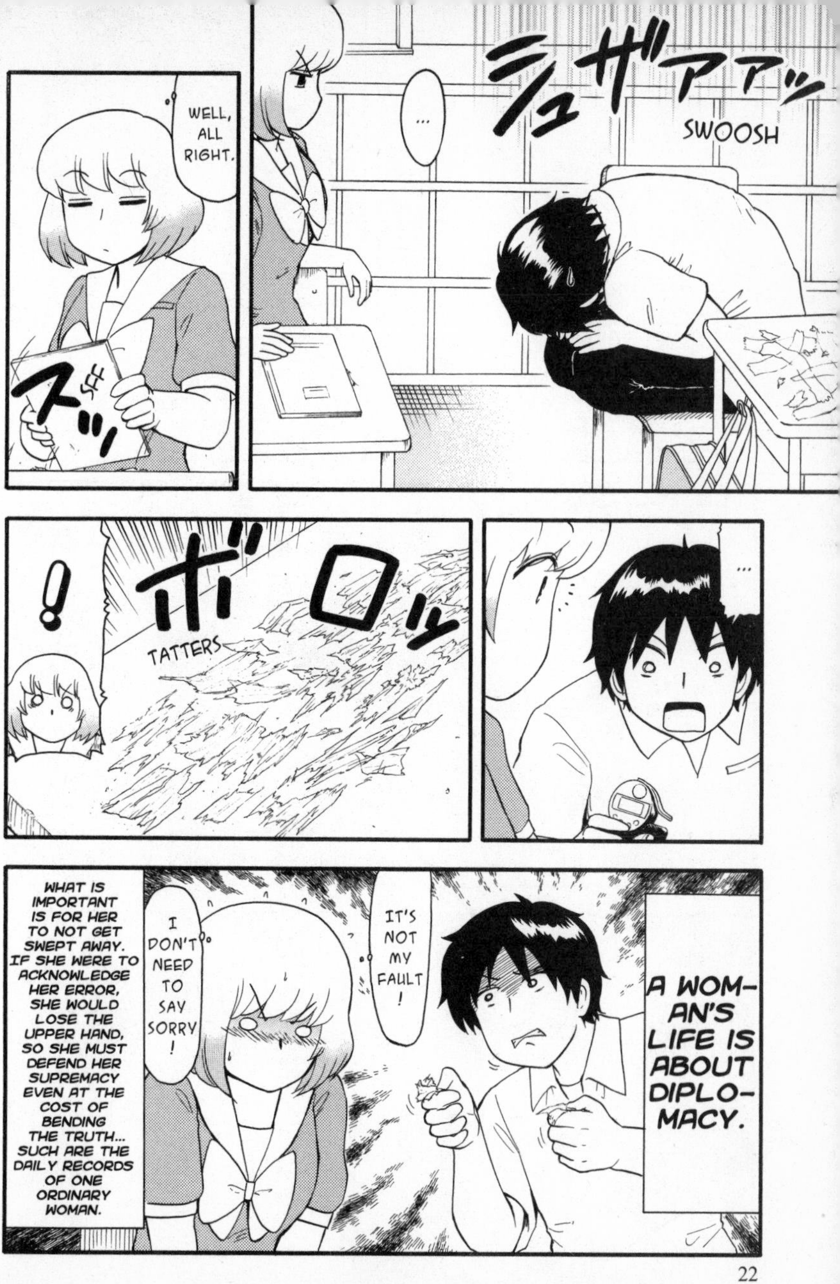
シュザアッ
SWOOSH
...
WELL, ALL RIGHT.
スッ
SFF
...
ボロッ
TATTERS
!
A WOMAN'S LIFE IS ABOUT DIPLOMACY.
IT'S NOT MY FAULT!
I DON'T NEED TO SAY SORRY!
WHAT IS IMPORTANT IS FOR HER TO NOT GET SWEPT AWAY. IF SHE WERE TO ACKNOWLEDGE HER ERROR, SHE WOULD LOSE THE UPPER HAND, SO SHE MUST DEFEND HER SUPREMACY EVEN AT THE COST OF BENDING THE TRUTH... SUCH ARE THE DAILY RECORDS OF ONE ORDINARY WOMAN.

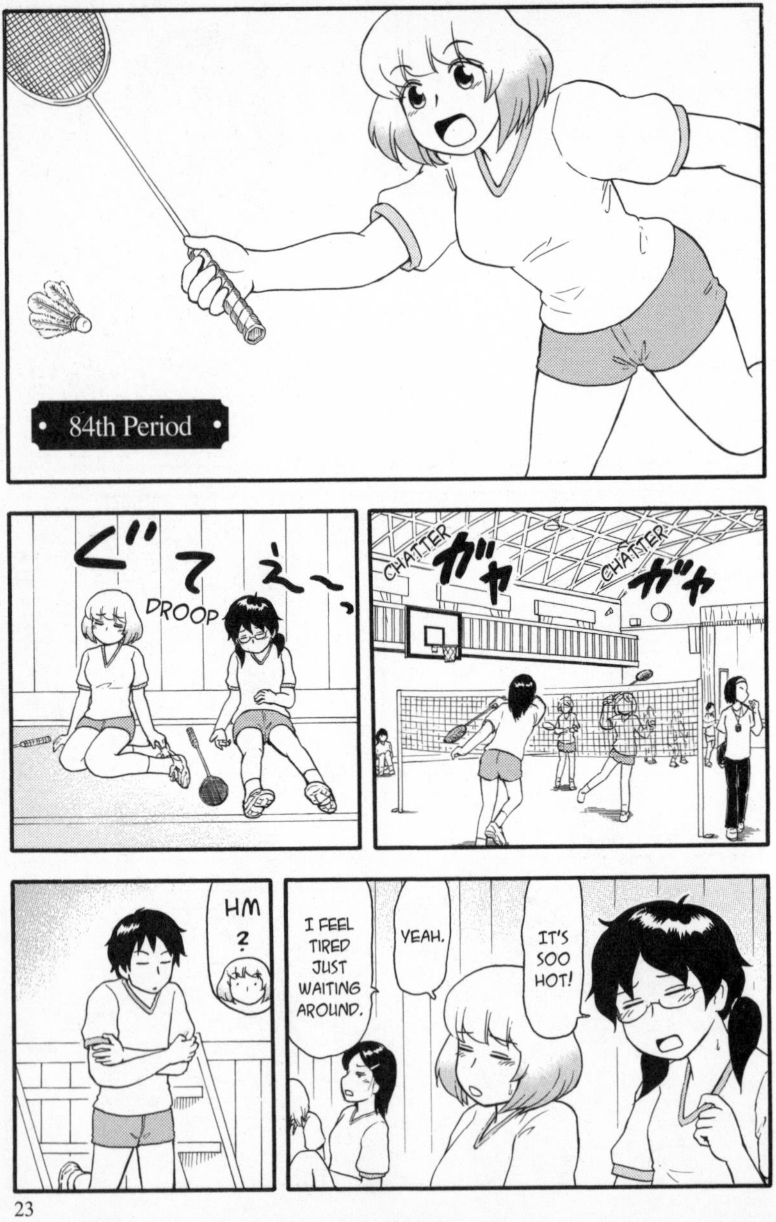
84th Period
CHATTER
ガヤ
CHATTER
ガヤ
ぐでぇ～
DROOP
IT'S SOO HOT!
YEAH.
I FEEL TIRED JUST WAITING AROUND.
HM?

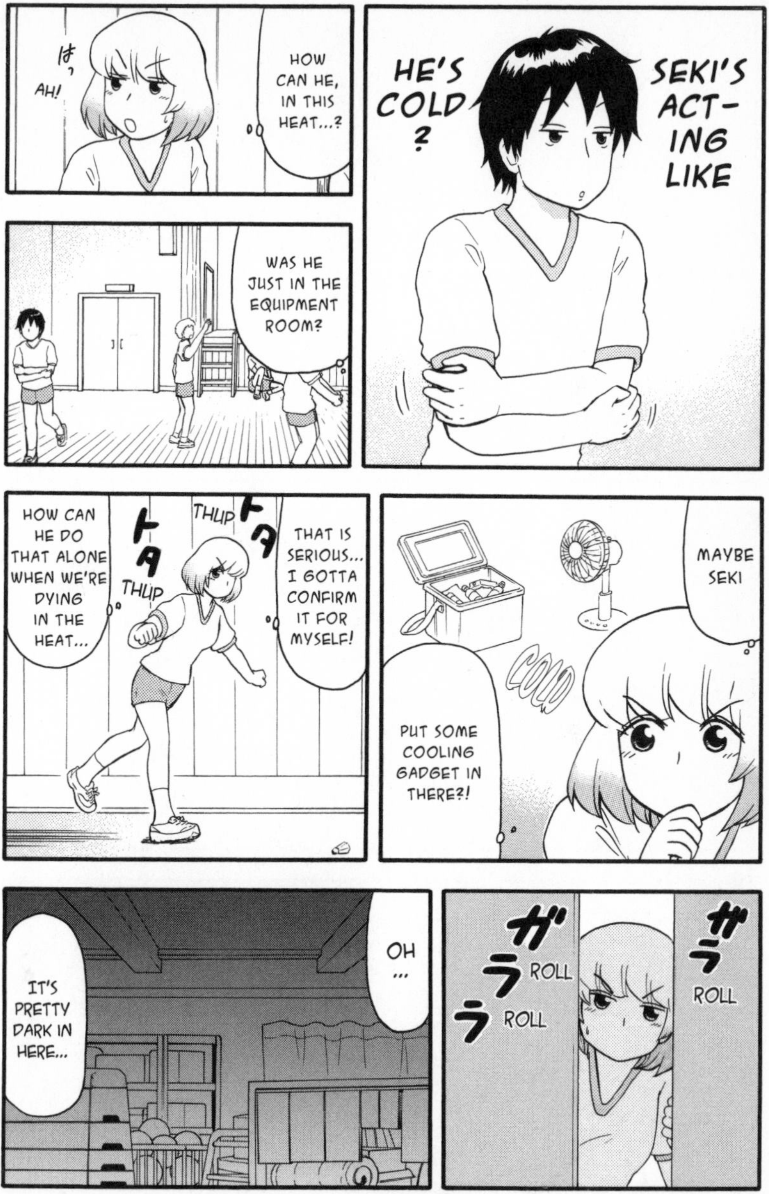
SEKI'S ACT-ING LIKE
HE'S COLD?
は、
AH!
HOW CAN HE, IN THIS HEAT...?
WAS HE JUST IN THE EQUIPMENT ROOM?
MAYBE SEKI
COLD
PUT SOME COOLING GADGET IN THERE?!
トタ
THUP
THAT IS SERIOUS... I GOTTA CONFIRM IT FOR MYSELF!
トタ
THUP
HOW CAN HE DO THAT ALONE WHEN WE'RE DYING IN THE HEAT...
ガラ
ROLL
ラ
ROLL
ラ
ROLL
OH...
IT'S PRETTY DARK IN HERE...

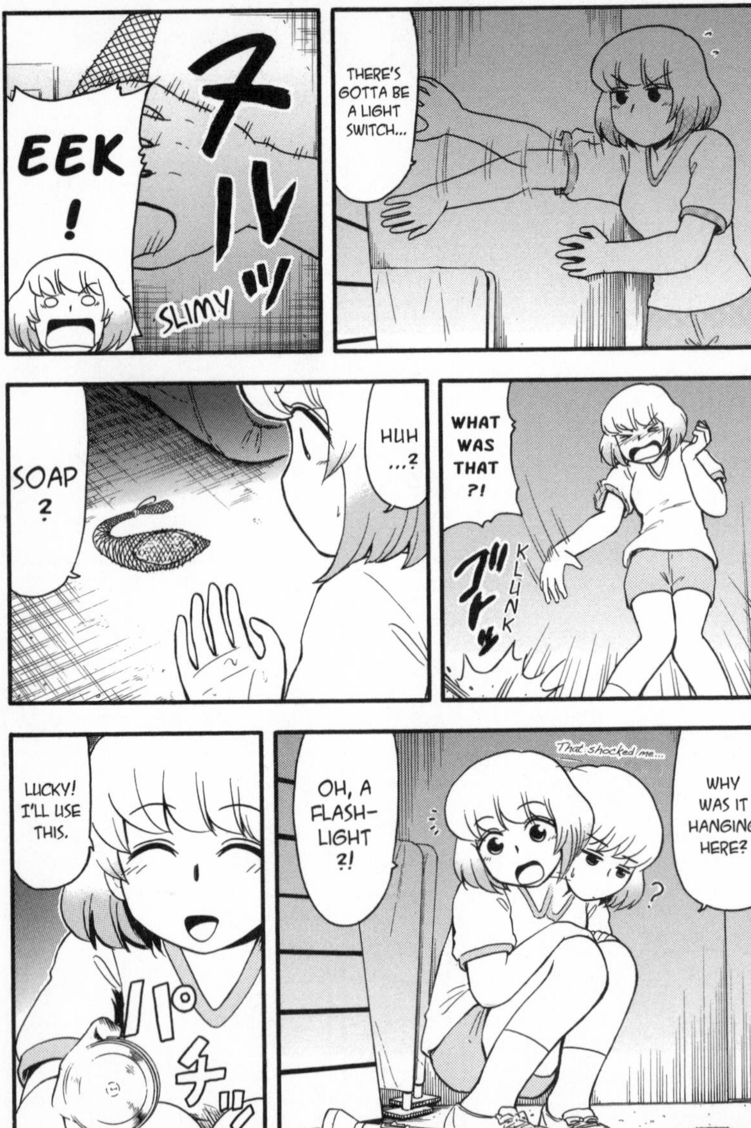
THERE'S GOTTA BE A LIGHT SWITCH...
EEK!
フルッ
SLIMY
WHAT WAS THAT?!
ゴトッ
KLUNK
HUH...?
SOAP?
WHY WAS IT HANGING HERE?
That shocked me...
OH, A FLASHLIGHT?!
LUCKY! I'LL USE THIS.
パチッ
KLIK

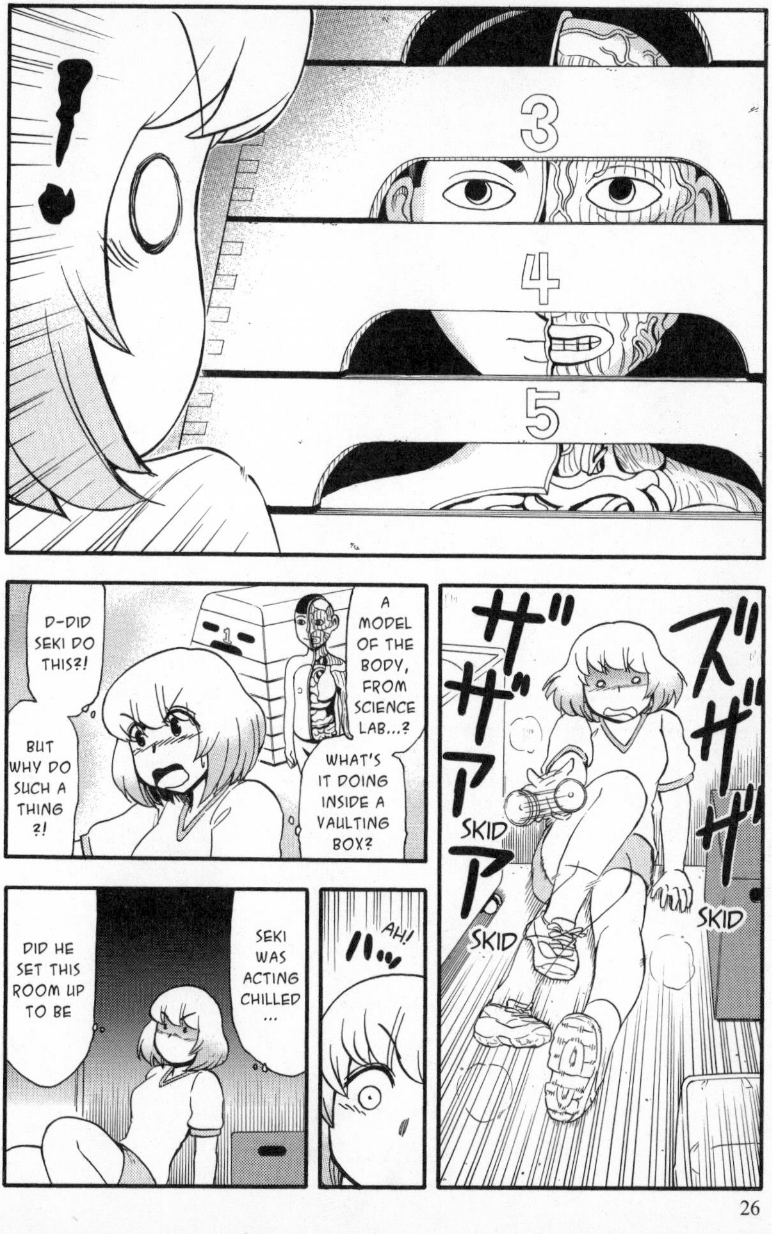
!
3
4
5
ズザザ
ザザア
SKID
SKID
SKID
A MODEL OF THE BODY, FROM SCIENCE LAB...?
WHAT'S IT DOING INSIDE A VAULTING BOX?
D-DID SEKI DO THIS?!
BUT WHY DO SUCH A THING ?!
ハッ
AH!
SEKI WAS ACTING CHILLED ...
DID HE SET THIS ROOM UP TO BE

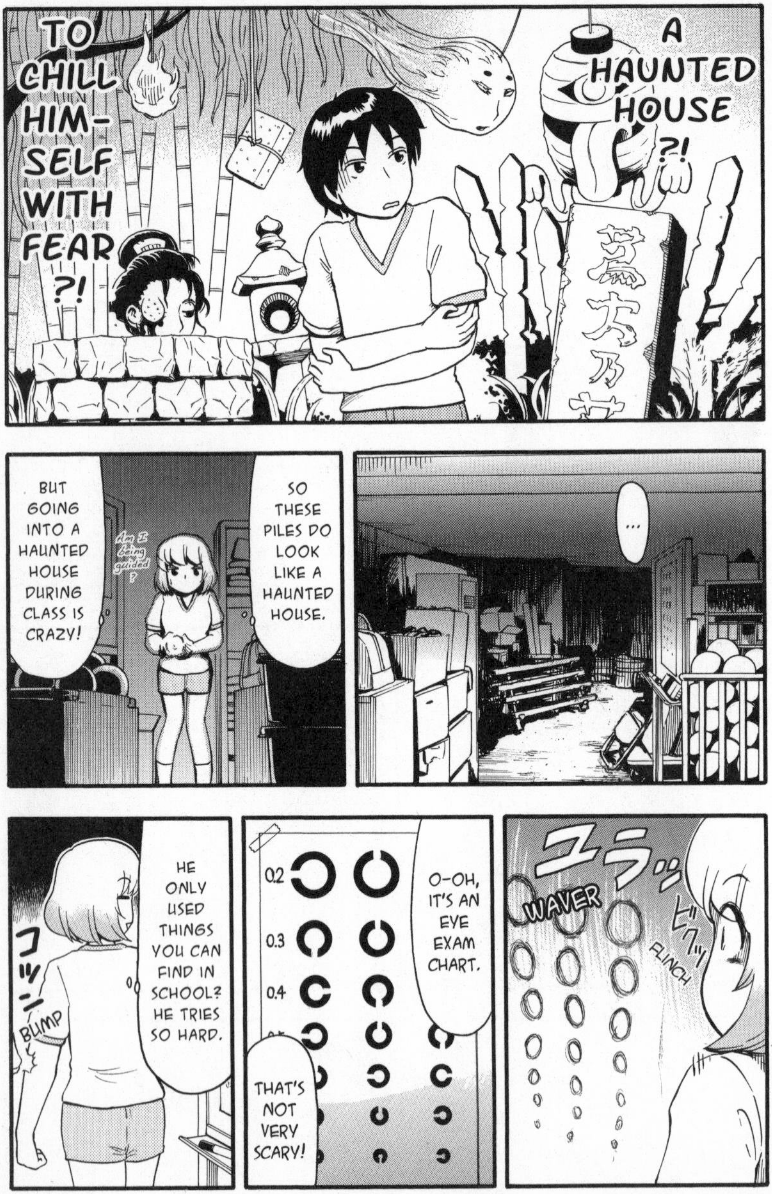
A HAUNTED HOUSE ?!
TO CHILL HIM-SELF WITH FEAR ?!
...
SO THESE PILES DO LOOK LIKE A HAUNTED HOUSE.
Am I being guided?
BUT GOING INTO A HAUNTED HOUSE DURING CLASS IS CRAZY!
ユラッ
WAVER
ビクッ
FLINCH
O-OH, IT'S AN EYE EXAM CHART.
0.2
0.3
0.4
THAT'S NOT VERY SCARY!
HE ONLY USED THINGS YOU CAN FIND IN SCHOOL? HE TRIES SO HARD.
コツン
BUMP

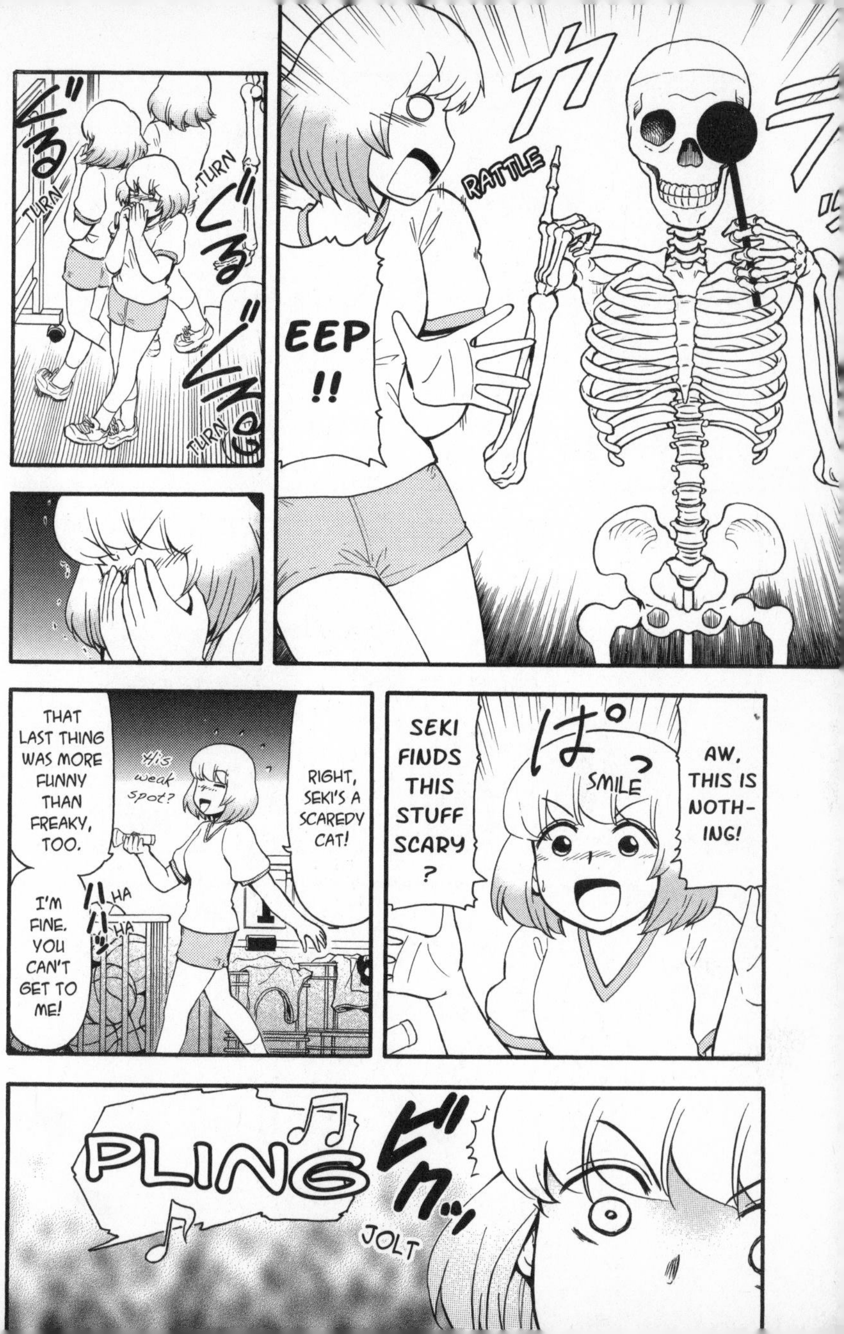
カラ
RATTLE
EEP!!
TURN
TURN
TURN
AW. THIS IS NOTH-ING!
ぱっ
SMILE
SEKI FINDS THIS STUFF SCARY?
RIGHT, SEKI'S A SCAREDY CAT!
His weak spot?
THAT LAST THING WAS MORE FUNNY THAN FREAKY, TOO.
HA HA
I'M FINE. YOU CAN'T GET TO ME!
JOLT
PLING

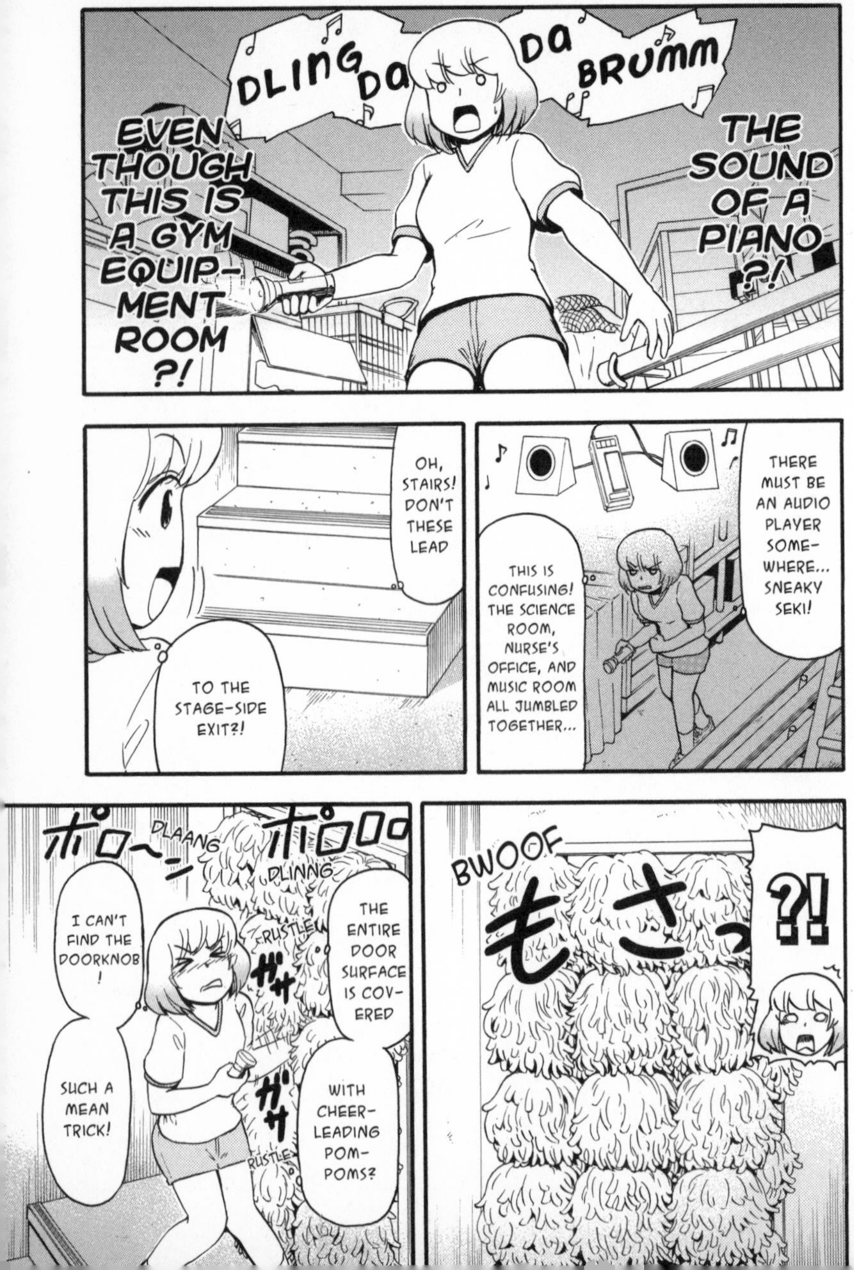

DLING DA DA BRUMM
THE SOUND OF A PIANO ?!
EVEN THOUGH THIS IS A GYM EQUIP-MENT ROOM ?!
THERE MUST BE AN AUDIO PLAYER SOME-WHERE... SNEAKY SEKI!
THIS IS CONFUSING! THE SCIENCE ROOM, NURSE'S OFFICE, AND MUSIC ROOM ALL JUMBLED TOGETHER...
OH, STAIRS! DON'T THESE LEAD
TO THE STAGE-SIDE EXIT?!
BWOOF
もさっ
?!
DLINNG
THE ENTIRE DOOR SURFACE IS COV-ERED
WITH CHEER-LEADING POM-POMS?
RUSTLE
ザザ
RUSTLE
ポロ～ン
DLAANG
I CAN'T FIND THE DOORKNOB!
SUCH A MEAN TRICK!

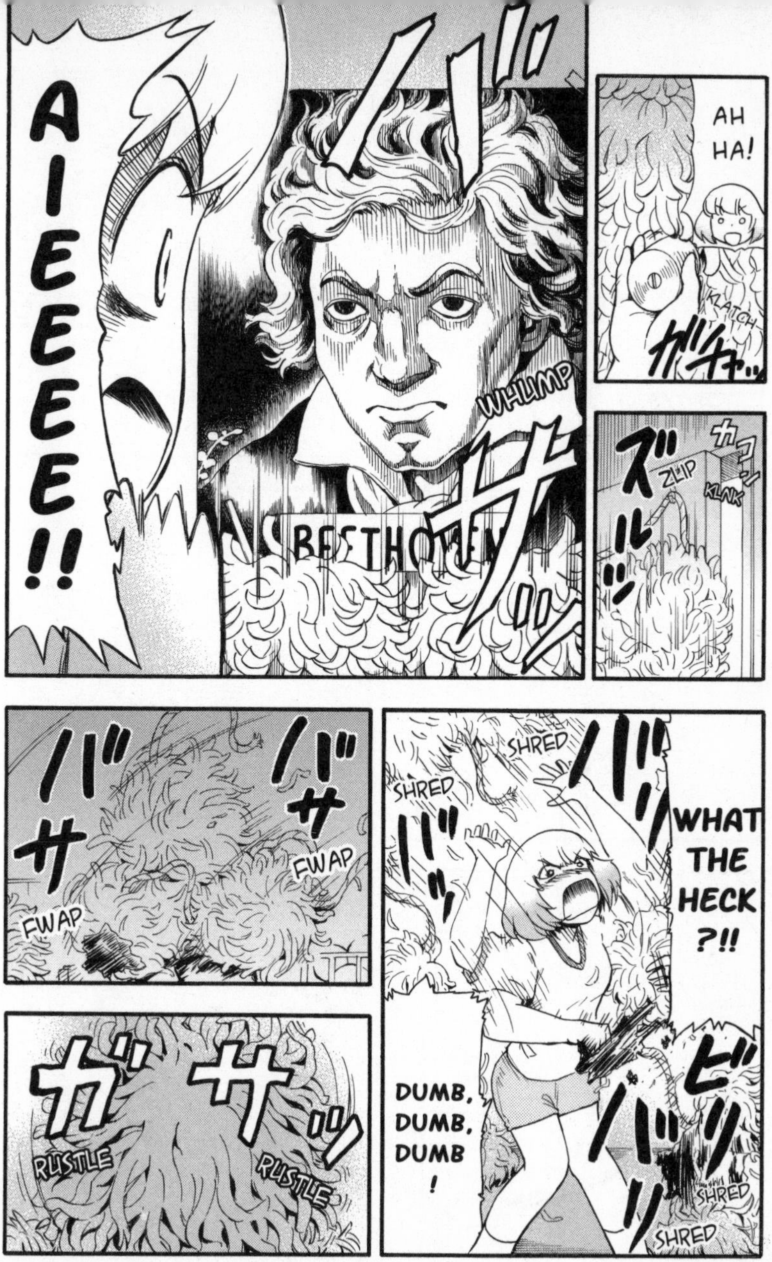
AH HA!
KLATCH
ガチャッ
ズルッ
ZLIP
カコッ
KLNK
WHLUMP
サッ
BEETHOVEN
AIEEEEE!!
WHAT THE HECK?!!
バリッ
SHRED
SHRED
バリッ
SHRED
ビリッ
バリッ
SHRED
DUMB, DUMB, DUMB!
バサ
FWAP
バサ
FWAP
ガサッ
RUSTLE
RUSTLE

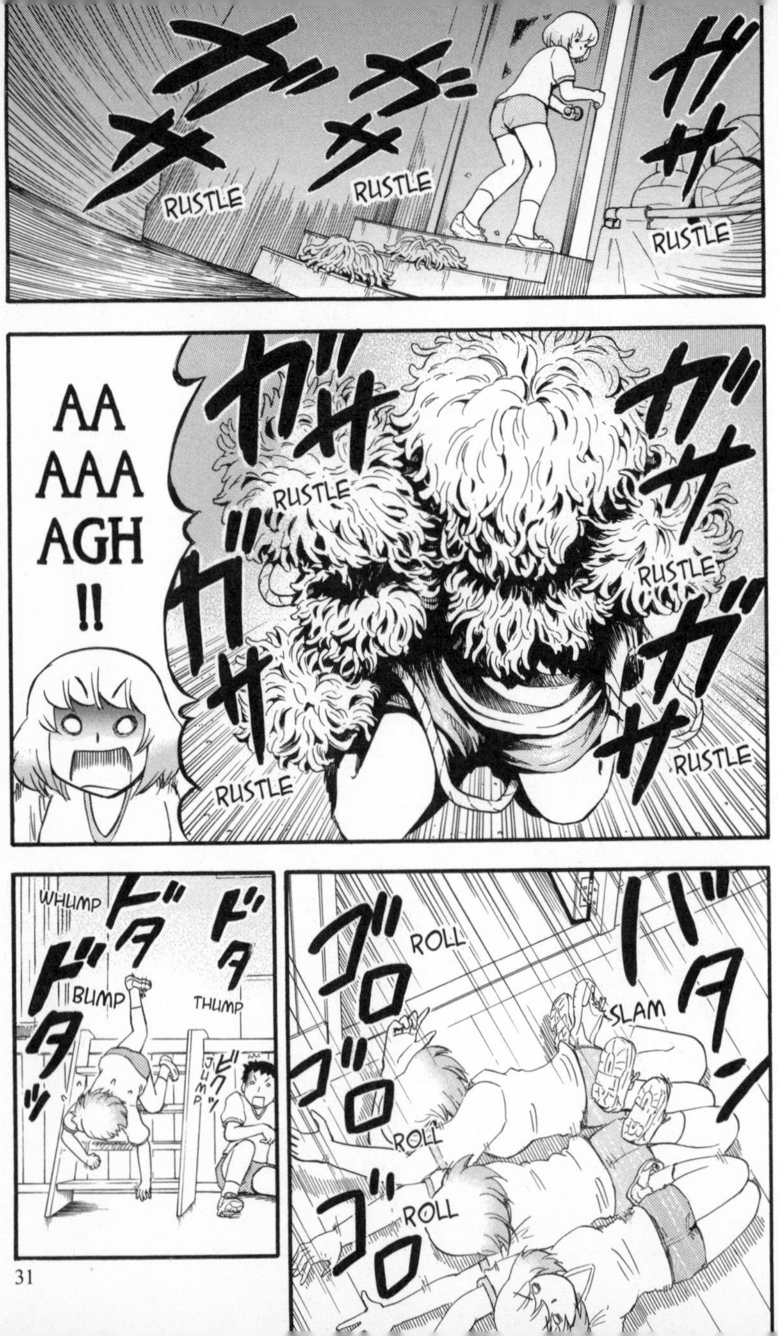
RUSTLE
RUSTLE
RUSTLE
RUSTLE
RUSTLE
AAAAAAGH!!
RUSTLE
RUSTLE
SLAM
ROLL
ROLL
ROLL
THUMP
JUMP
WHUMP
BUMP

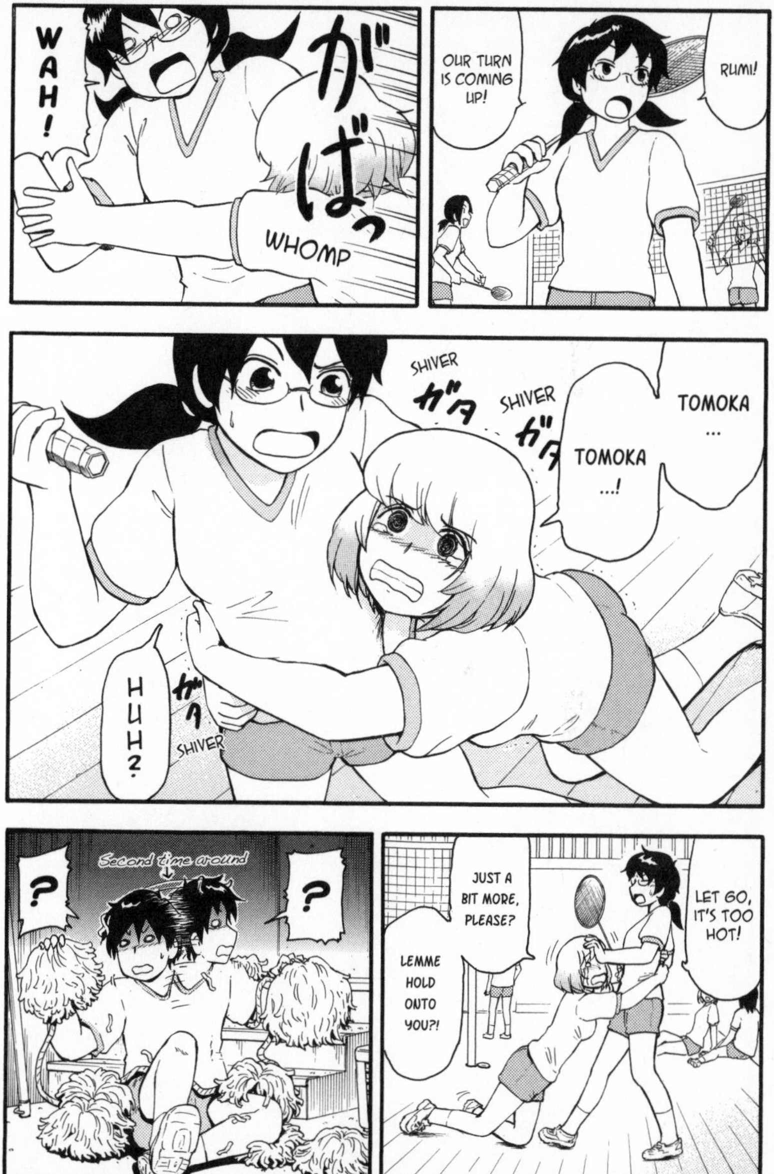
RUMI!
OUR TURN IS COMING UP!
がばっ
WHOMP
WAH!
TOMOKA ...
TOMOKA ...!
SHIVER
ガタ
SHIVER
ガタ
HUH?
ガタ
SHIVER
LET GO, IT'S TOO HOT!
JUST A BIT MORE, PLEASE?
LEMME HOLD ONTO YOU?!
?
Second time around
?

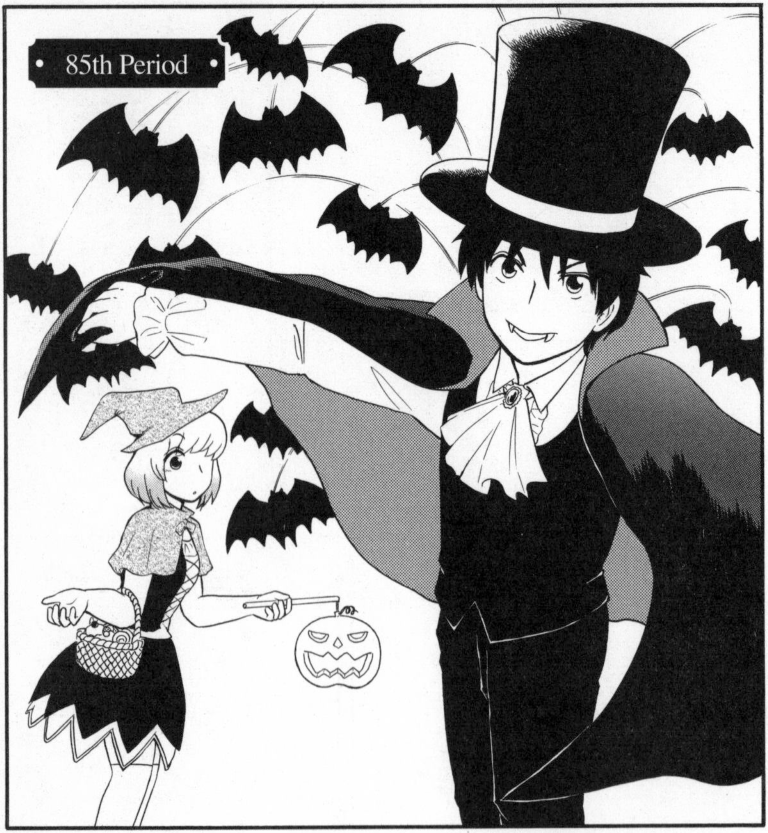
85th Period

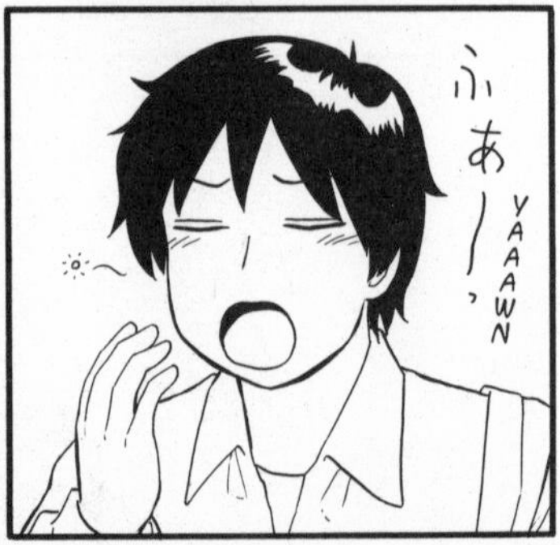
ふあ〜っ
YAAAWN

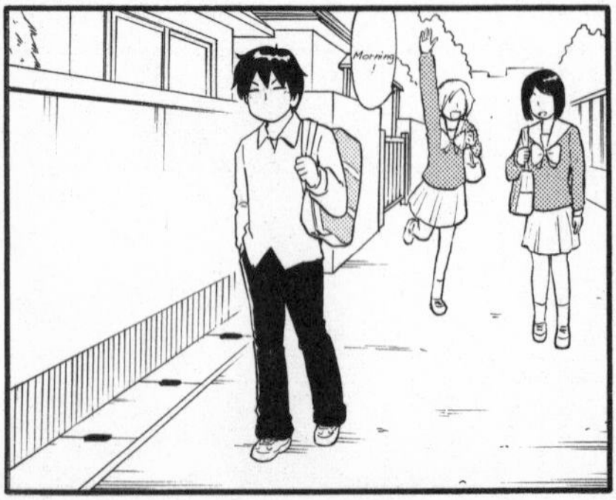
Morning!

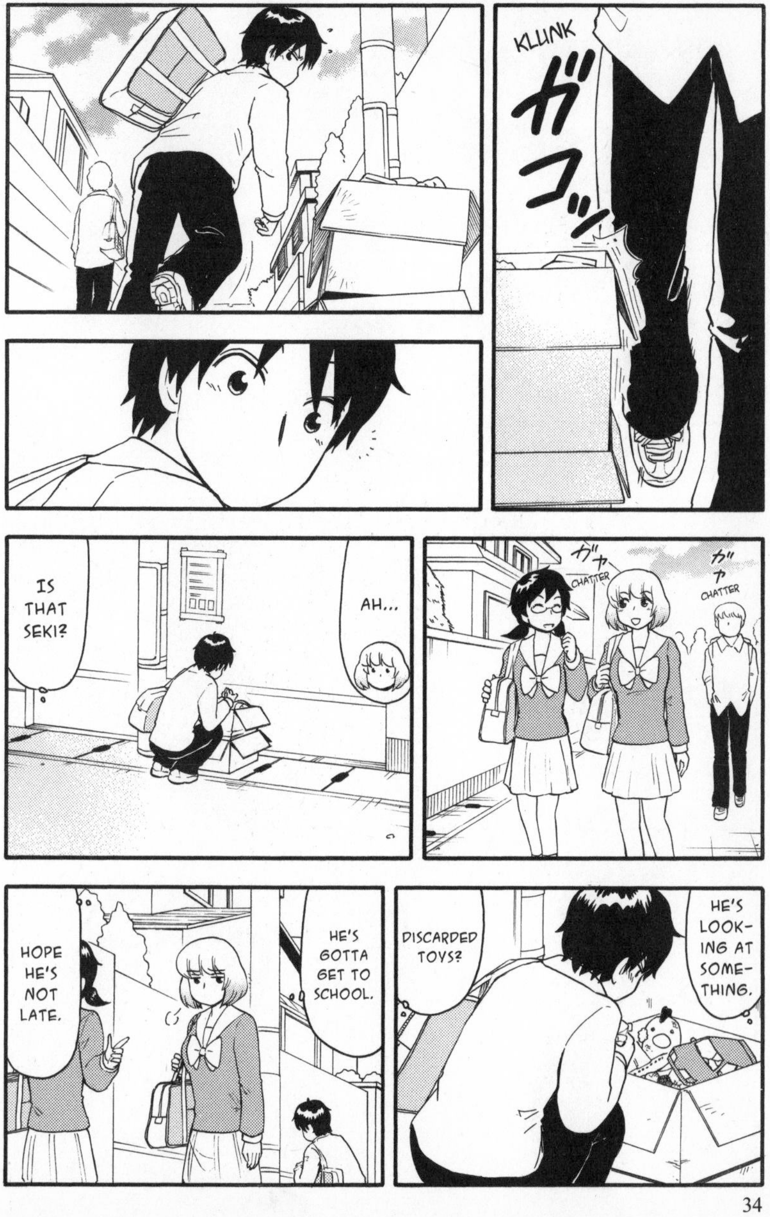
KLUNK
ガコッ
ガヤ
CHATTER
ガヤ
CHATTER
AH...
IS THAT SEKI?
HE'S LOOKING AT SOMETHING.
DISCARDED TOYS?
HE'S GOTTA GET TO SCHOOL.
HOPE HE'S NOT LATE.

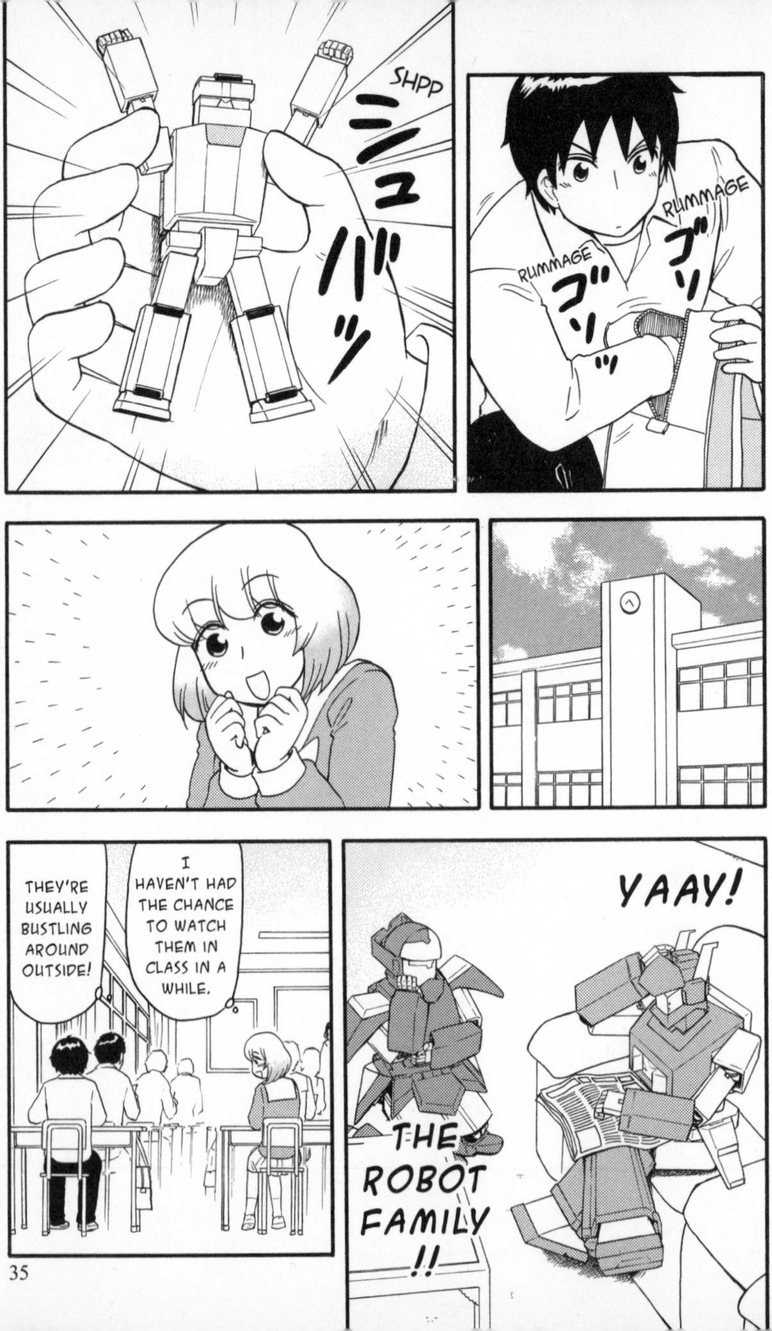
RUMMAGE
ゴソ
RUMMAGE
ゴソッ
SHPP
シュバッ
YAAY!
THE ROBOT FAMILY!!
I HAVEN'T HAD THE CHANCE TO WATCH THEM IN CLASS IN A WHILE.
THEY'RE USUALLY BUSTLING AROUND OUTSIDE!

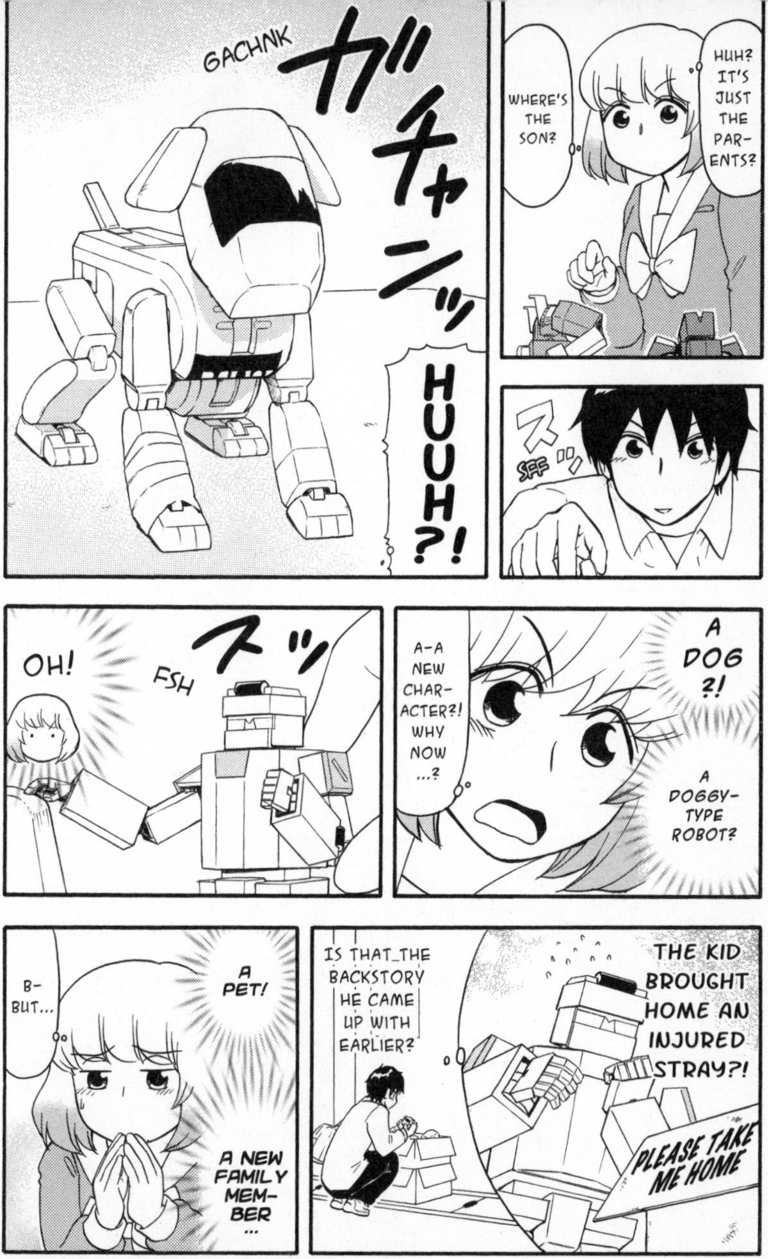
HUH? IT'S JUST THE PARENTS?
WHERE'S THE SON?
SFF
GACHNK
HUUUH?!
A DOG?!
A DOGGY-TYPE ROBOT?
A-A NEW CHARACTER?! WHY NOW ...?
OH!
FSH
THE KID BROUGHT HOME AN INJURED STRAY?!
IS THAT THE BACKSTORY HE CAME UP WITH EARLIER?
PLEASE TAKE ME HOME
A PET!
A NEW FAMILY MEMBER ...
B-BUT...

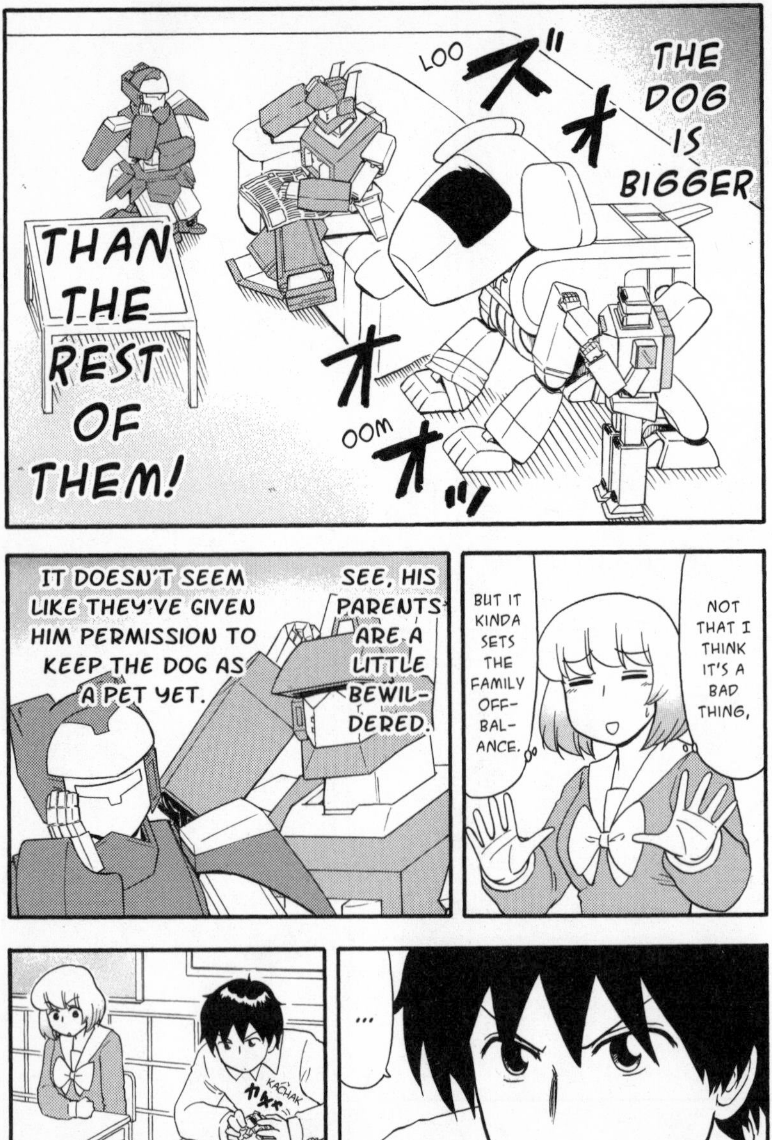
THE DOG IS BIGGER
LOO
ズオ
オ
OOM
オッ
THAN THE REST OF THEM!
NOT THAT I THINK IT'S A BAD THING,
BUT IT KINDA SETS THE FAMILY OFF-BALANCE.
SEE, HIS PARENTS ARE A LITTLE BEWILDERED.
IT DOESN'T SEEM LIKE THEY'VE GIVEN HIM PERMISSION TO KEEP THE DOG AS A PET YET.
...
KACHAK
KACHAK

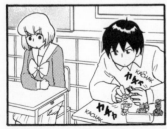

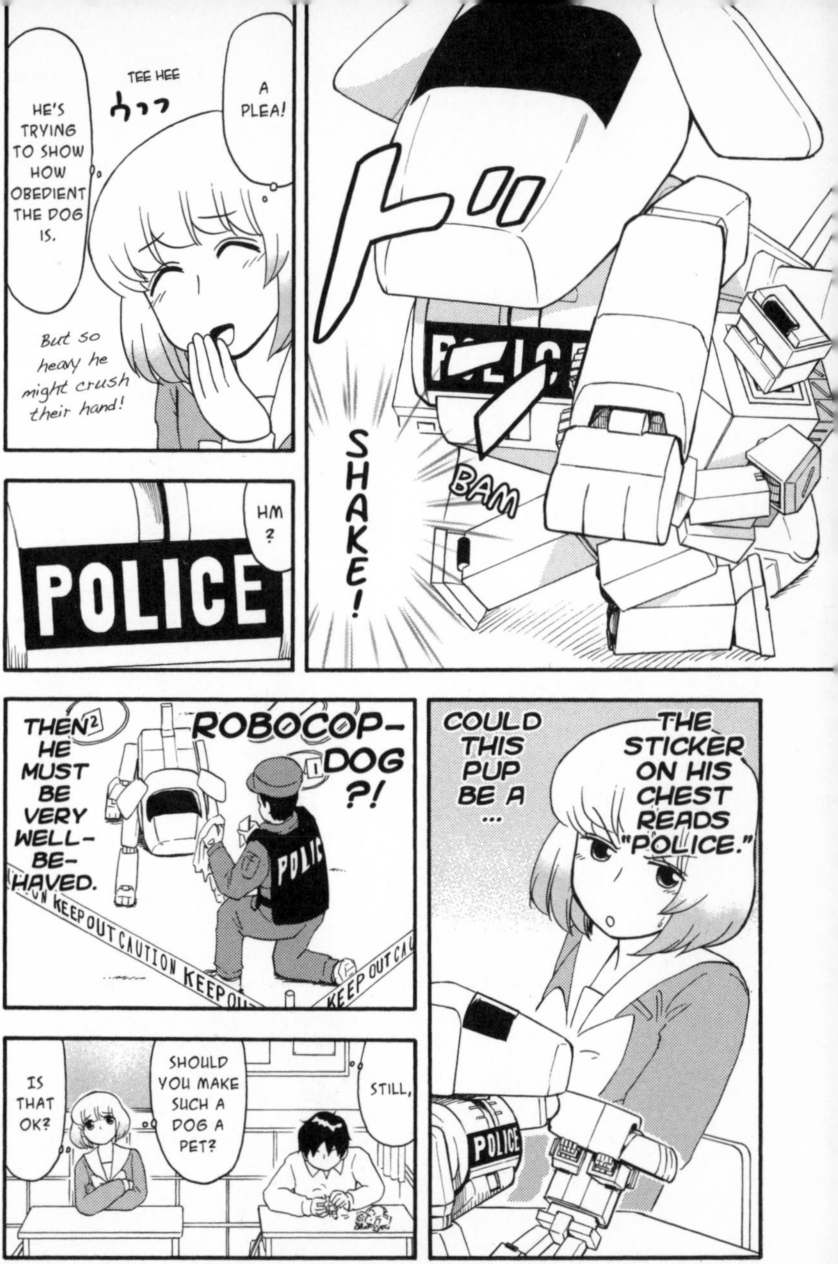
SHAKE!
BAM
POLICE
A PLEA!
TEE HEE
HE'S TRYING TO SHOW HOW OBEDIENT THE DOG IS.
But so heavy he might crush their hand!
HM?
POLICE
THE STICKER ON HIS CHEST READS "POLICE."
COULD THIS PUP BE A ...
POLICE
ROBOCOP-DOG?!
THEN HE MUST BE VERY WELL-BE-HAVED.
POLICE
KEEP OUT CAUTION
STILL,
SHOULD YOU MAKE SUCH A DOG A PET?
IS THAT OK?

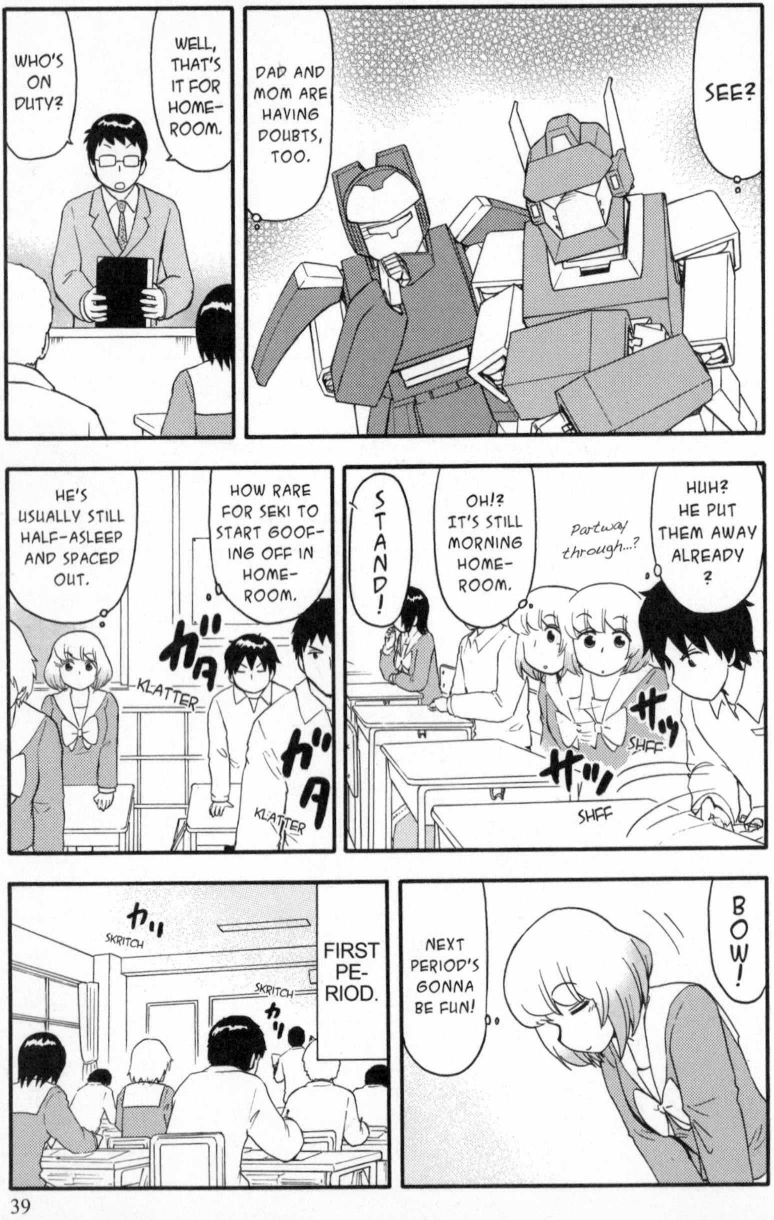
SEE?
DAD AND MOM ARE HAVING DOUBTS, TOO.
WELL, THAT'S IT FOR HOME-ROOM.
WHO'S ON DUTY?
HUH? HE PUT THEM AWAY ALREADY?
Partway through...?
OH!? IT'S STILL MORNING HOME-ROOM.
STAND!
SHFF
SHFF
HOW RARE FOR SEKI TO START GOOF-ING OFF IN HOME-ROOM.
HE'S USUALLY STILL HALF-ASLEEP AND SPACED OUT.
KLATTER
KLATTER
BOW!
NEXT PERIOD'S GONNA BE FUN!
FIRST PE-RIOD.
SKRITCH
SKRITCH

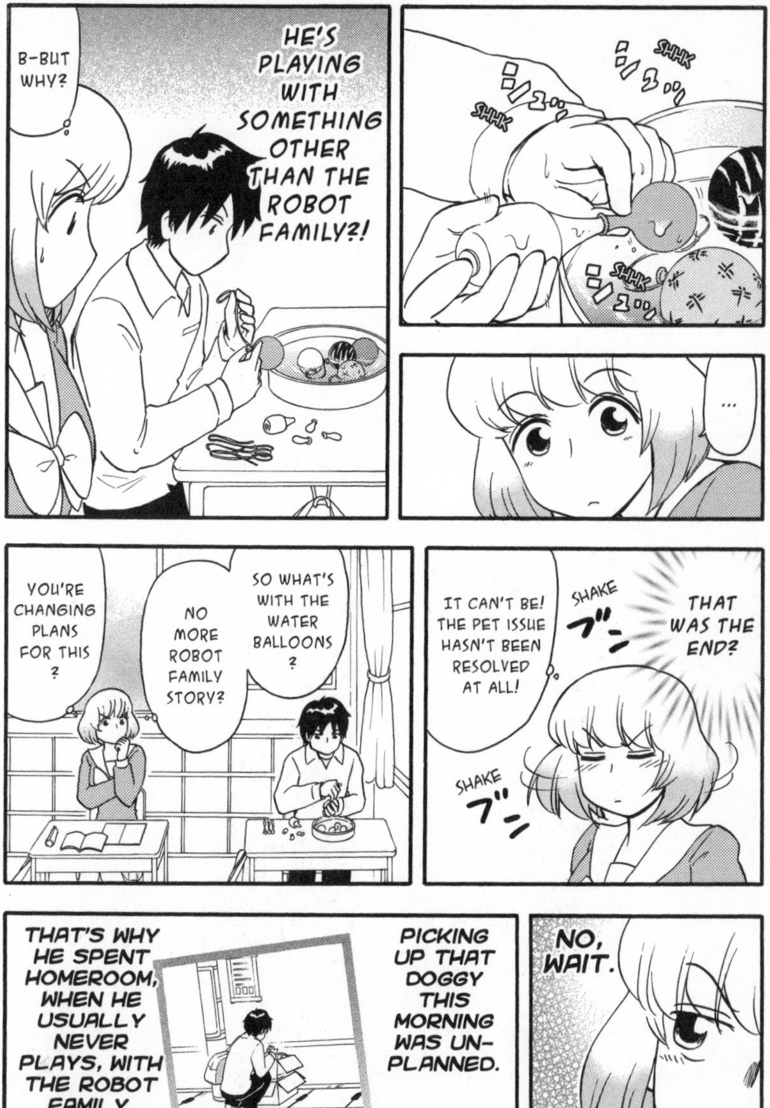
SHHK
SHHK
SHHK
...
B-BUT WHY?
HE'S PLAYING WITH SOMETHING OTHER THAN THE ROBOT FAMILY?!
THAT WAS THE END?
SHAKE
IT CAN'T BE! THE PET ISSUE HASN'T BEEN RESOLVED AT ALL!
SHAKE
SO WHAT'S WITH THE WATER BALLOONS?
NO MORE ROBOT FAMILY STORY?
YOU'RE CHANGING PLANS FOR THIS?
NO, WAIT.
PICKING UP THAT DOGGY THIS MORNING WAS UN-PLANNED.
THAT'S WHY HE SPENT HOMEROOM, WHEN HE USUALLY NEVER PLAYS, WITH THE ROBOT FAMILY.

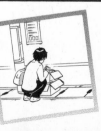

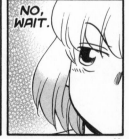

IT'S HIGHLY LIKELY HE'LL BRING THEM BACK OUT BETWEEN CLASSES!

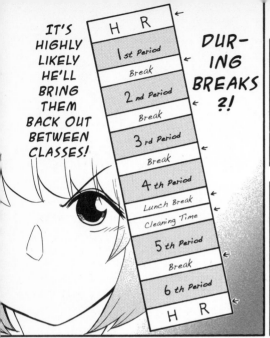

H	R
1st Period	
Break	
2nd Period	
Break	
3rd Period	
Break	
4th Period	
Lunch Break	
Cleaning Time	
5th Period	
Break	
6th Period	
H	R

DUR- ING BREAKS ?!

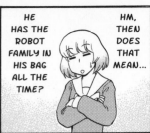

HE HAS THE ROBOT FAMILY IN HIS BAG ALL THE TIME?

HM, THEN DOES THAT MEAN...

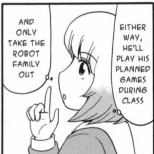

AND ONLY TAKE THE ROBOT FAMILY OUT

EITHER WAY, HE'LL PLAY HIS PLANNED GAMES DURING CLASS

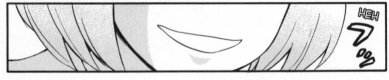

HEH

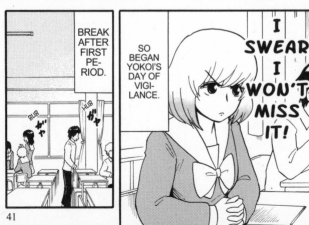

BREAK AFTER FIRST PE- RIOD.

BUB GA

HUB GA

SO BEGAN YOKOI'S DAY OF VIGI- LANCE.

I SWEAR I WON'T MISS IT!

41

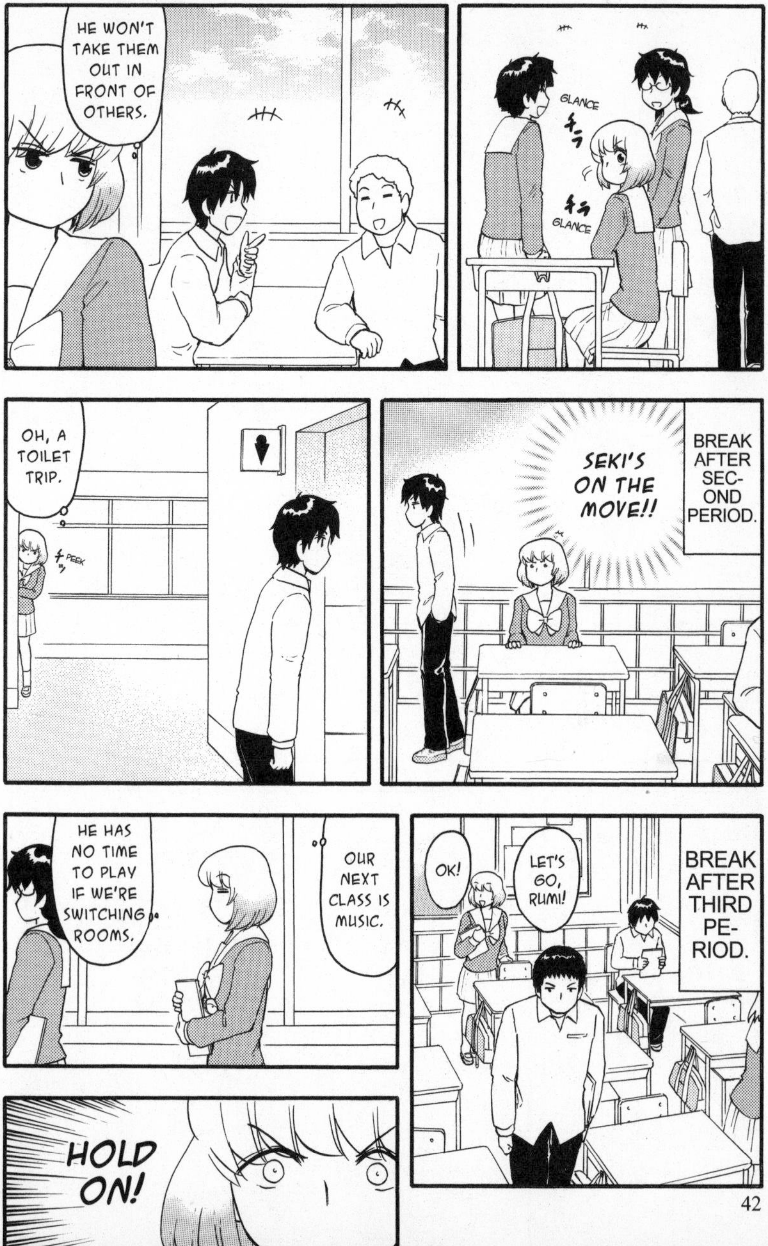
GLANCE
GLANCE
HE WON'T TAKE THEM OUT IN FRONT OF OTHERS.
BREAK AFTER SECOND PERIOD.
SEKI'S ON THE MOVE!!
OH, A TOILET TRIP.
PEEK
BREAK AFTER THIRD PERIOD.
LET'S GO, RUMI!
OK!
OUR NEXT CLASS IS MUSIC.
HE HAS NO TIME TO PLAY IF WE'RE SWITCHING ROOMS.
HOLD ON!

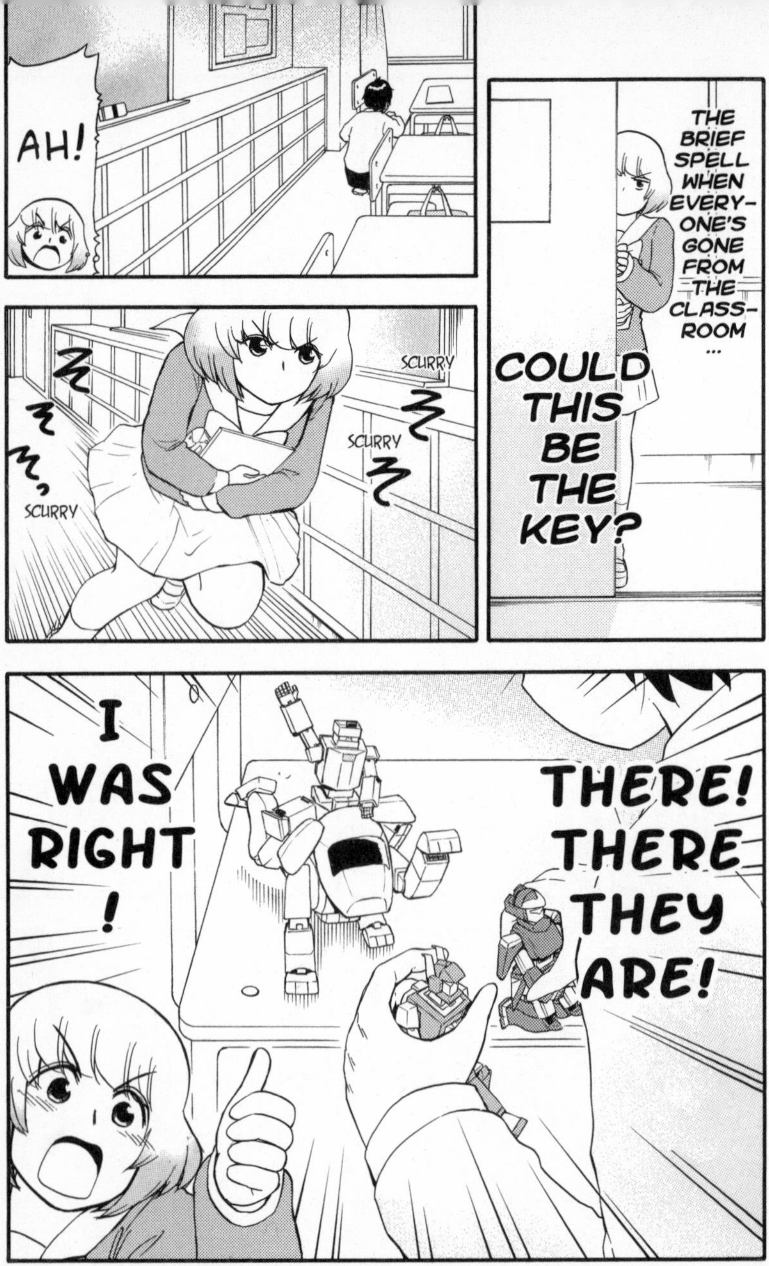
THE BRIEF SPELL WHEN EVERYONE'S GONE FROM THE CLASSROOM ...
COULD THIS BE THE KEY?
AH!
SCURRY
SCURRY
SCURRY
THERE! THERE THEY ARE!
I WAS RIGHT!

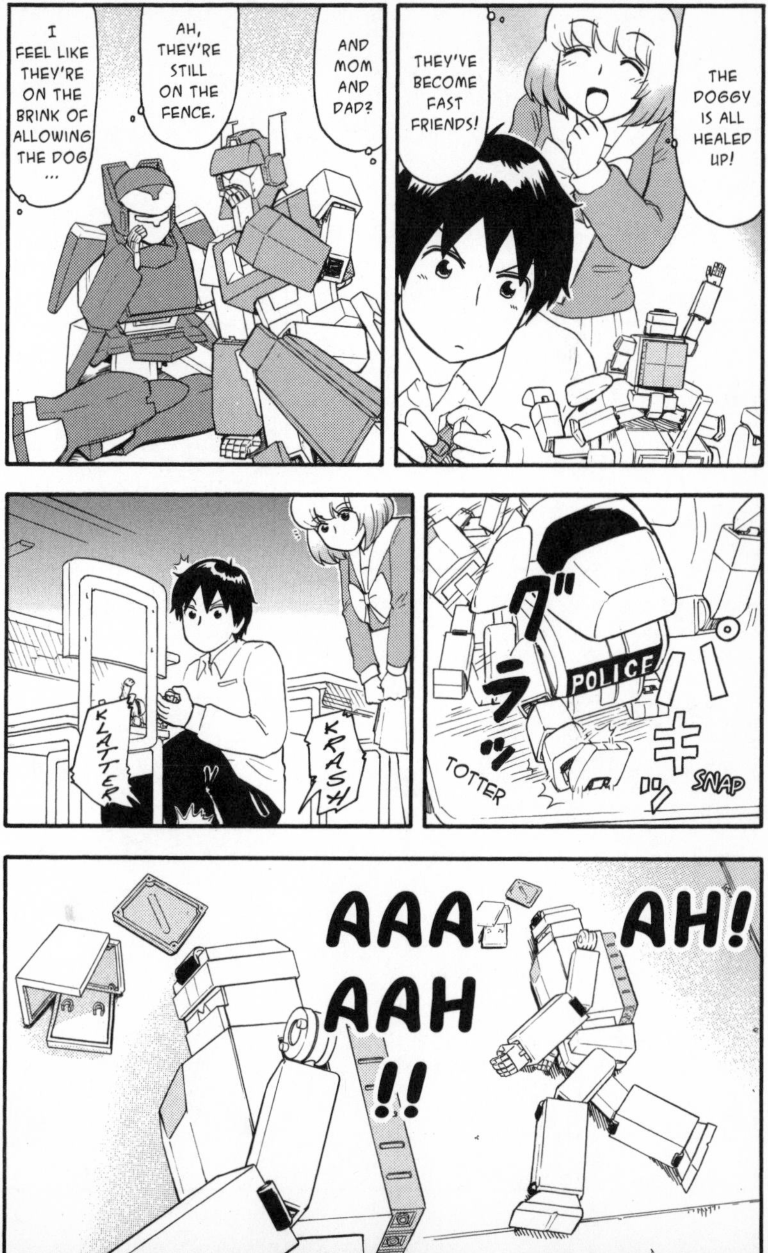
THE DOGGY IS ALL HEALED UP!
THEY'VE BECOME FAST FRIENDS!
AND MOM AND DAD?
AH, THEY'RE STILL ON THE FENCE.
I FEEL LIKE THEY'RE ON THE BRINK OF ALLOWING THE DOG ...
グラッ
TOTTER
ハキッ
SNAP
KRASH
KLATTER
AAA AH!
AAH
!!

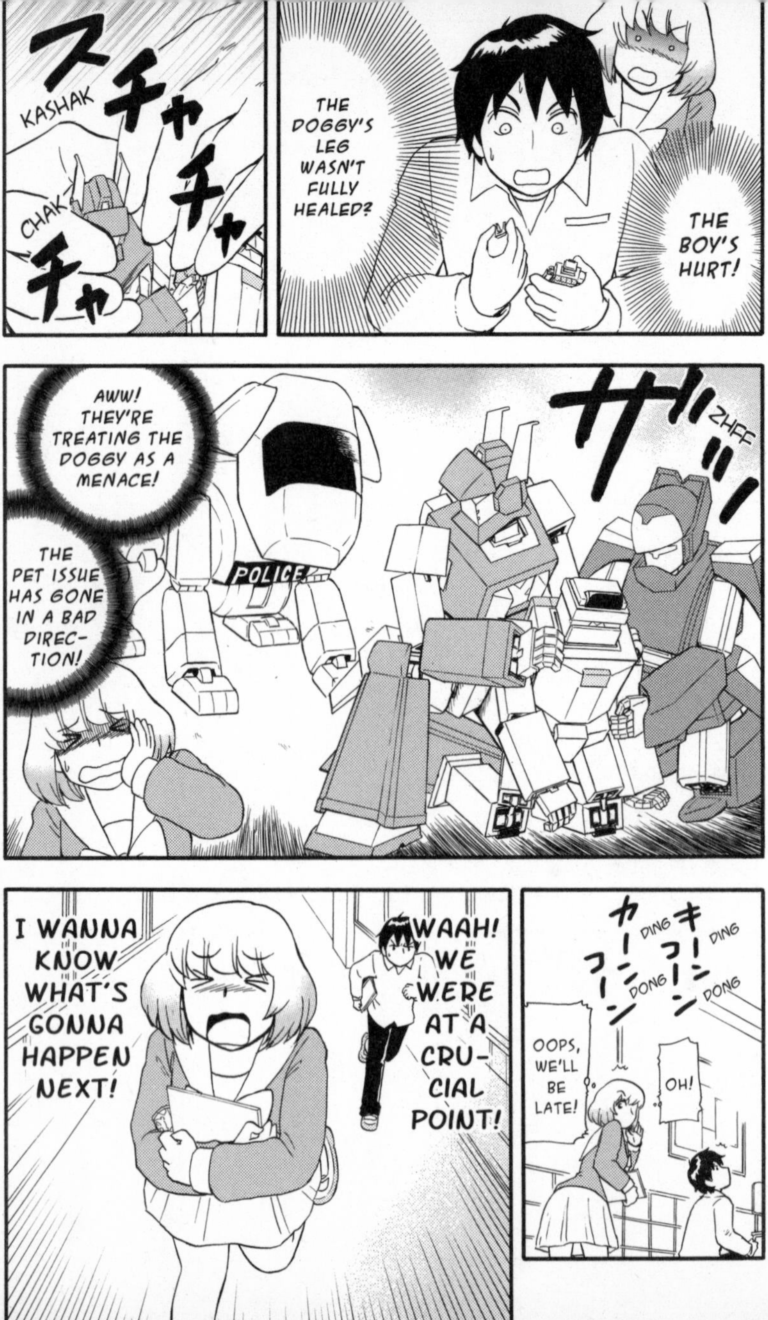
THE DOGGY'S LEG WASN'T FULLY HEALED?
THE BOY'S HURT!
スチャチャチャ
KASHAK
CHAK
ザッ
ZHFF
AWW! THEY'RE TREATING THE DOGGY AS A MENACE!
POLICE
THE PET ISSUE HAS GONE IN A BAD DIREC-TION!
キーンコーン
DING DONG
カーンコーン
DING DONG
OH!
OOPS, WE'LL BE LATE!
WAAH! WE WERE AT A CRU-CIAL POINT!
I WANNA KNOW WHAT'S GONNA HAPPEN NEXT!

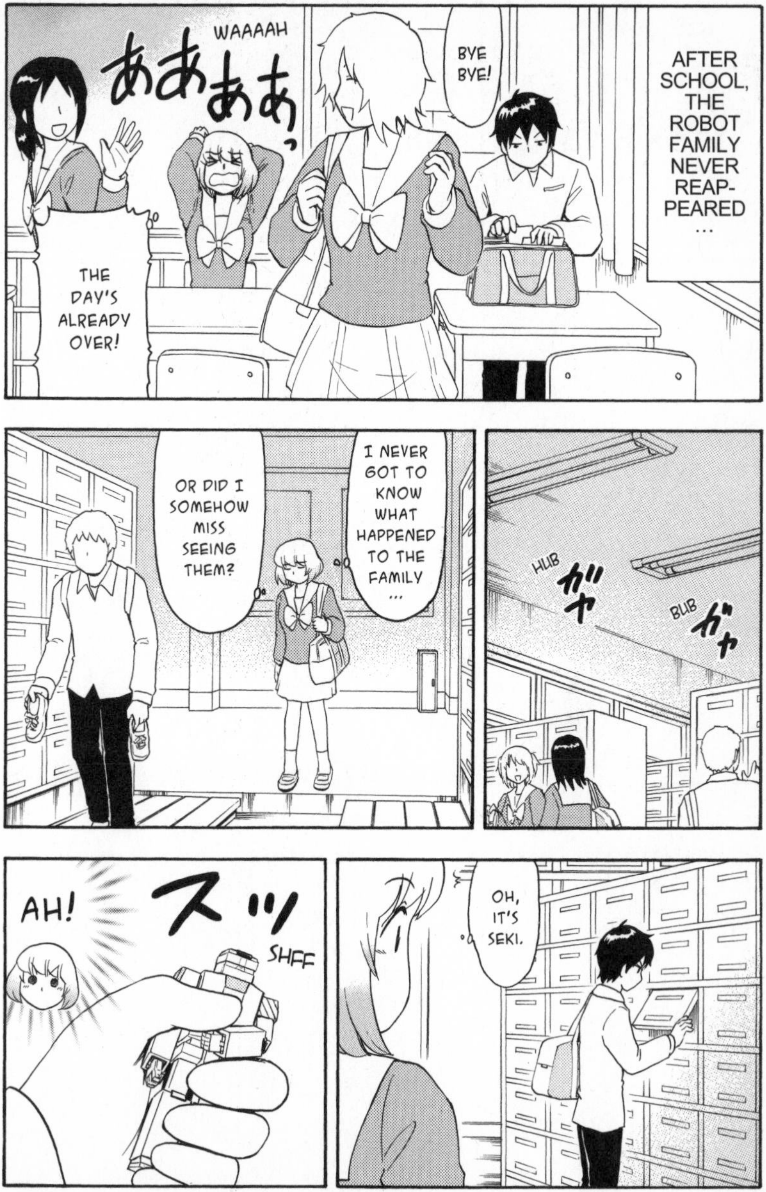

AFTER SCHOOL, THE ROBOT FAMILY NEVER REAP-PEARED ...
BYE BYE!
WAAAAH
ああああっ
THE DAY'S ALREADY OVER!
HUB
ガヤ
BUB
ガヤ
I NEVER GOT TO KNOW WHAT HAPPENED TO THE FAMILY ...
OR DID I SOMEHOW MISS SEEING THEM?
OH, IT'S SEKI.
スッ
SHFF
AH!

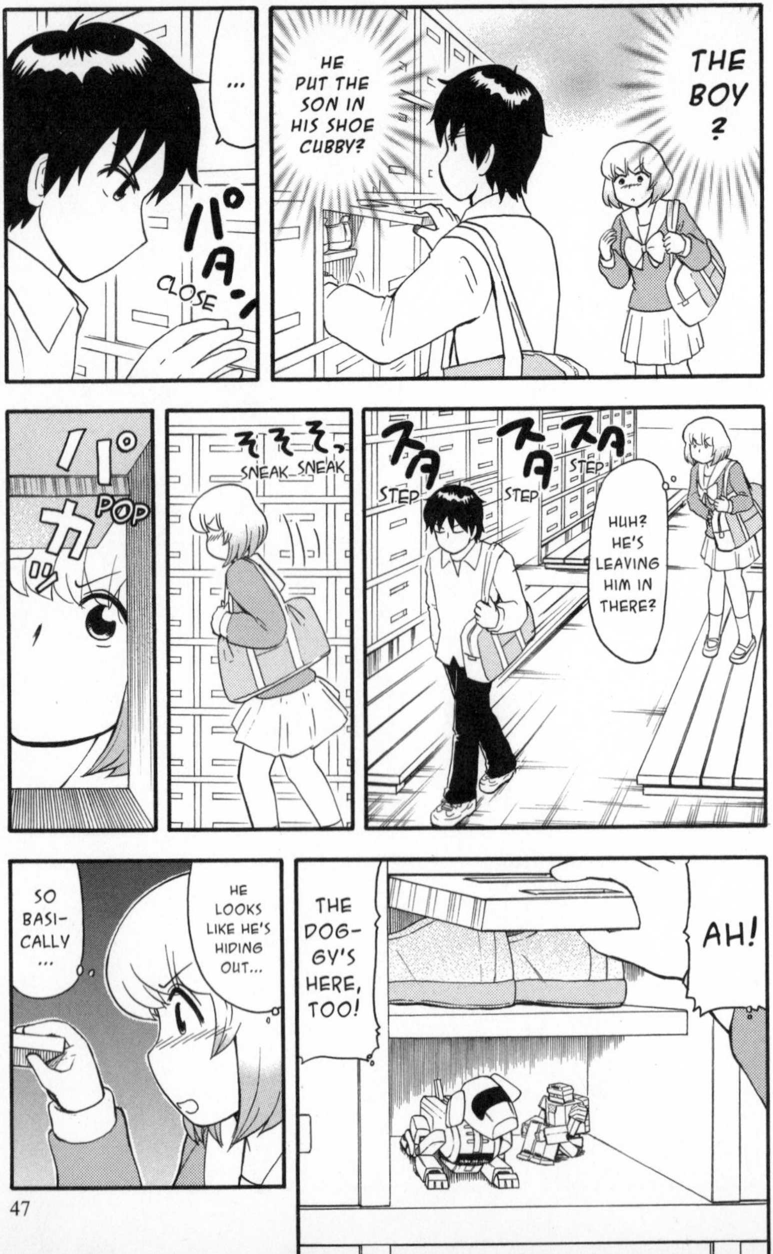
THE BOY?
HE PUT THE SON IN HIS SHOE CUBBY?
...
パタン
CLOSE
スタ
STEP
HUH? HE'S LEAVING HIM IN THERE?
スタ
STEP
スタ
STEP
そそそっ
SNEAK SNEAK
パカッ
POP
AH!
THE DOG-GY'S HERE, TOO!
HE LOOKS LIKE HE'S HIDING OUT...
SO BASI-CALLY ...

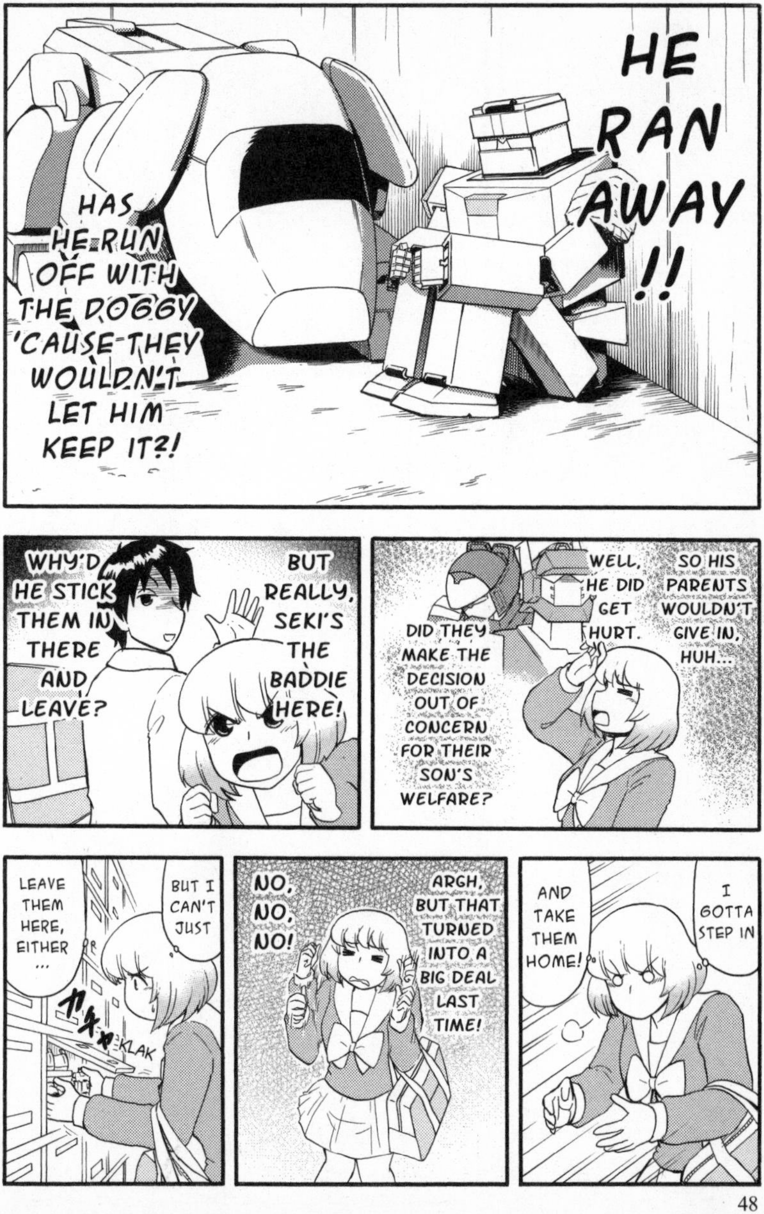
HE RAN AWAY!!
HAS HE RUN OFF WITH THE DOGGY 'CAUSE THEY WOULDN'T LET HIM KEEP IT?!
SO HIS PARENTS WOULDN'T GIVE IN, HUH...
WELL, HE DID GET HURT.
DID THEY MAKE THE DECISION OUT OF CONCERN FOR THEIR SON'S WELFARE?
BUT REALLY, SEKI'S THE BADDIE HERE!
WHY'D HE STICK THEM IN THERE AND LEAVE?
I GOTTA STEP IN
AND TAKE THEM HOME!
ARGH, BUT THAT TURNED INTO A BIG DEAL LAST TIME!
NO, NO, NO!
BUT I CAN'T JUST
LEAVE THEM HERE, EITHER ...
KLAK

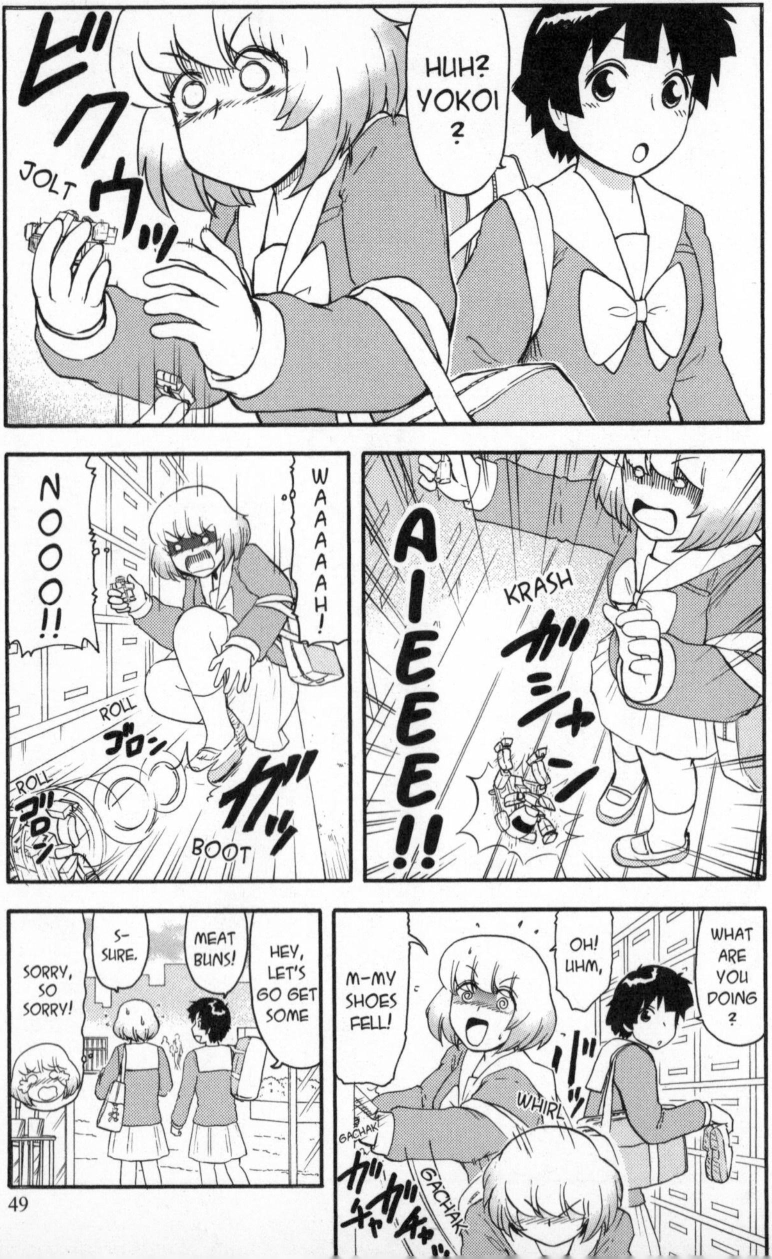
ビクウッ
JOLT
HUH? YOKOI?
AIEEE!!
KRASH
ガシャーン
WAAAAAAH!
NOOOO!!
ROLL
ゴロン
ROLL
ゴロン
ガッ
BOOT
WHAT ARE YOU DOING?
OH! UHM,
M-MY SHOES FELL!
WHIRL
GACHAK
GACHAK
HEY, LET'S GO GET SOME
MEAT BUNS!
S-SURE.
SORRY, SO SORRY!

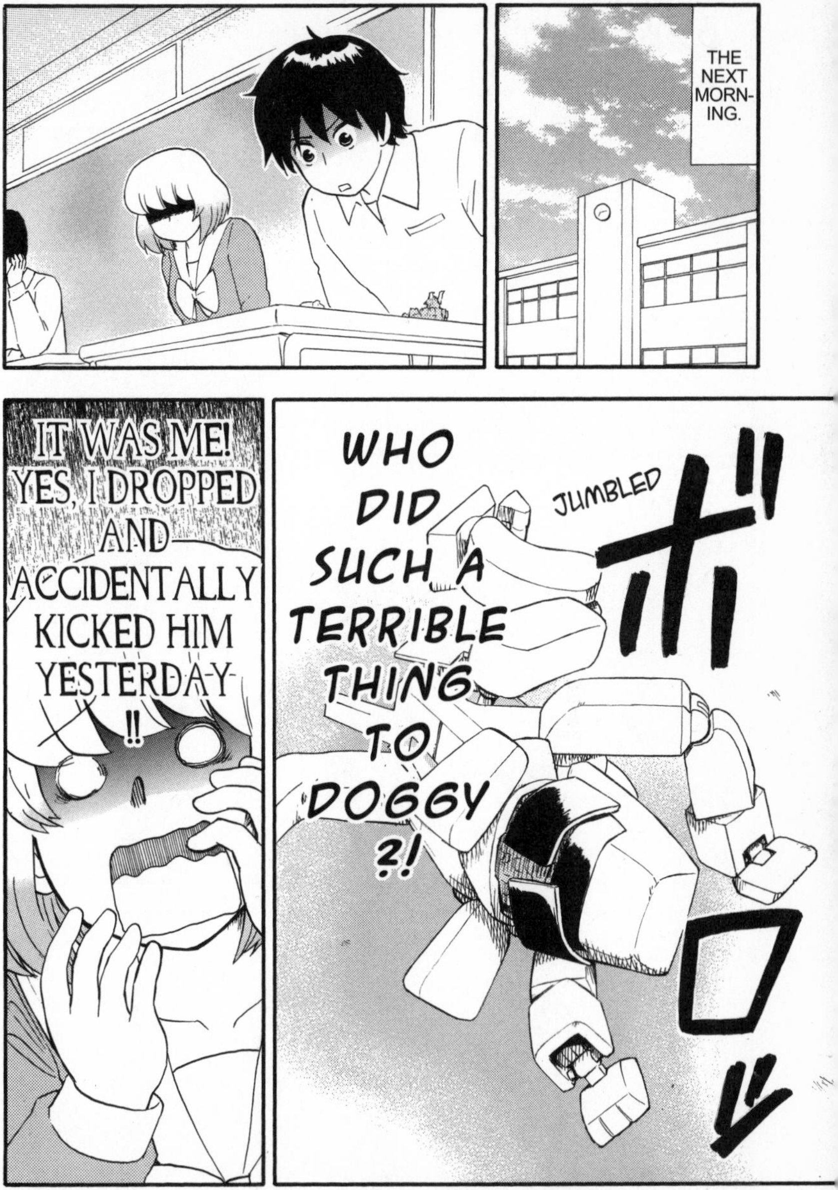
THE NEXT MORN-ING.
WHO DID SUCH A TERRIBLE THING TO DOGGY ?!
JUMBLED
IT WAS ME! YES, I DROPPED AND ACCIDENTALLY KICKED HIM YESTERDAY !!

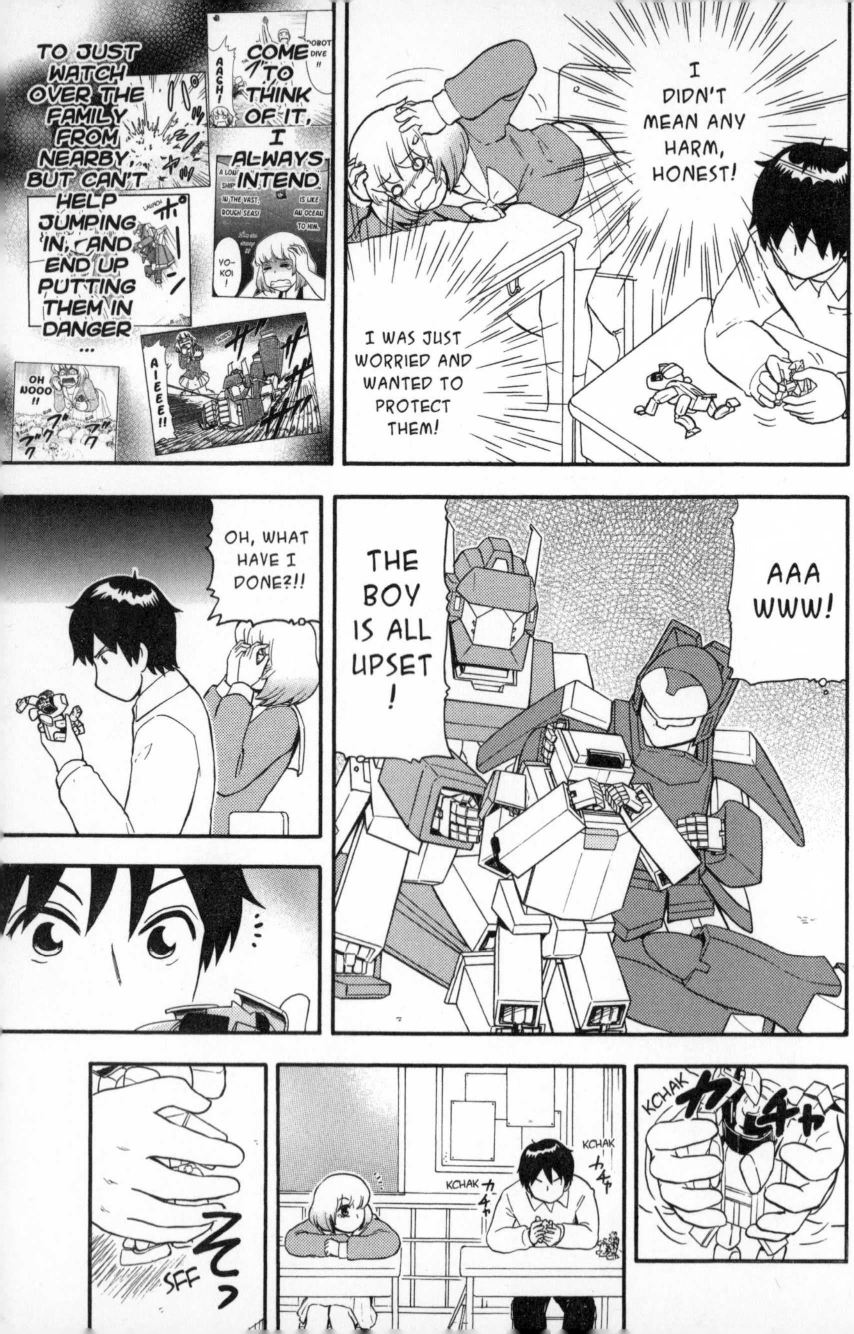
I DIDN'T MEAN ANY HARM, HONEST!
I WAS JUST WORRIED AND WANTED TO PROTECT THEM!
COME TO THINK OF IT, I ALWAYS INTEND
TO JUST WATCH OVER THE FAMILY FROM NEARBY, BUT CAN'T HELP JUMPING IN, AND END UP PUTTING THEM IN DANGER...
ROBOT DIVE !!
AAGH!
A LONE SHIP IN THE VAST, ROUGH SEAS!
IS LIKE AN OCEAN TO HIM.
YO-KOI!
LAUNCH
AIEEE!!
OH NOOO !!
AAA WWW!
THE BOY IS ALL UPSET!
OH, WHAT HAVE I DONE?!!
KCHAK
KCHAK
KCHAK
SFF

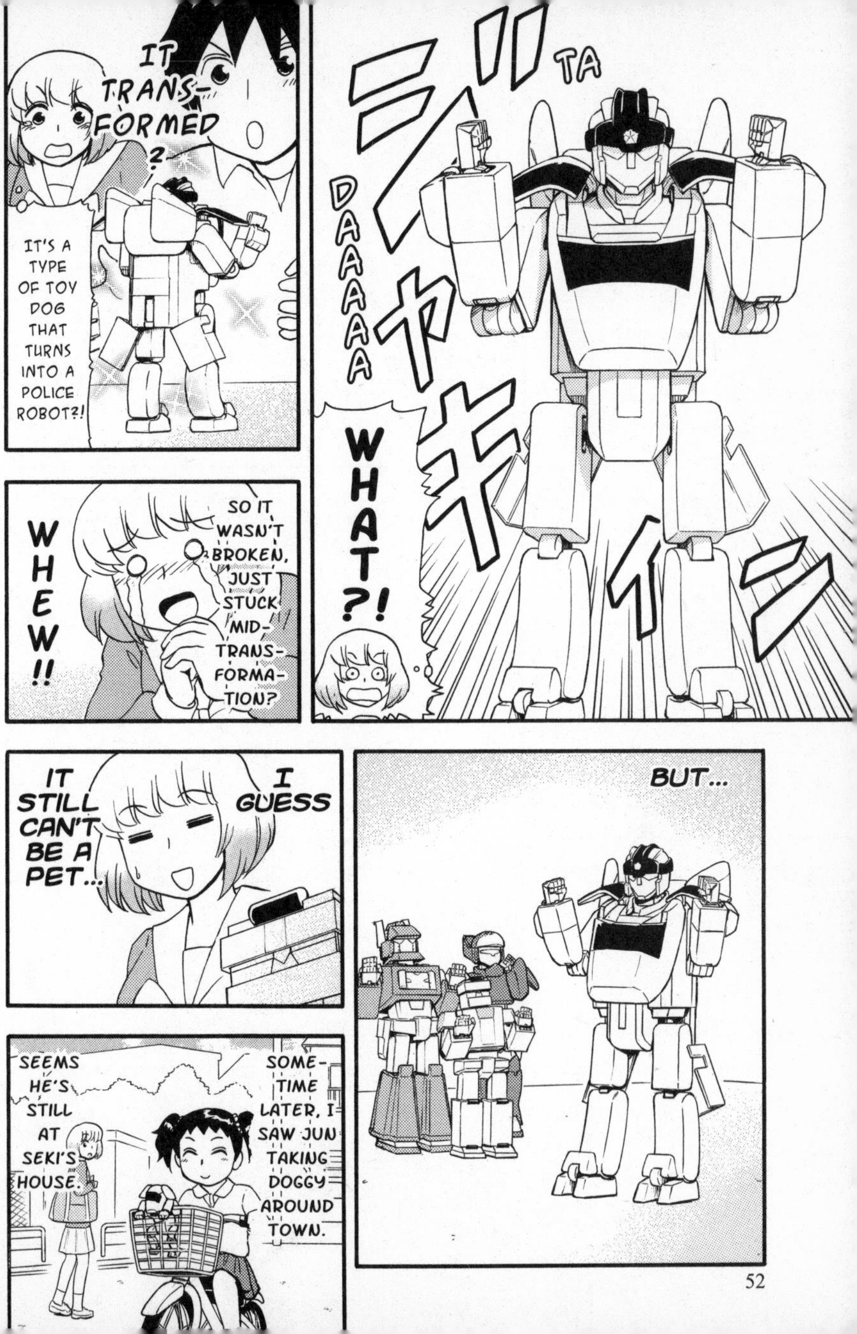

ジャキイン
TA DAAAAAA
WHAT?!
IT TRANSFORMED?
IT'S A TYPE OF TOY DOG THAT TURNS INTO A POLICE ROBOT?!
SO IT WASN'T BROKEN, JUST STUCK MID-TRANSFORMATION?
WHEW!!
BUT...
I GUESS
IT STILL CAN'T BE A PET...
SOMETIME LATER, I SAW JUN TAKING DOGGY AROUND TOWN.
SEEMS HE'S STILL AT SEKI'S HOUSE.

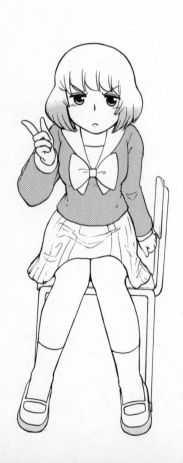

My Neighbor Seki

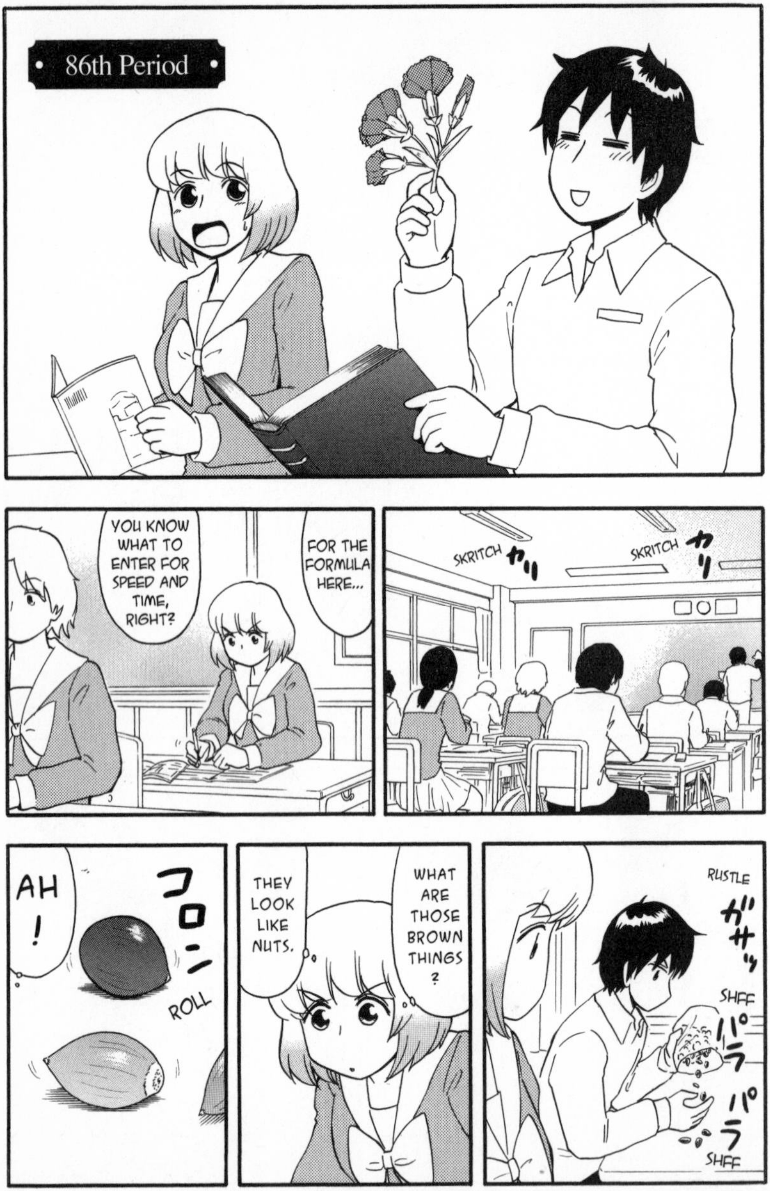
86th Period
SKRITCH カリ
SKRITCH カリ
FOR THE FORMULA HERE...
YOU KNOW WHAT TO ENTER FOR SPEED AND TIME, RIGHT?
RUSTLE ガサッ
SHFF パラ
パラ SHFF
WHAT ARE THOSE BROWN THINGS?
THEY LOOK LIKE NUTS.
AH!
コロン ROLL

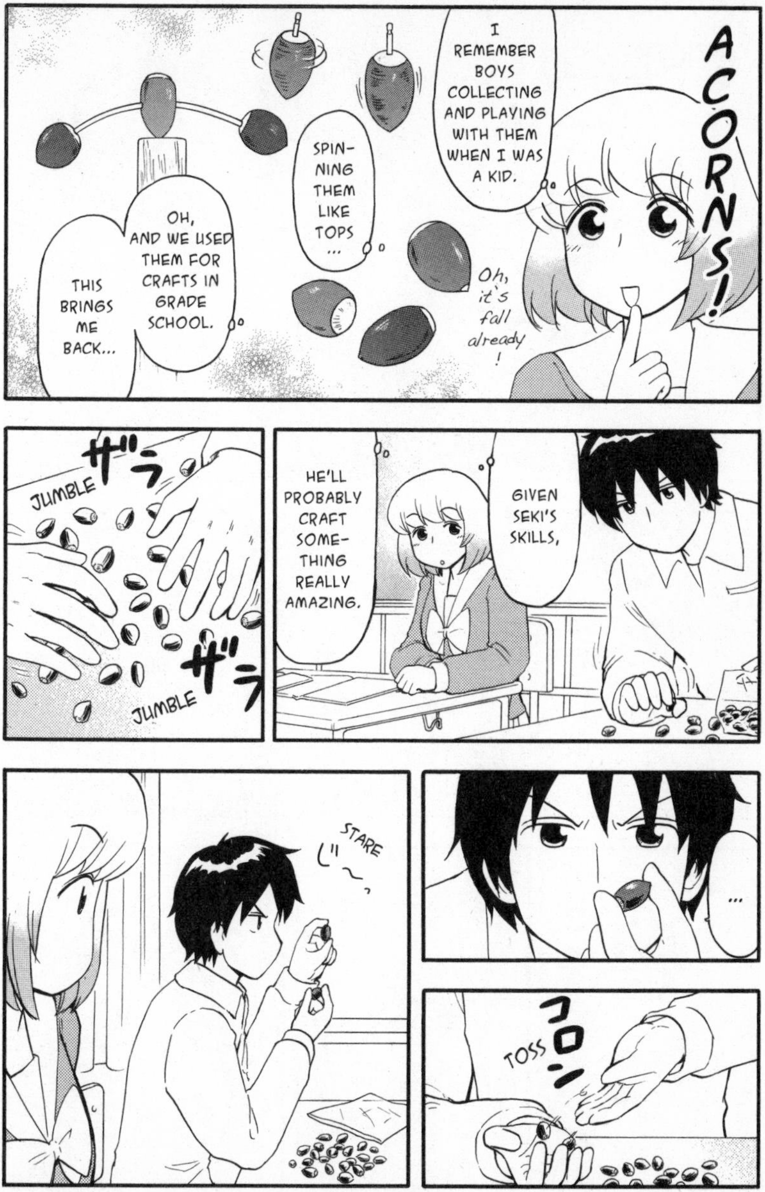
ACORNS!
I REMEMBER BOYS COLLECTING AND PLAYING WITH THEM WHEN I WAS A KID.
Oh, it's fall already!
SPIN-NING THEM LIKE TOPS ...
OH, AND WE USED THEM FOR CRAFTS IN GRADE SCHOOL.
THIS BRINGS ME BACK...
GIVEN SEKI'S SKILLS,
HE'LL PROBABLY CRAFT SOME-THING REALLY AMAZING.
ザラ JUMBLE
ザラ JUMBLE
...
コロン TOSS
じ~ STARE

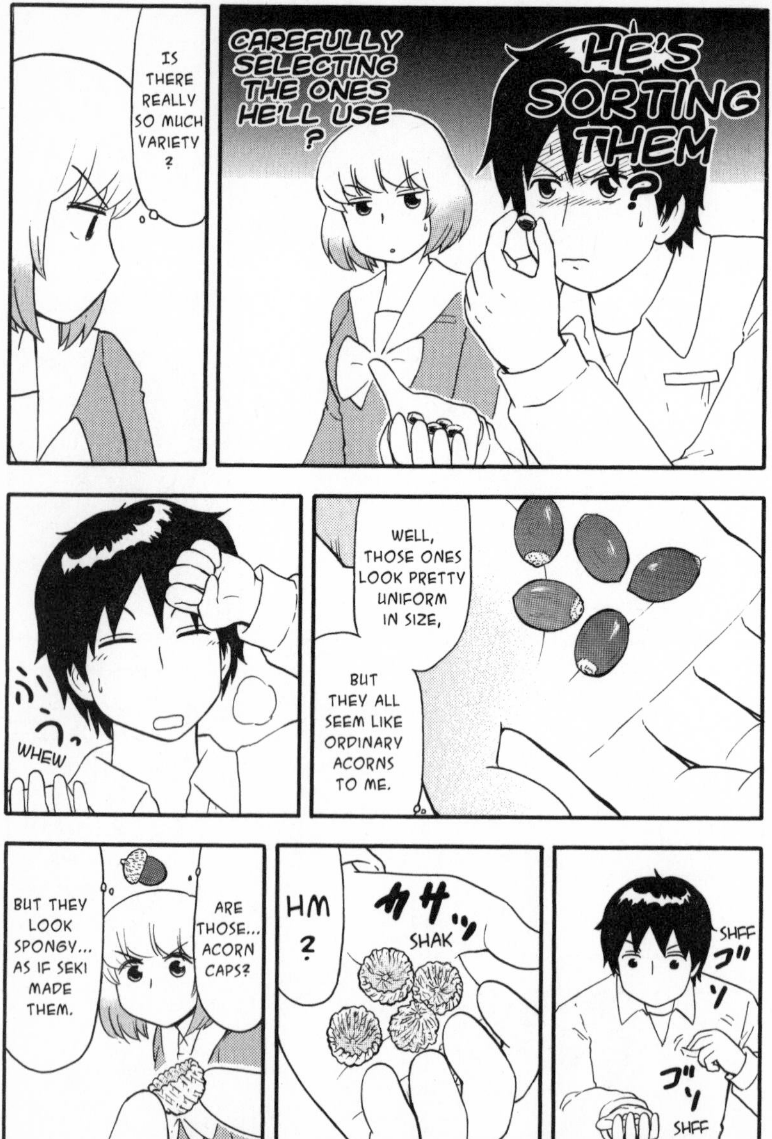
HE'S SORTING THEM?
CAREFULLY SELECTING THE ONES HE'LL USE?
IS THERE REALLY SO MUCH VARIETY?
WELL, THOSE ONES LOOK PRETTY UNIFORM IN SIZE,
BUT THEY ALL SEEM LIKE ORDINARY ACORNS TO ME.
WHEW
SHFF
ゴソ
ゴソ
SHFF
カサッ
SHAK
HM?
ARE THOSE... ACORN CAPS?
BUT THEY LOOK SPONGY... AS IF SEKI MADE THEM.

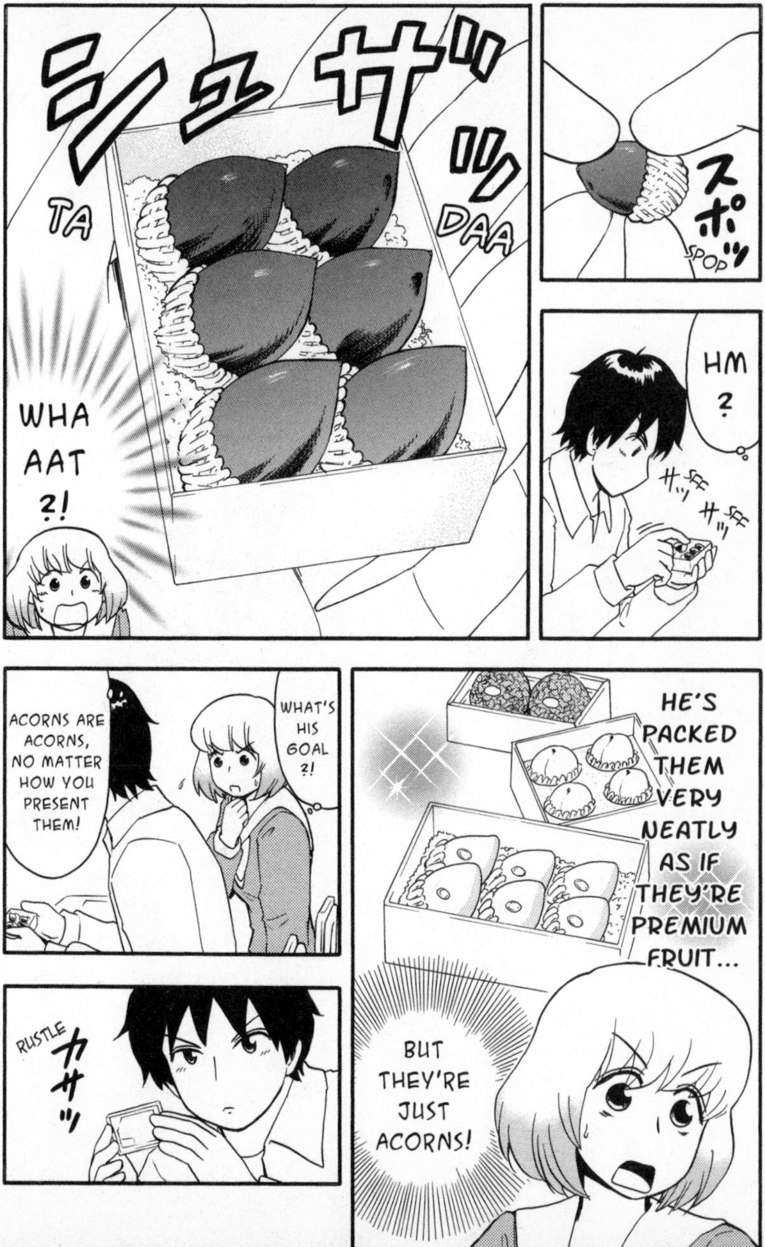
スポッ
SPOP
HM?
サッ SFF
サッ SFF
シュザッ
TA DAA
WHAAAT?!
HE'S PACKED THEM VERY NEATLY AS IF THEY'RE PREMIUM FRUIT...
BUT THEY'RE JUST ACORNS!
WHAT'S HIS GOAL?!
ACORNS ARE ACORNS, NO MATTER HOW YOU PRESENT THEM!
RUSTLE
カサッ

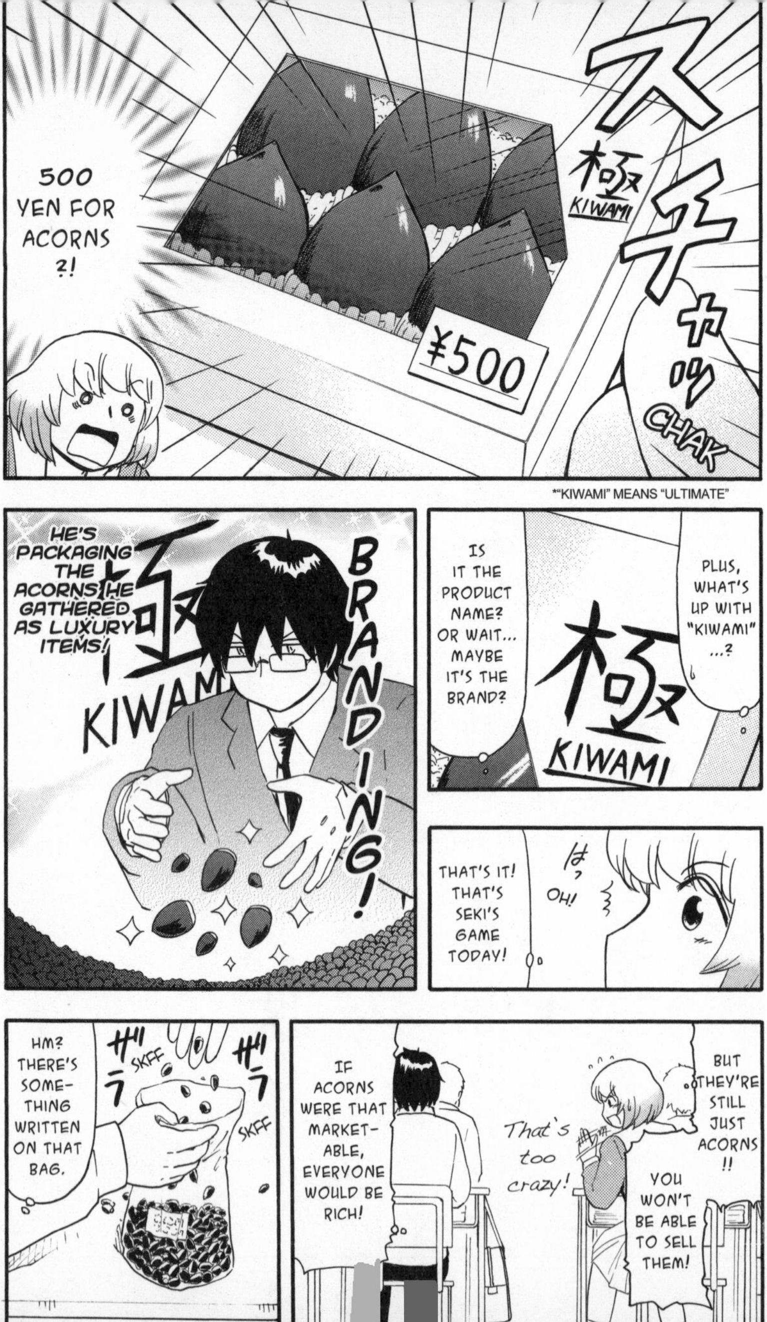
スチャッ
極
KIWAMI
¥500
500 YEN FOR ACORNS ?!
CHAK
*"KIWAMI" MEANS "ULTIMATE"
PLUS, WHAT'S UP WITH "KIWAMI" ...?
極
KIWAMI
IS IT THE PRODUCT NAME? OR WAIT... MAYBE IT'S THE BRAND?
はっ
OH!
THAT'S IT! THAT'S SEKI'S GAME TODAY!
BRANDING!
極
KIWAMI
HE'S PACKAGING THE ACORNS HE GATHERED AS LUXURY ITEMS!
BUT THEY'RE STILL JUST ACORNS!!
YOU WON'T BE ABLE TO SELL THEM!
That's too crazy!
IF ACORNS WERE THAT MARKET-ABLE, EVERYONE WOULD BE RICH!
ザラ
SKFF
ザラ
SKFF
HM? THERE'S SOME-THING WRITTEN ON THAT BAG.

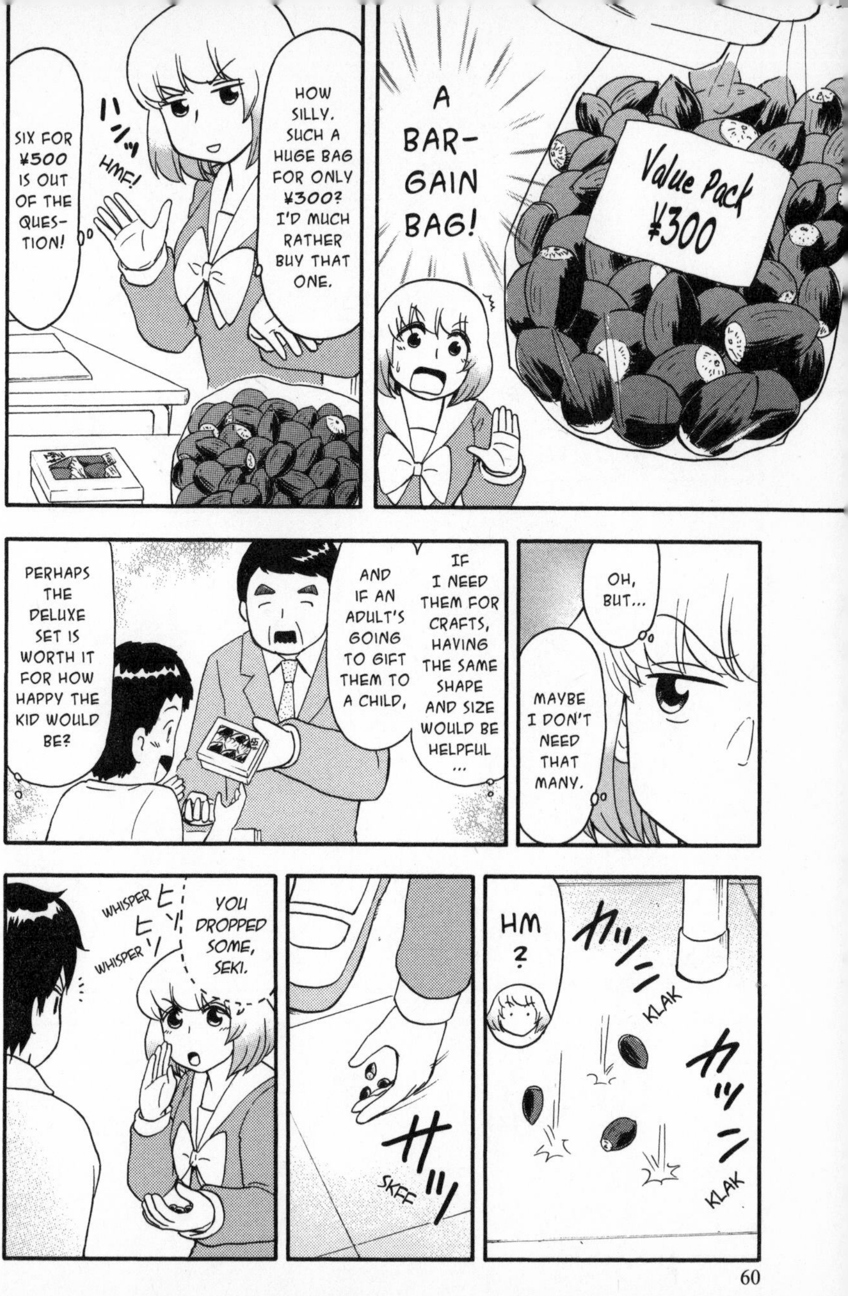
A BAR-GAIN BAG!
Value Pack ¥300
HOW SILLY. SUCH A HUGE BAG FOR ONLY ¥300? I'D MUCH RATHER BUY THAT ONE.
ハッ HMF!
SIX FOR ¥500 IS OUT OF THE QUES-TION!
OH, BUT...
MAYBE I DON'T NEED THAT MANY.
IF I NEED THEM FOR CRAFTS, HAVING THE SAME SHAPE AND SIZE WOULD BE HELPFUL ...
AND IF AN ADULT'S GOING TO GIFT THEM TO A CHILD,
PERHAPS THE DELUXE SET IS WORTH IT FOR HOW HAPPY THE KID WOULD BE?
HM ?
カッ KLAK
カッ KLAK
サッ SKFF
ヒソ WHISPER
ヒソ WHISPER
YOU DROPPED SOME, SEKI.

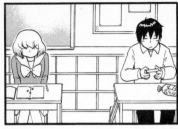

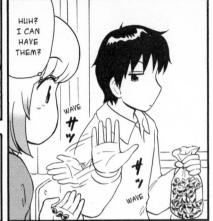

HUH? I CAN HAVE THEM?
WAVE
サッ
サッ
WAVE
チラッ
GLANCE
IF YOU'RE GONNA GIVE ME SOME,
I'D RATHER HAVE THE "KIWAMI"...
¥500
OH!
ハッ
DON'T BE DUPED! THEY'RE ALL THE SAME, REMEMBER?!
I CAN'T FALL FOR SEKI'S BUSINESS SCHEME!
DON'T BE A FOOLISH CONSUMER WHO SPENDS MONEY ON THE SAME PRODUCT THAT'S JUST PACKAGED DIFFER-ENTLY!

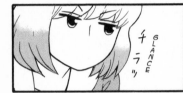

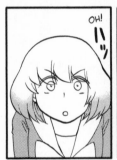

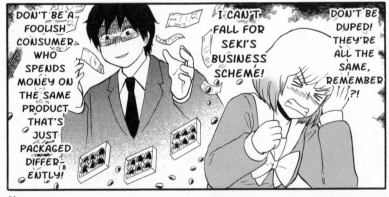

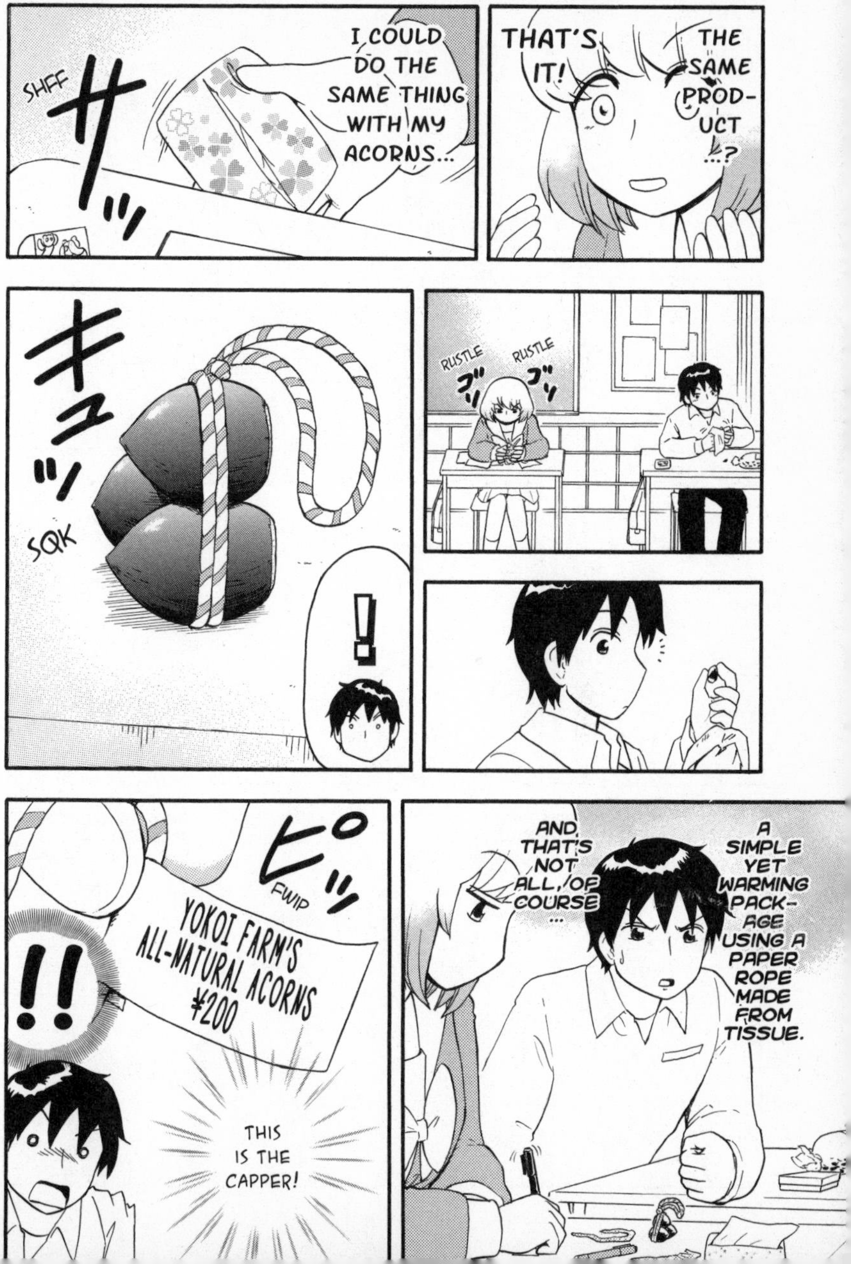

THE SAME PRODUCT ...?
THAT'S IT!
SHFF
I COULD DO THE SAME THING WITH MY ACORNS...
RUSTLE
RUSTLE
SQK
!
A SIMPLE YET WARMING PACKAGE USING A PAPER ROPE MADE FROM TISSUE.
AND THAT'S NOT ALL, OF COURSE ...
FWIP
YOKOI FARM'S ALL-NATURAL ACORNS ¥200
!!
THIS IS THE CAPPER!

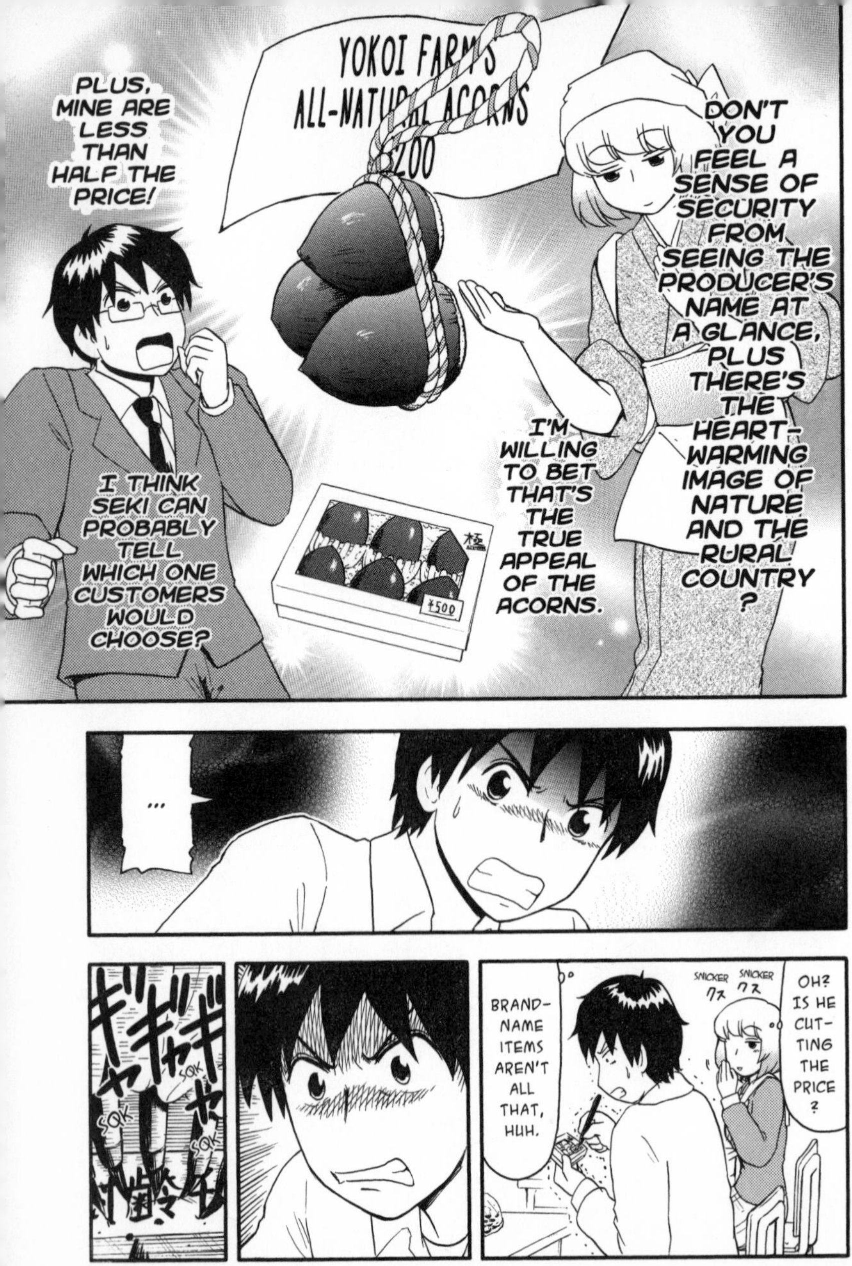

YOKOI FARM'S ALL-NATURAL ACORNS ¥200
DON'T YOU FEEL A SENSE OF SECURITY FROM SEEING THE PRODUCER'S NAME AT A GLANCE, PLUS THERE'S THE HEART-WARMING IMAGE OF NATURE AND THE RURAL COUNTRY?
I'M WILLING TO BET THAT'S THE TRUE APPEAL OF THE ACORNS.
¥500
PLUS, MINE ARE LESS THAN HALF THE PRICE!
I THINK SEKI CAN PROBABLY TELL WHICH ONE CUSTOMERS WOULD CHOOSE?
...
OH? IS HE CUTTING THE PRICE?
SNICKER クス SNICKER クス
BRAND-NAME ITEMS AREN'T ALL THAT, HUH.
SQK SQK SQK

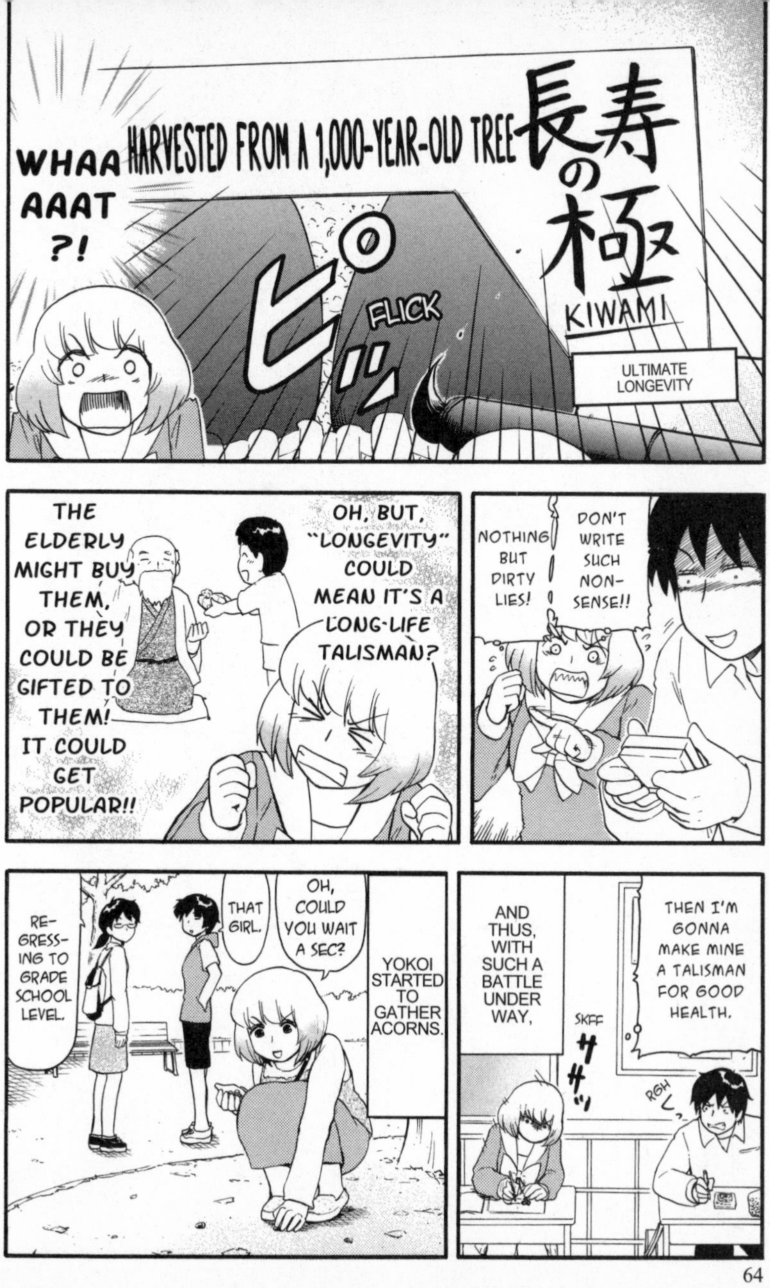

長寿の極
KIWAMI
ULTIMATE LONGEVITY
HARVESTED FROM A 1,000-YEAR-OLD TREE
ピッ
FLICK
WHAAAAAT?!
DON'T WRITE SUCH NON-SENSE!!
NOTHING BUT DIRTY LIES!
OH, BUT, "LONGEVITY" COULD MEAN IT'S A LONG-LIFE TALISMAN?
THE ELDERLY MIGHT BUY THEM, OR THEY COULD BE GIFTED TO THEM! IT COULD GET POPULAR!!
THEN I'M GONNA MAKE MINE A TALISMAN FOR GOOD HEALTH.
AND THUS, WITH SUCH A BATTLE UNDER WAY,
SKFF
サササッ
RGH
YOKOI STARTED TO GATHER ACORNS.
OH, COULD YOU WAIT A SEC?
THAT GIRL.
RE-GRESSING TO GRADE SCHOOL LEVEL.

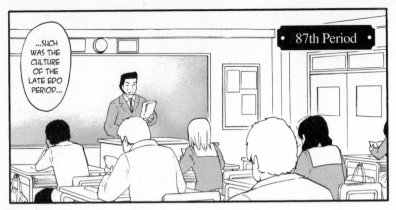

• 87th Period •

...SUCH WAS THE CULTURE OF THE LATE EDO PERIOD...

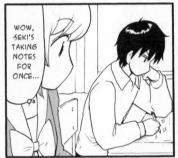

WOW, SEKI'S TAKING NOTES FOR ONCE...

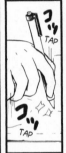

フッ TAP

フッ TAP

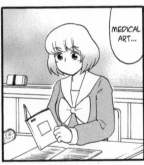

MEDICAL ART...

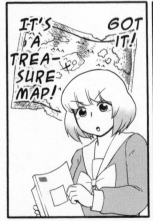

IT'S A TREASURE MAP!

GOT IT!

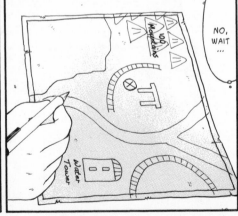

NO, WAIT...

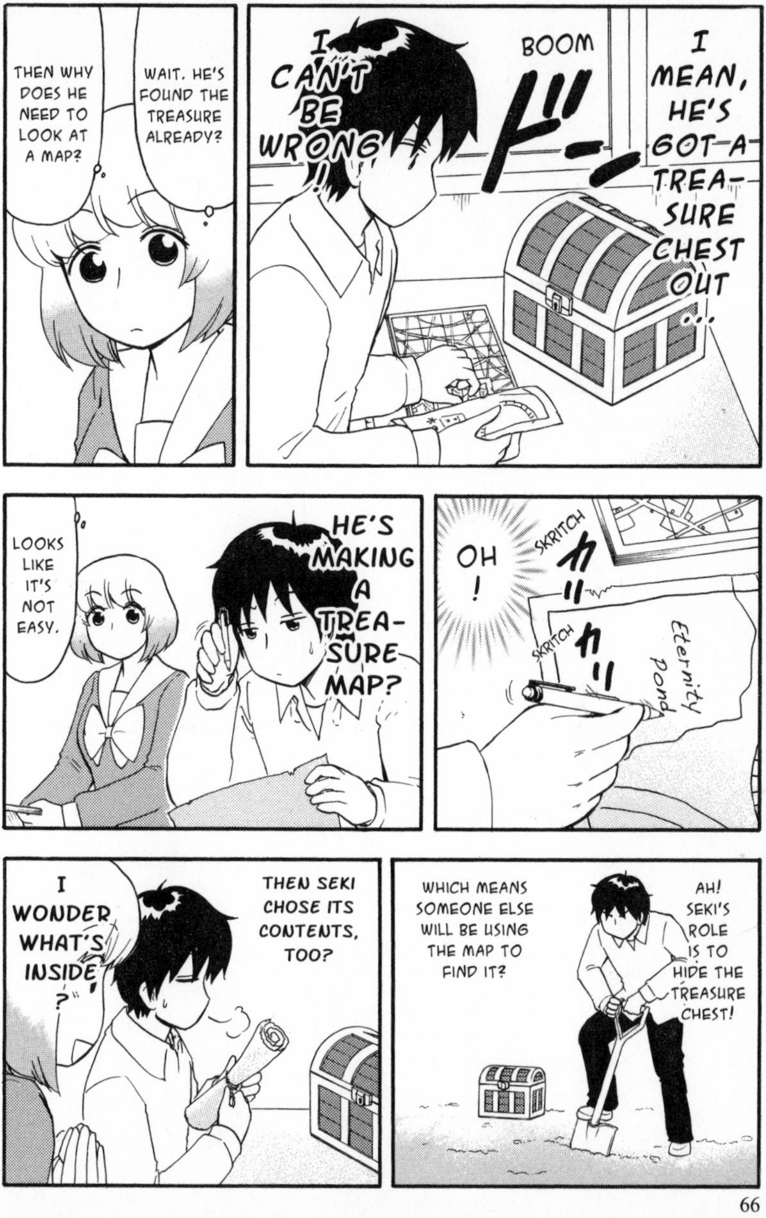
I MEAN, HE'S GOT A TREASURE CHEST OUT...
BOOM
I CAN'T BE WRONG!!
WAIT. HE'S FOUND THE TREASURE ALREADY?
THEN WHY DOES HE NEED TO LOOK AT A MAP?
OH!
SKRITCH
SKRITCH
Eternity Pond
HE'S MAKING A TREASURE MAP?
LOOKS LIKE IT'S NOT EASY.
AH! SEKI'S ROLE IS TO HIDE THE TREASURE CHEST!
WHICH MEANS SOMEONE ELSE WILL BE USING THE MAP TO FIND IT?
THEN SEKI CHOSE ITS CONTENTS, TOO?
I WONDER WHAT'S INSIDE?

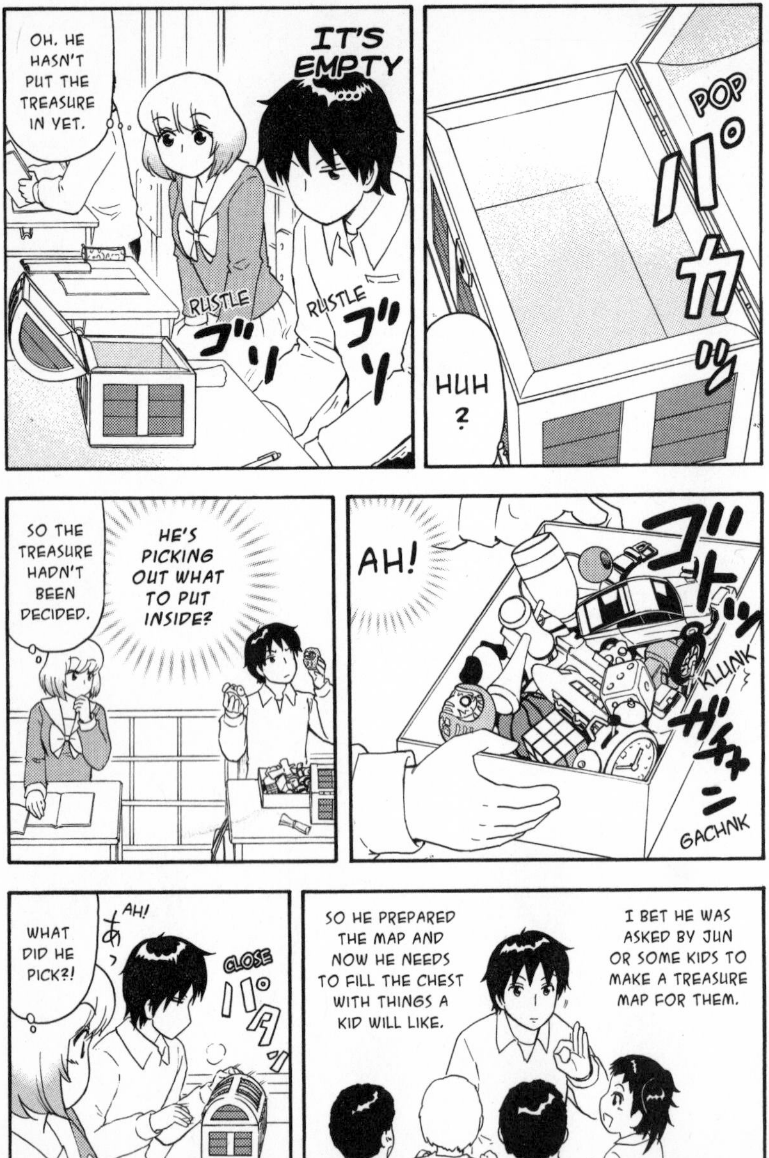
POP
パカッ
HUH?
IT'S EMPTY
...
OH. HE HASN'T PUT THE TREASURE IN YET.
RUSTLE
ゴソ
RUSTLE
ゴソ
AH!
ゴトッ
KLUNK
ガチャン
GACHNK
HE'S PICKING OUT WHAT TO PUT INSIDE?
SO THE TREASURE HADN'T BEEN DECIDED.
I BET HE WAS ASKED BY JUN OR SOME KIDS TO MAKE A TREASURE MAP FOR THEM.
SO HE PREPARED THE MAP AND NOW HE NEEDS TO FILL THE CHEST WITH THINGS A KID WILL LIKE.
AH!
あっ
CLOSE
パタッ
WHAT DID HE PICK?!

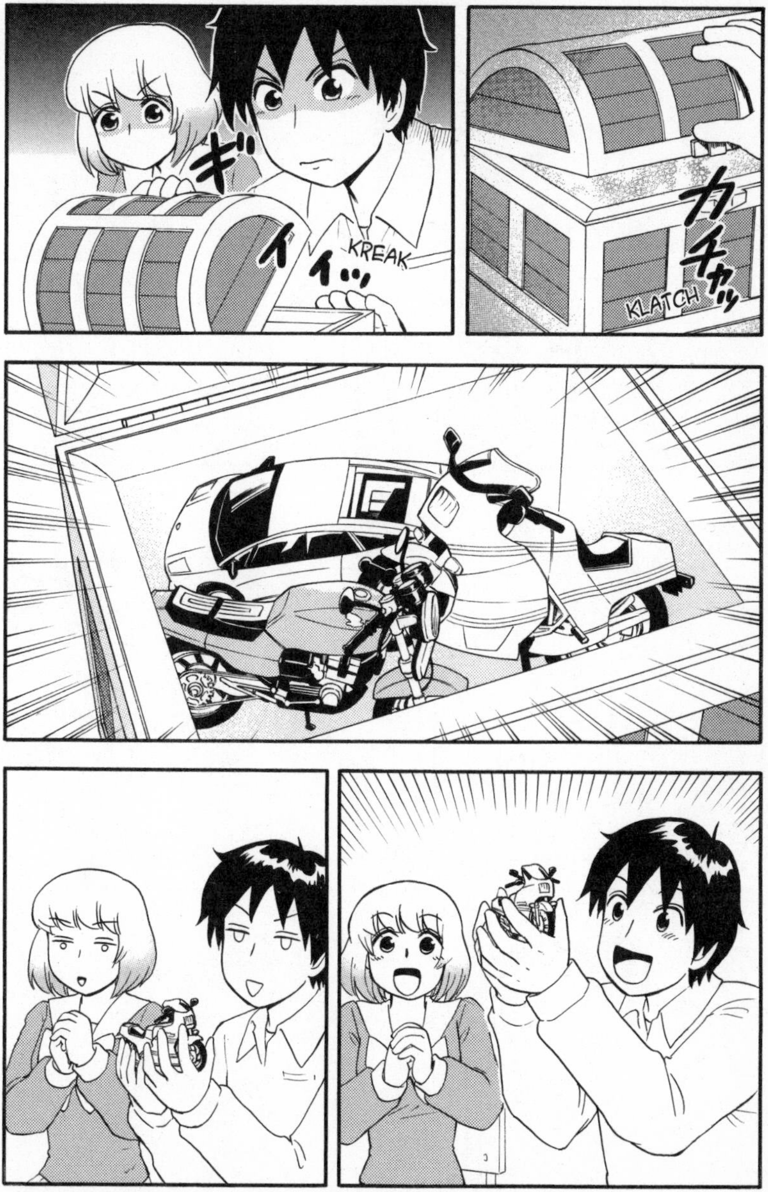
カチャッ
KLATCH
ギイイッ
KREAK

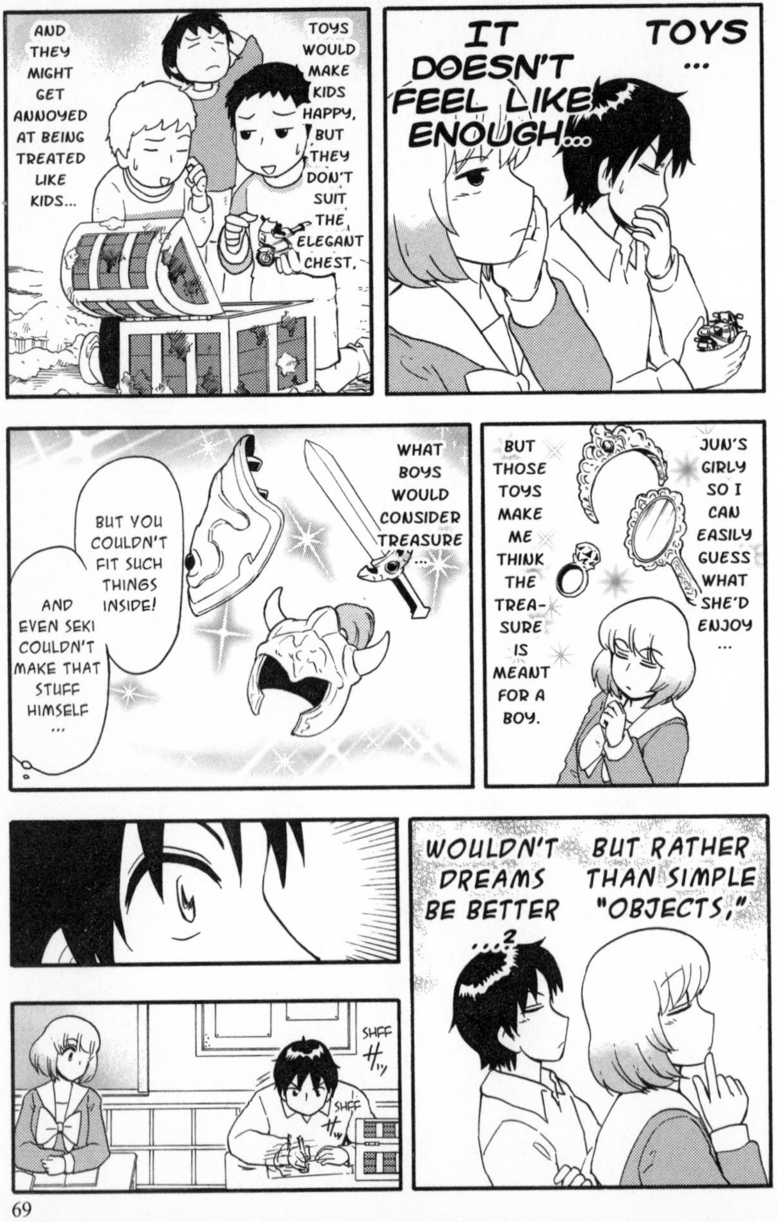
TOYS ...
IT DOESN'T FEEL LIKE ENOUGH...
TOYS WOULD MAKE KIDS HAPPY, BUT THEY DON'T SUIT THE ELEGANT CHEST.
AND THEY MIGHT GET ANNOYED AT BEING TREATED LIKE KIDS...
JUN'S GIRLY SO I CAN EASILY GUESS WHAT SHE'D ENJOY ...
BUT THOSE TOYS MAKE ME THINK THE TREA-SURE IS MEANT FOR A BOY.
WHAT BOYS WOULD CONSIDER TREASURE ...
BUT YOU COULDN'T FIT SUCH THINGS INSIDE!
AND EVEN SEKI COULDN'T MAKE THAT STUFF HIMSELF ...
BUT RATHER THAN SIMPLE "OBJECTS,"
WOULDN'T DREAMS BE BETTER ...?
SHFF
SHFF

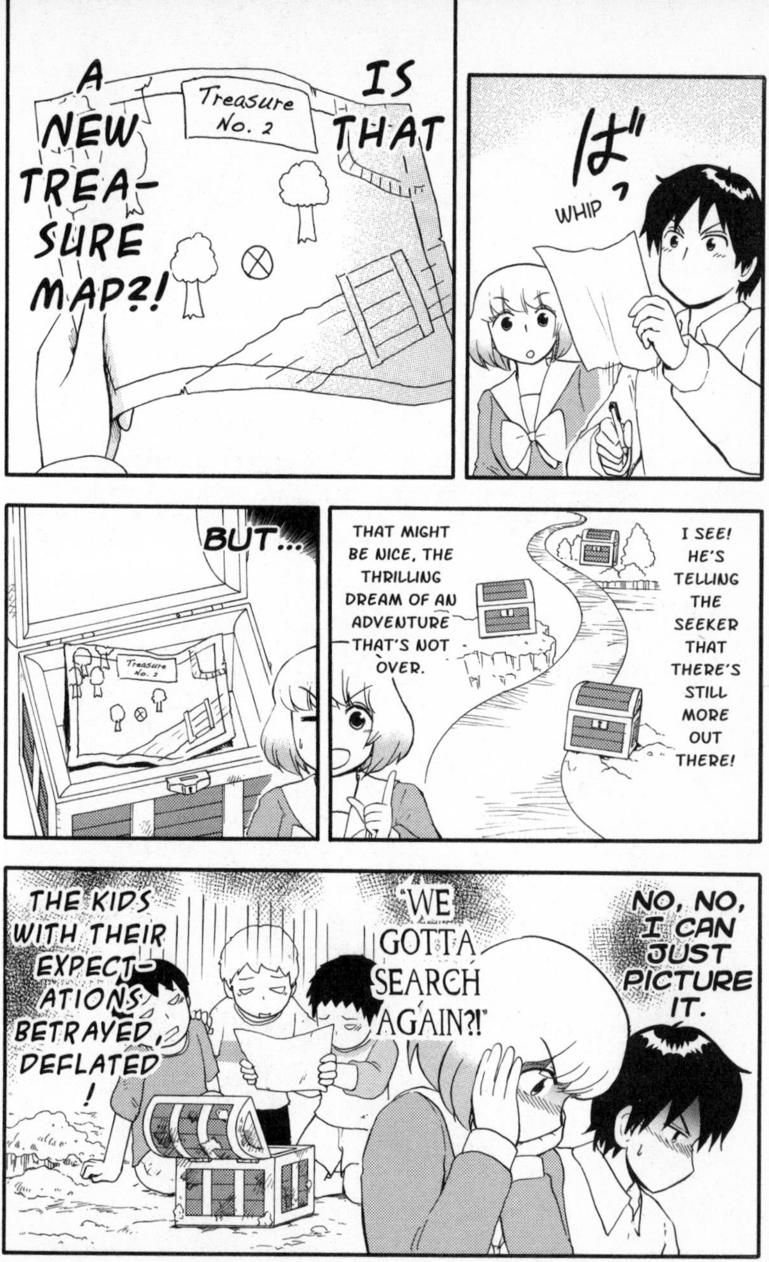
ばっ
WHIP
IS THAT
A NEW TREASURE MAP?!
Treasure No. 2
I SEE! HE'S TELLING THE SEEKER THAT THERE'S STILL MORE OUT THERE!
THAT MIGHT BE NICE, THE THRILLING DREAM OF AN ADVENTURE THAT'S NOT OVER.
BUT...
Treasure No. 2
NO, NO, I CAN JUST PICTURE IT.
"WE GOTTA SEARCH AGAIN?!"
THE KIDS WITH THEIR EXPECTATIONS BETRAYED, DEFLATED!

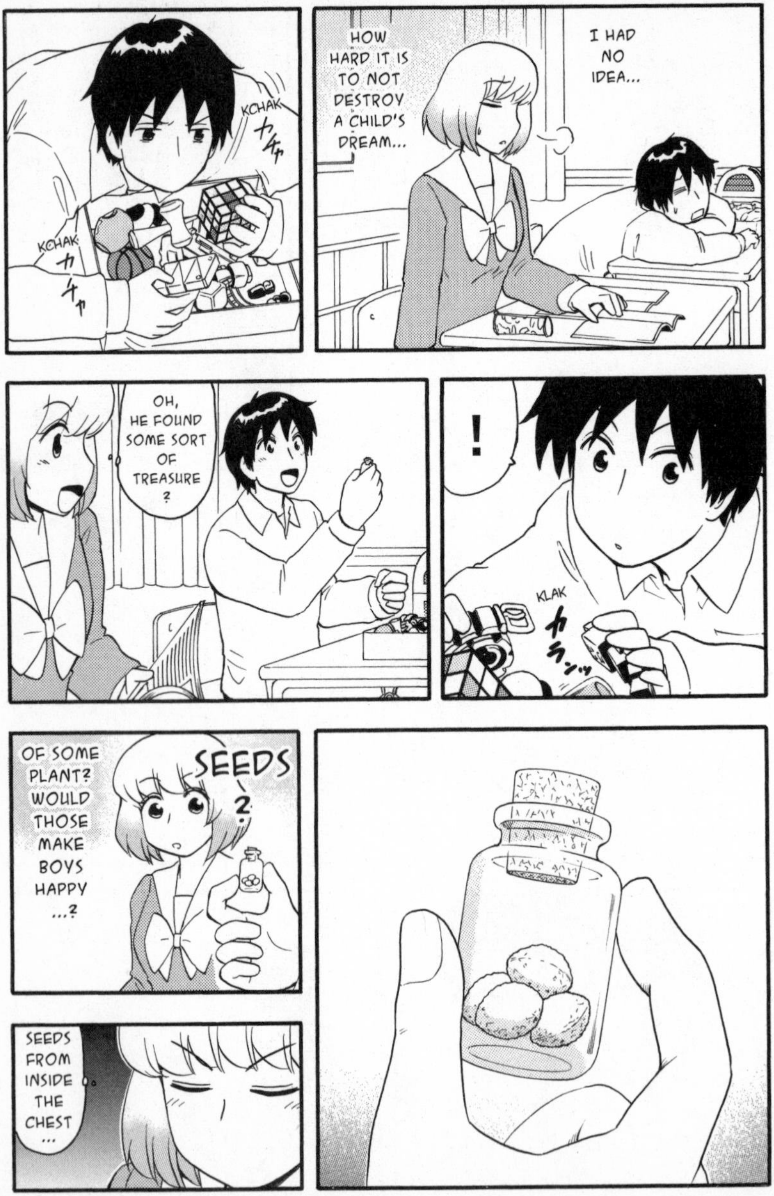
I HAD NO IDEA...
HOW HARD IT IS TO NOT DESTROY A CHILD'S DREAM...
KCHAK
KCHAK
!
KLAK
OH, HE FOUND SOME SORT OF TREASURE?
SEEDS?
OF SOME PLANT? WOULD THOSE MAKE BOYS HAPPY...?
SEEDS FROM INSIDE THE CHEST...

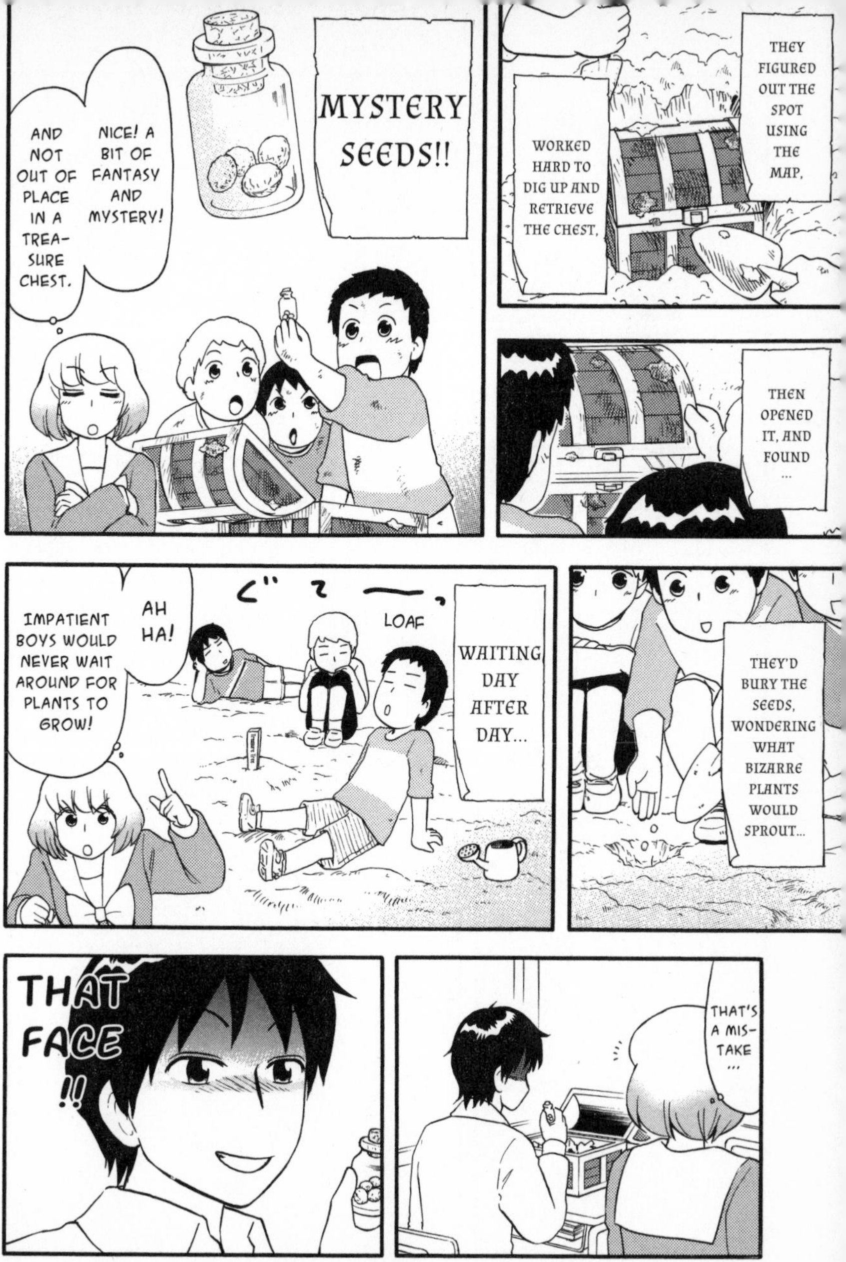
THEY FIGURED OUT THE SPOT USING THE MAP,
WORKED HARD TO DIG UP AND RETRIEVE THE CHEST,
THEN OPENED IT, AND FOUND ...
MYSTERY SEEDS!!
NICE! A BIT OF FANTASY AND MYSTERY!
AND NOT OUT OF PLACE IN A TREASURE CHEST.
THEY'D BURY THE SEEDS, WONDERING WHAT BIZARRE PLANTS WOULD SPROUT...
WAITING DAY AFTER DAY...
ぐでーー
LOAF
AH HA!
IMPATIENT BOYS WOULD NEVER WAIT AROUND FOR PLANTS TO GROW!
THAT'S A MISTAKE ...
THAT FACE !!

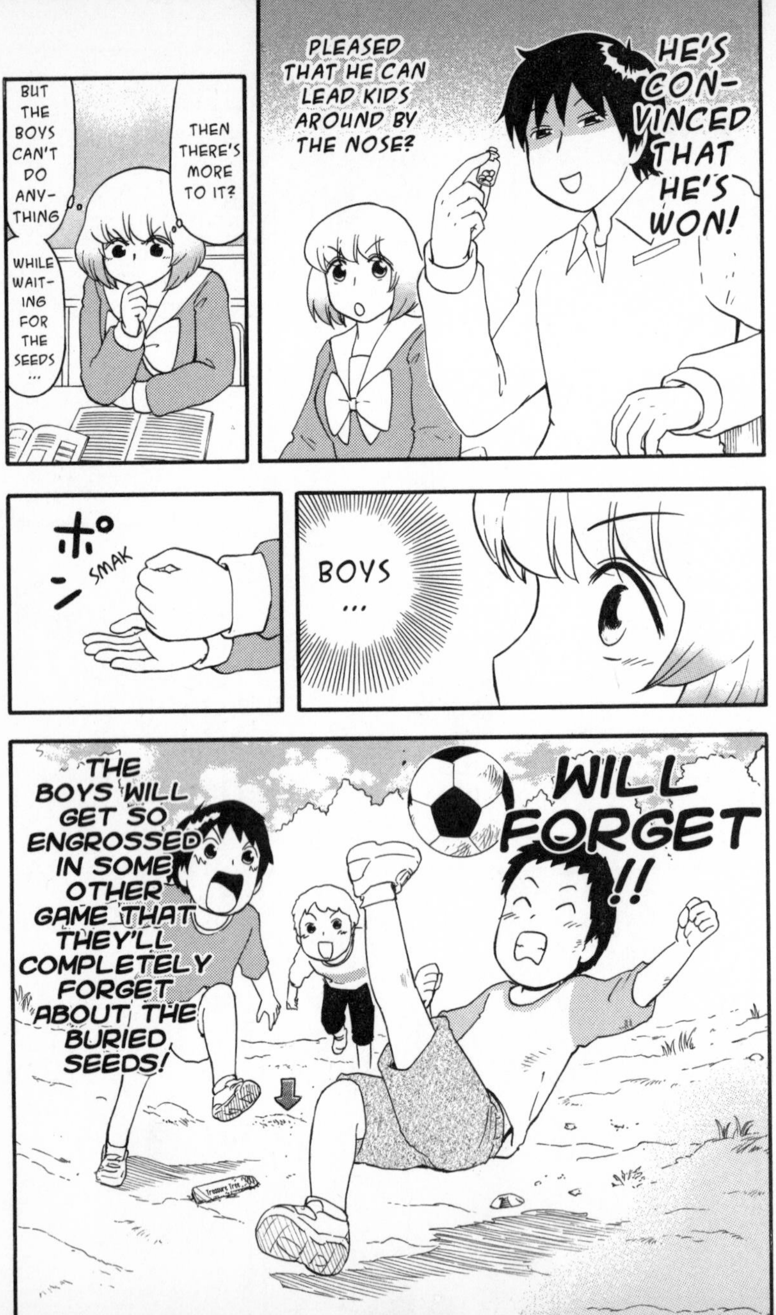

HE'S CON-VINCED THAT HE'S WON!
PLEASED THAT HE CAN LEAD KIDS AROUND BY THE NOSE?
THEN THERE'S MORE TO IT?
BUT THE BOYS CAN'T DO ANY-THING
WHILE WAIT-ING FOR THE SEEDS ...
BOYS ...
ポン
SMAK
WILL FORGET!!
THE BOYS WILL GET SO ENGROSSED IN SOME OTHER GAME THAT THEY'LL COMPLETELY FORGET ABOUT THE BURIED SEEDS!
Treasure Tree

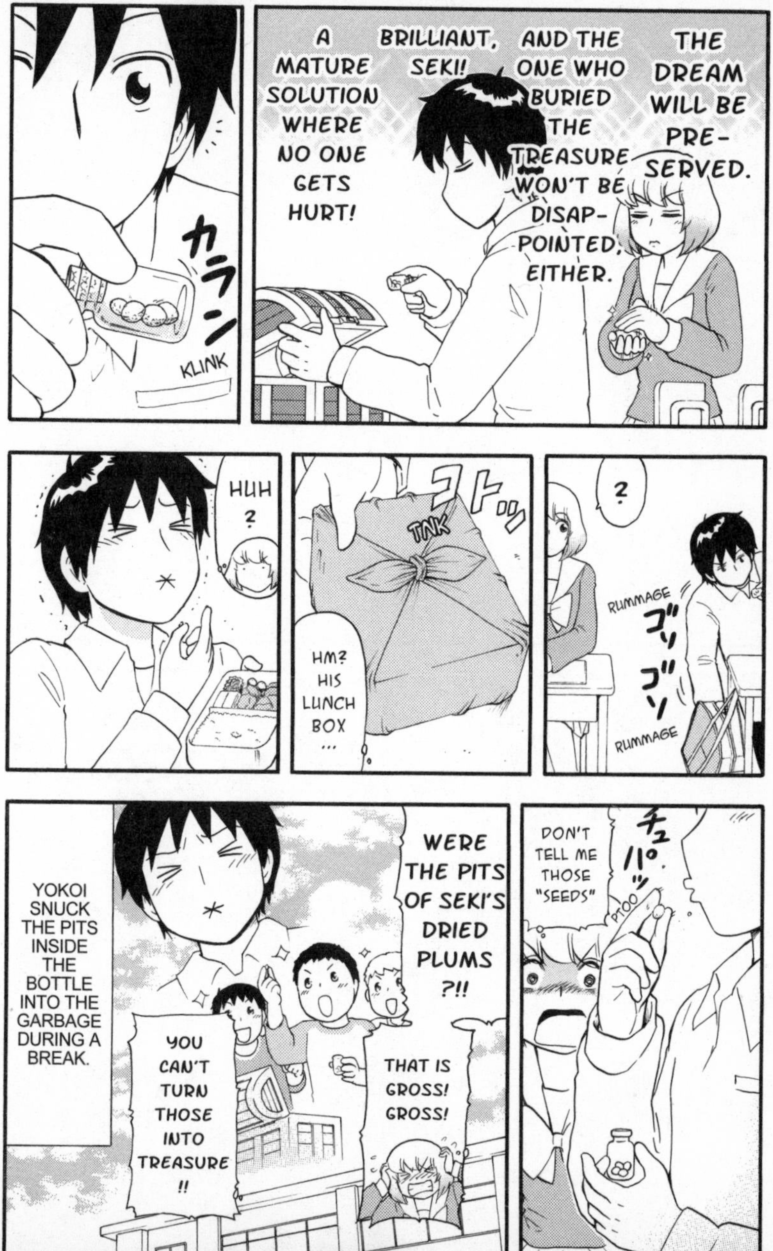
A MATURE SOLUTION WHERE NO ONE GETS HURT!
BRILLIANT, SEKI!
AND THE ONE WHO BURIED THE TREASURE WON'T BE DISAP-POINTED, EITHER.
THE DREAM WILL BE PRE-SERVED.
カラン
KLINK
?
ゴソ
RUMMAGE
ゴソ
RUMMAGE
コトッ
TNK
HM? HIS LUNCH BOX ...
HUH ?
チュパッ
PTOO
DON'T TELL ME THOSE "SEEDS"
WERE THE PITS OF SEKI'S DRIED PLUMS ?!!
THAT IS GROSS! GROSS!
YOU CAN'T TURN THOSE INTO TREASURE !!
YOKOI SNUCK THE PITS INSIDE THE BOTTLE INTO THE GARBAGE DURING A BREAK.

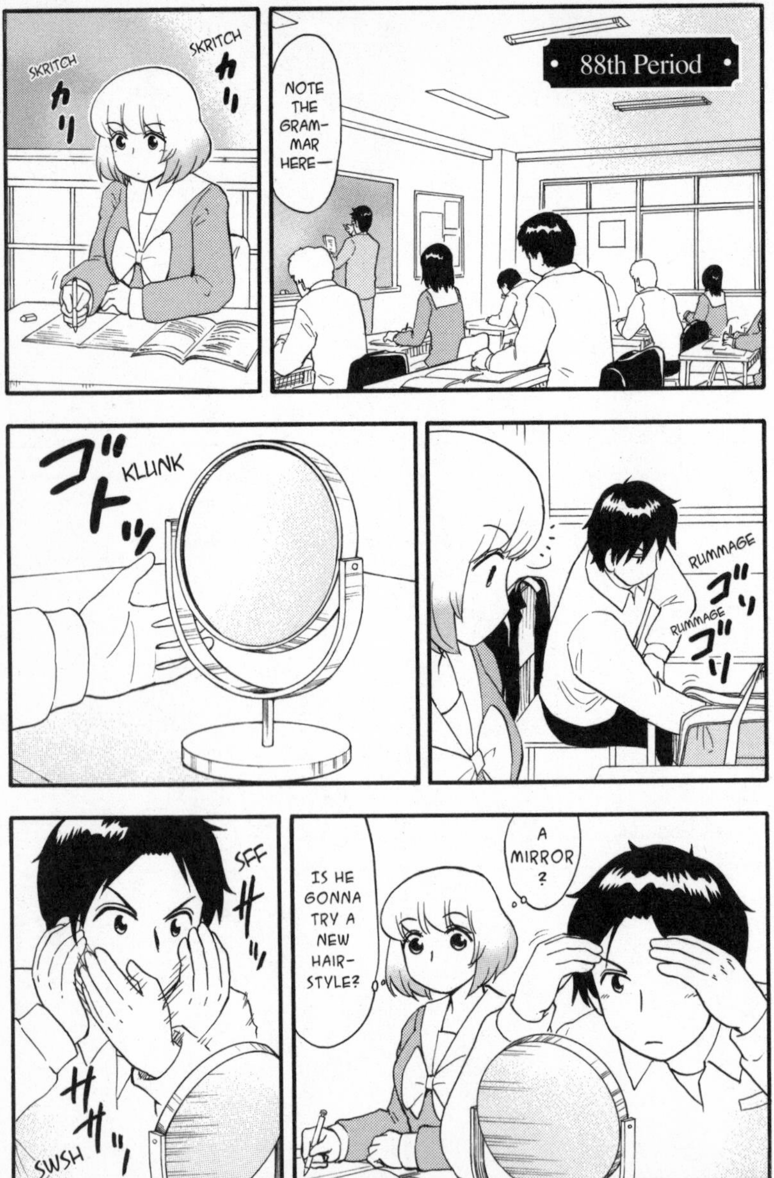
• 88th Period •
NOTE THE GRAM-MAR HERE—
SKRITCH
SKRITCH
RUMMAGE
RUMMAGE
KLUNK
A MIRROR?
IS HE GONNA TRY A NEW HAIR-STYLE?
SFF
SWSH

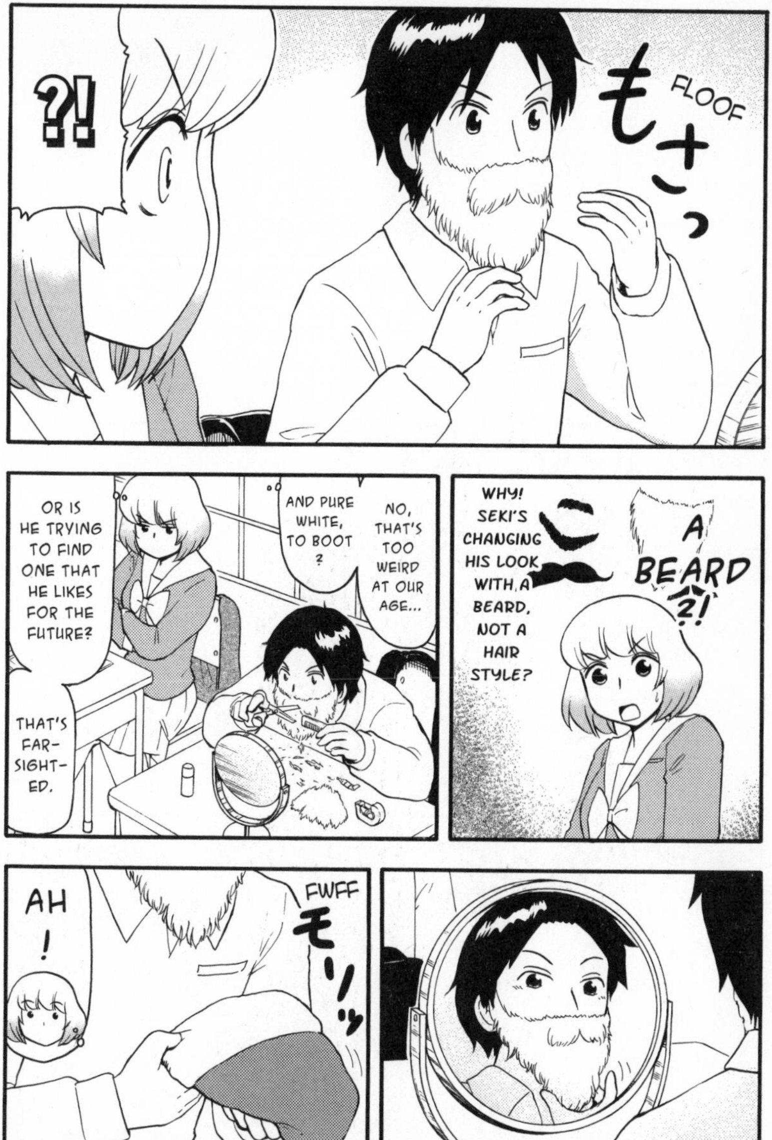
もさっ
FLOOF
?!
WHY! SEKI'S CHANGING HIS LOOK WITH A BEARD, NOT A HAIR STYLE?
A BEARD?!
NO, THAT'S TOO WEIRD AT OUR AGE...
AND PURE WHITE, TO BOOT?
OR IS HE TRYING TO FIND ONE THAT HE LIKES FOR THE FUTURE?
THAT'S FAR-SIGHTED.
モリッ
FWFF
AH!

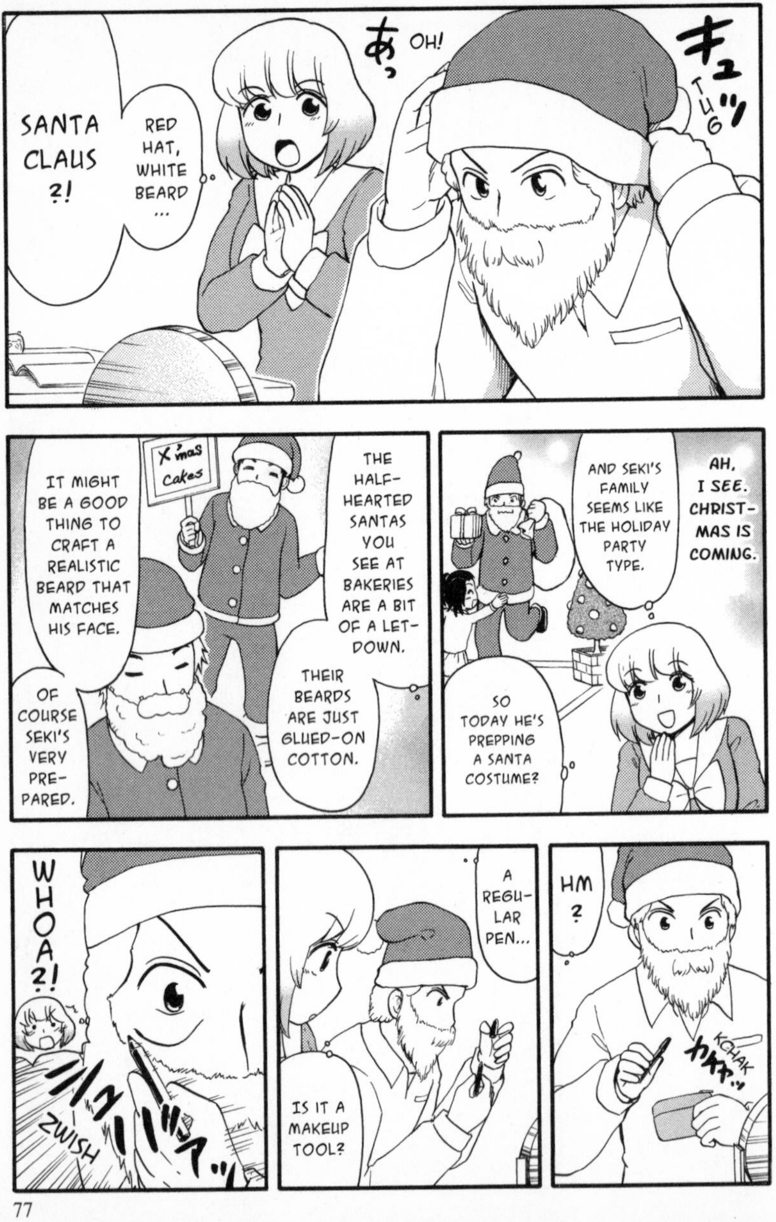
キュッ
TUG
あっ
OH!
RED HAT, WHITE BEARD...
SANTA CLAUS?!
AH, I SEE. CHRISTMAS IS COMING.
AND SEKI'S FAMILY SEEMS LIKE THE HOLIDAY PARTY TYPE.
SO TODAY HE'S PREPPING A SANTA COSTUME?
THE HALF-HEARTED SANTAS YOU SEE AT BAKERIES ARE A BIT OF A LET-DOWN.
X'mas Cakes
IT MIGHT BE A GOOD THING TO CRAFT A REALISTIC BEARD THAT MATCHES HIS FACE.
THEIR BEARDS ARE JUST GLUED-ON COTTON.
OF COURSE SEKI'S VERY PRE-PARED.
HM?
カチャッ
KCHAK
A REGU-LAR PEN...
IS IT A MAKEUP TOOL?
WHOA?!
ZWISH

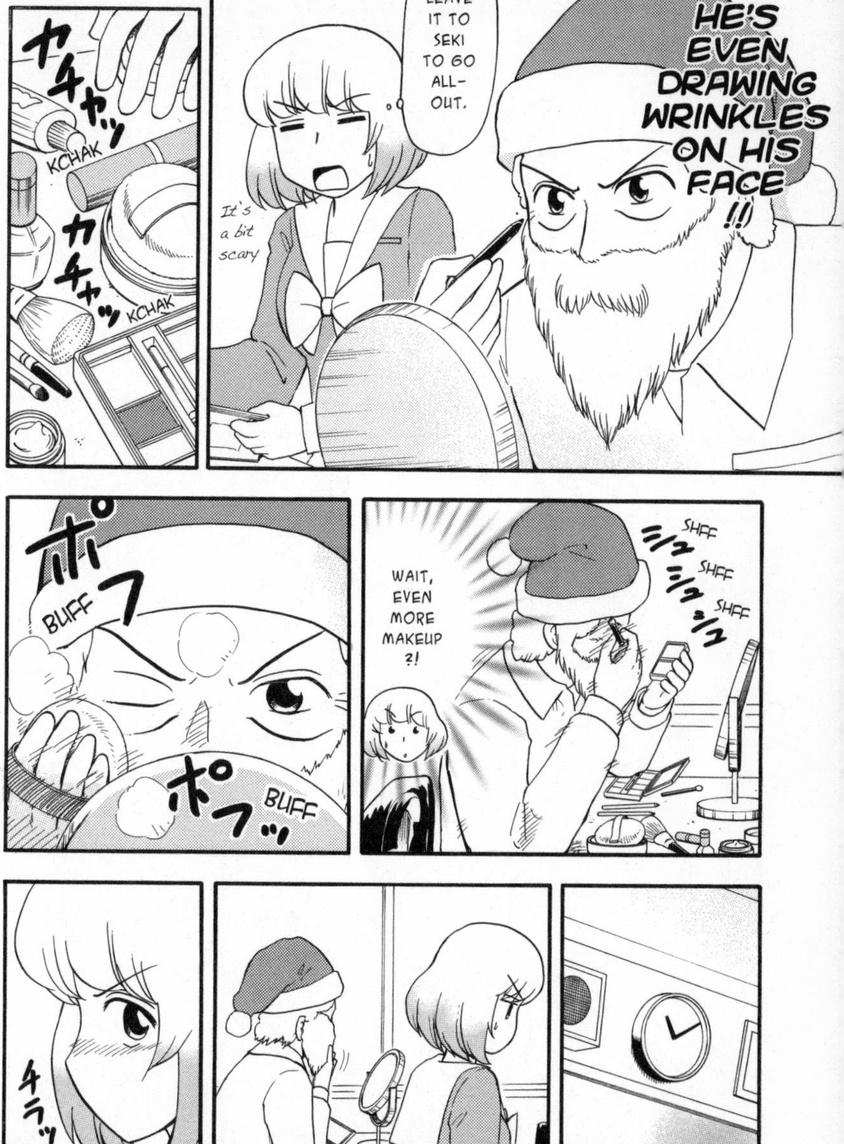
HE'S EVEN DRAWING WRINKLES ON HIS FACE!!
LEAVE IT TO SEKI TO GO ALL-OUT.
It's a bit scary
カチャッ
KCHAK
カチャッ
KCHAK
シュ
SHFF
シュ
SHFF
シュ
SHFF
WAIT, EVEN MORE MAKEUP?!
ポフ
BUFF
ポフッ
BUFF
チラッ
GLANCE

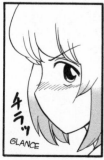

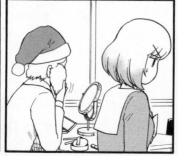

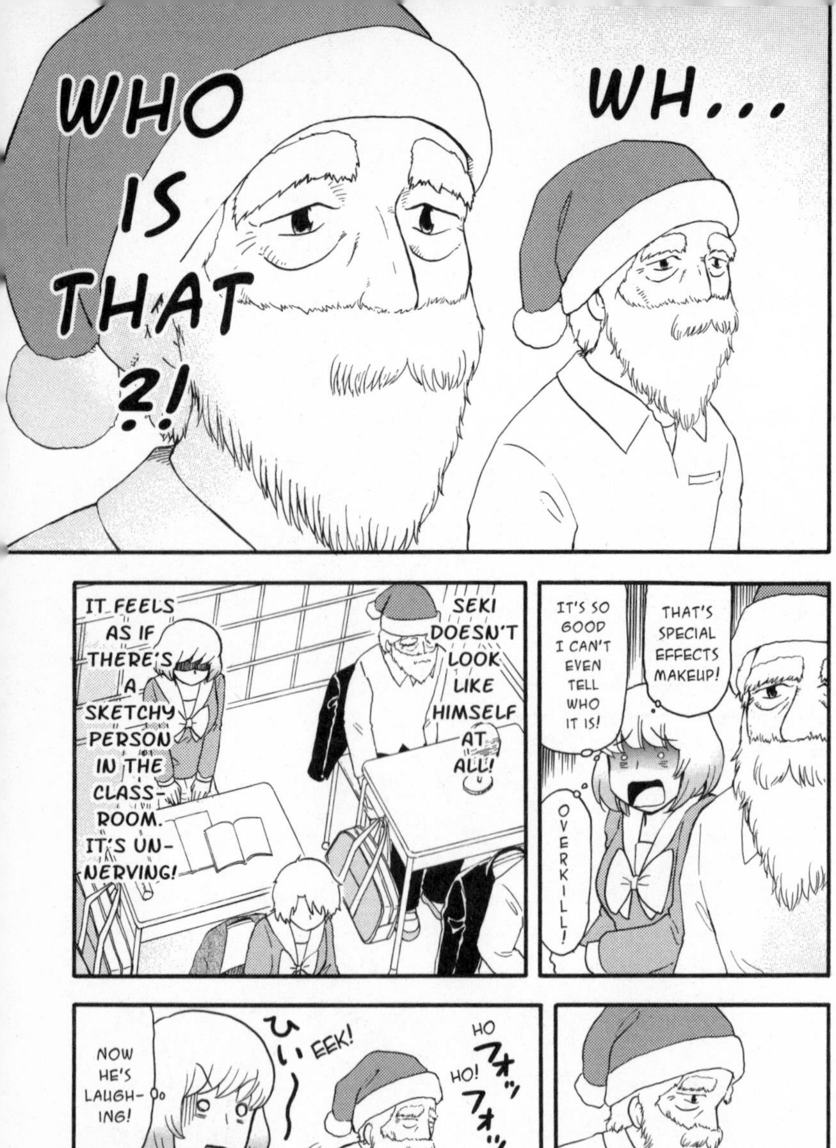
WH...
WHO IS THAT?!
THAT'S SPECIAL EFFECTS MAKEUP!
IT'S SO GOOD I CAN'T EVEN TELL WHO IT IS!
OVERKILL!
SEKI DOESN'T LOOK LIKE HIMSELF AT ALL!
IT FEELS AS IF THERE'S A SKETCHY PERSON IN THE CLASS-ROOM. IT'S UN-NERVING!
フォッフォッ HO HO!
ひぃ〜〜っ EEK!
NOW HE'S LAUGHING!

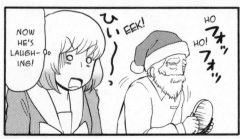

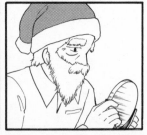

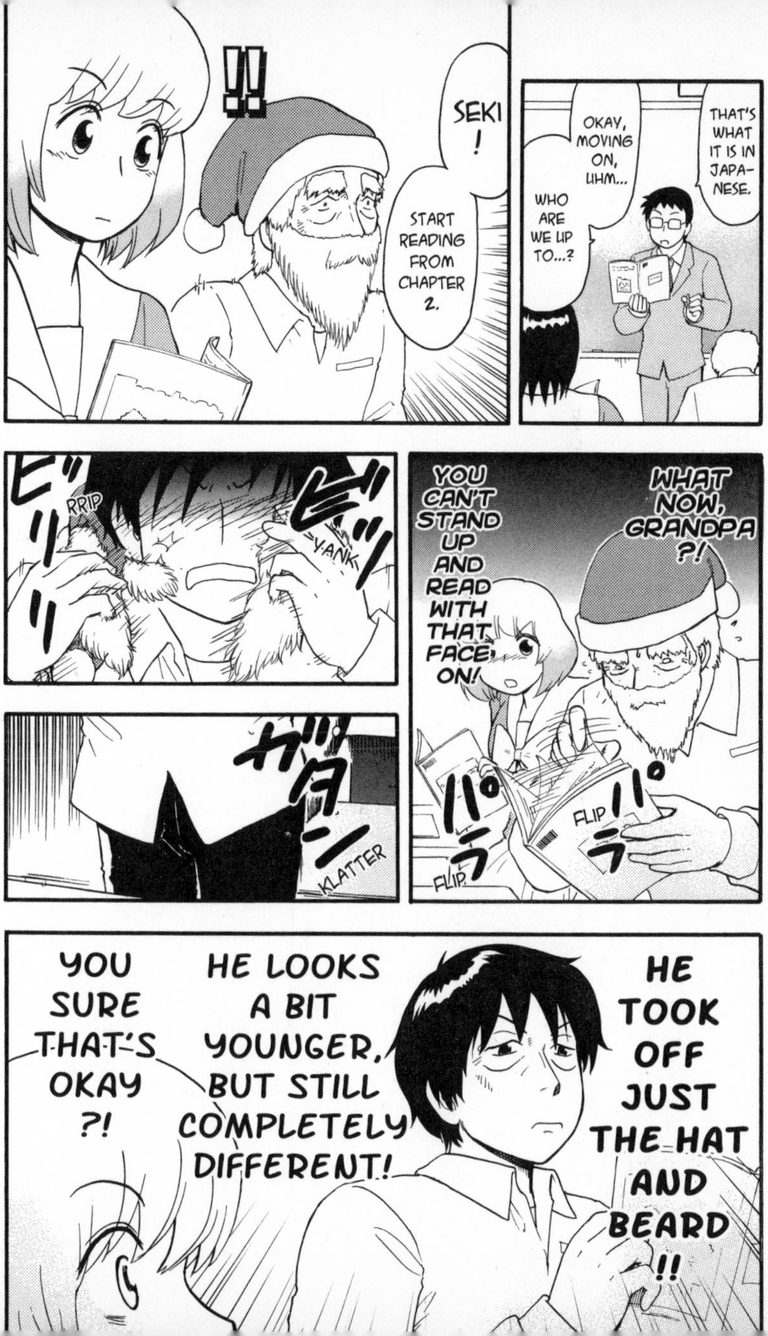
THAT'S WHAT IT IS IN JAPANESE.
OKAY, MOVING ON, UHM...
WHO ARE WE UP TO...?
SEKI!
START READING FROM CHAPTER 2.
!!
WHAT NOW, GRANDPA?!
YOU CAN'T STAND UP AND READ WITH THAT FACE ON!
FLIP
FLIP
YANK
RRIP
KLATTER
HE TOOK OFF JUST THE HAT AND BEARD!!
HE LOOKS A BIT YOUNGER, BUT STILL COMPLETELY DIFFERENT!
YOU SURE THAT'S OKAY?!

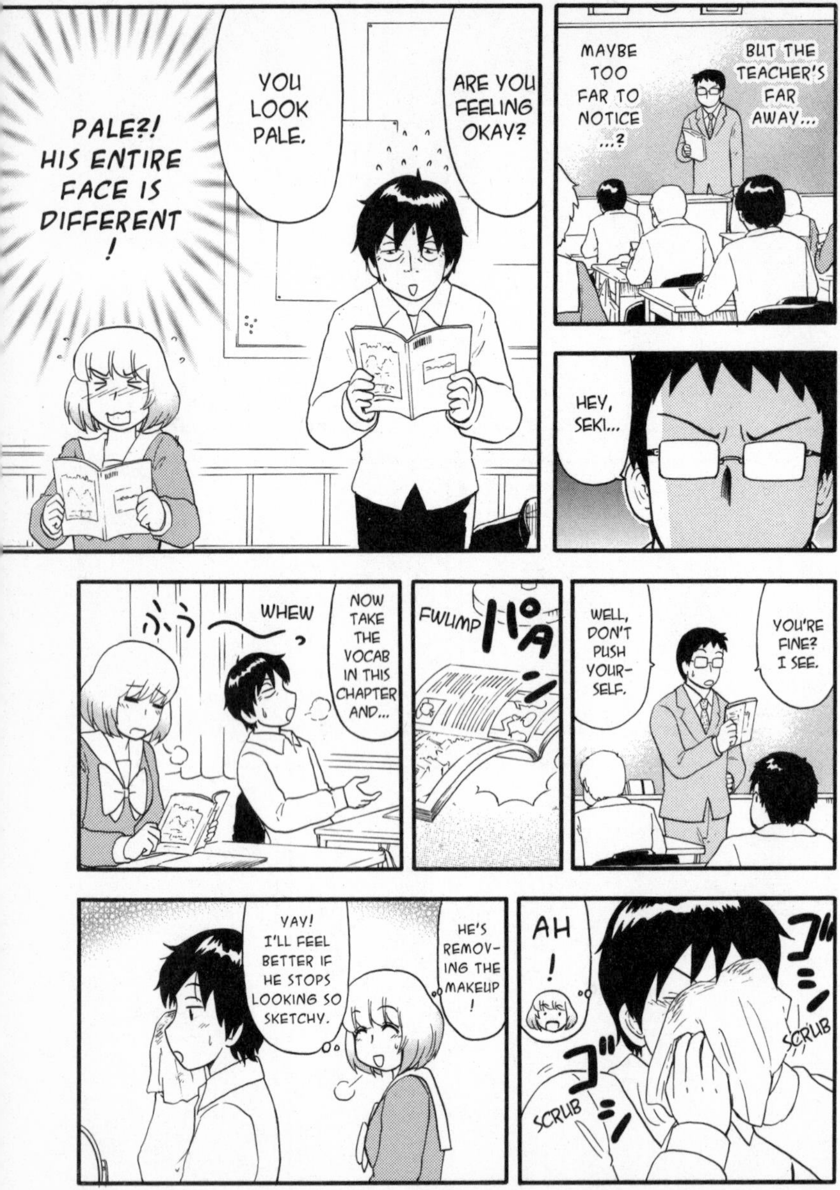
BUT THE TEACHER'S FAR AWAY...
MAYBE TOO FAR TO NOTICE ...?
HEY, SEKI...
ARE YOU FEELING OKAY?
YOU LOOK PALE.
PALE?! HIS ENTIRE FACE IS DIFFERENT !
YOU'RE FINE? I SEE.
WELL, DON'T PUSH YOUR-SELF.
パン
FWUMP
NOW TAKE THE VOCAB IN THIS CHAPTER AND...
WHEW
ふう
AH !
ゴシ
SCRUB
ゴシ
SCRUB
HE'S REMOV-ING THE MAKEUP !
YAY! I'LL FEEL BETTER IF HE STOPS LOOKING SO SKETCHY.

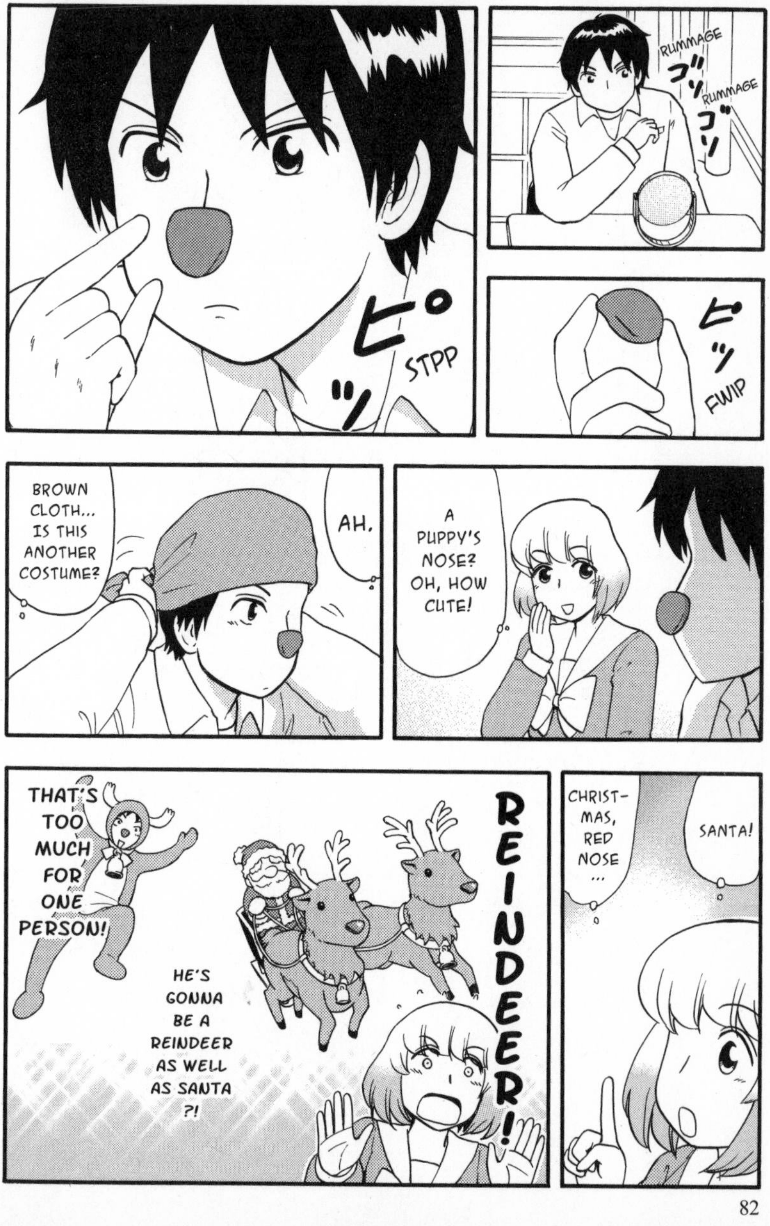
RUMMAGE
ゴソ
RUMMAGE
ゴソ
ピッ
FWIP
ピッ
STPP
A PUPPY'S NOSE? OH, HOW CUTE!
AH.
BROWN CLOTH... IS THIS ANOTHER COSTUME?
SANTA!
CHRISTMAS, RED NOSE ...
REINDEER!
HE'S GONNA BE A REINDEER AS WELL AS SANTA ?!
THAT'S TOO MUCH FOR ONE PERSON!

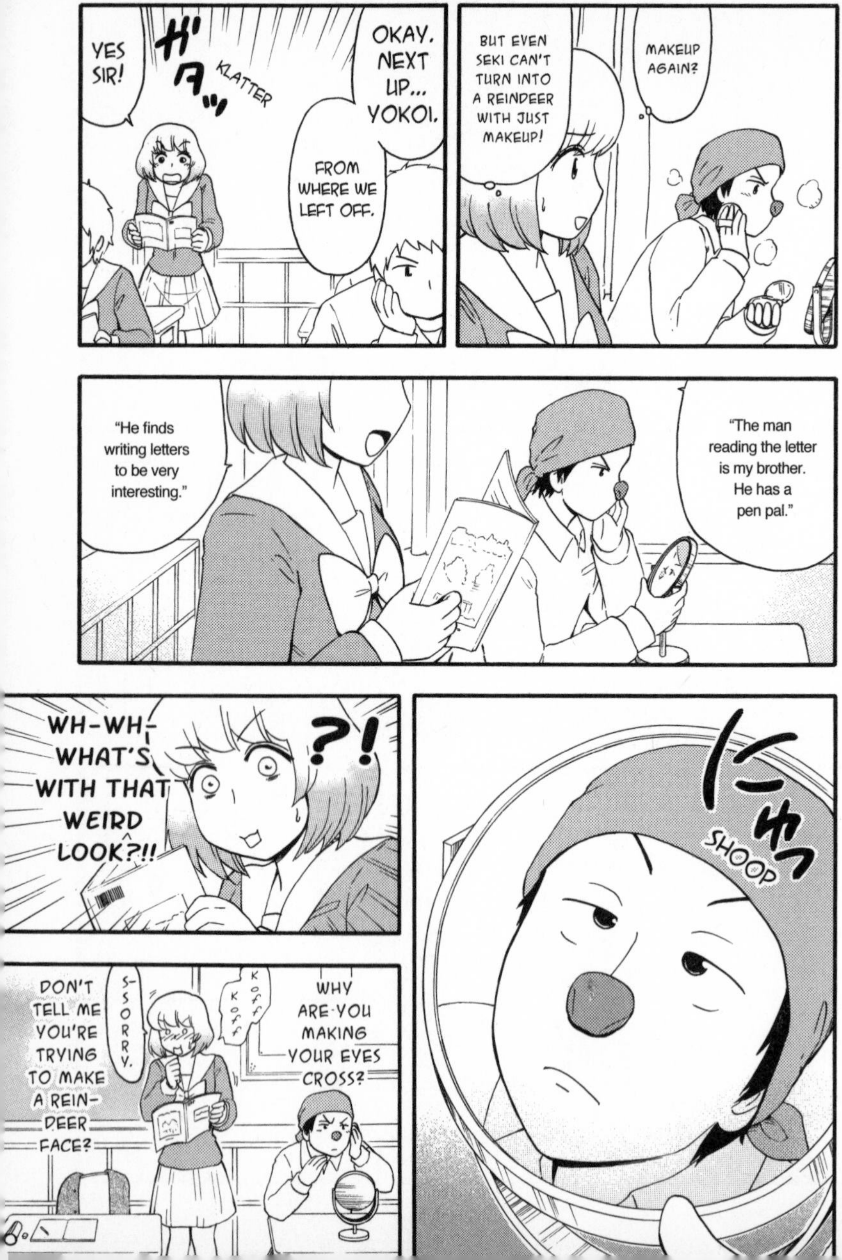
MAKEUP AGAIN?
BUT EVEN SEKI CAN'T TURN INTO A REINDEER WITH JUST MAKEUP!
OKAY. NEXT UP... YOKOI.
FROM WHERE WE LEFT OFF.
ガタッ
KLATTER
YES SIR!
"The man reading the letter is my brother. He has a pen pal."
"He finds writing letters to be very interesting."
にゅっ
SHOOP
?!
WH-WH-WHAT'S WITH THAT WEIRD LOOK?!!
WHY ARE YOU MAKING YOUR EYES CROSS?
KOFF KOFF
S-SORRY.
DON'T TELL ME YOU'RE TRYING TO MAKE A REIN-DEER FACE?

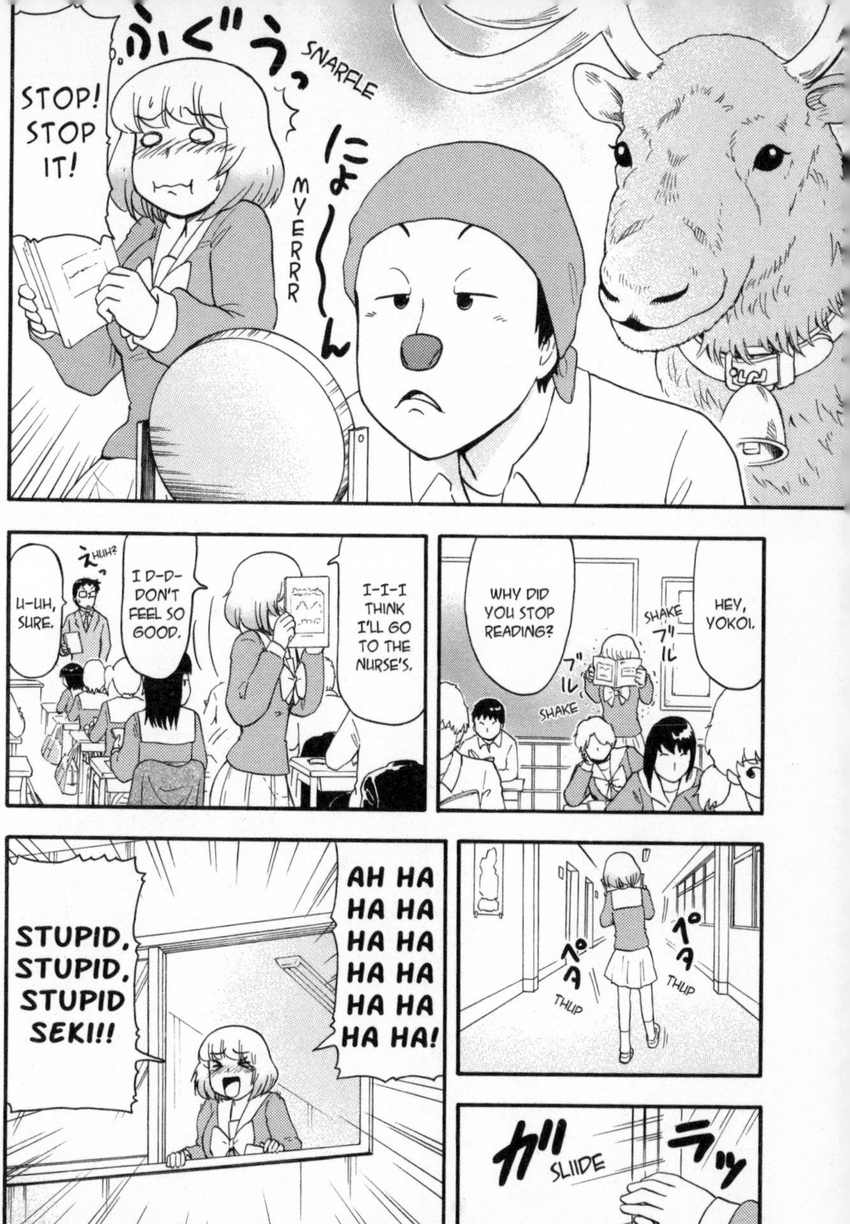
にょーーん
MYERRR
ふぐうっ
SNARFLE
STOP! STOP IT!
HEY, YOKOI.
ブル
SHAKE
ブル
SHAKE
WHY DID YOU STOP READING?
I-I-I THINK I'LL GO TO THE NURSE'S.
I D-D-DON'T FEEL SO GOOD.
え
HUH?
U-UH, SURE.
ペタ
THUP
ペタ
THUP
ガラッ
SLIIDE
AH HA HA HA HA HA HA HA HA HA HA HA!
STUPID, STUPID, STUPID SEKI!!

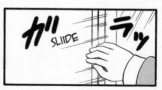

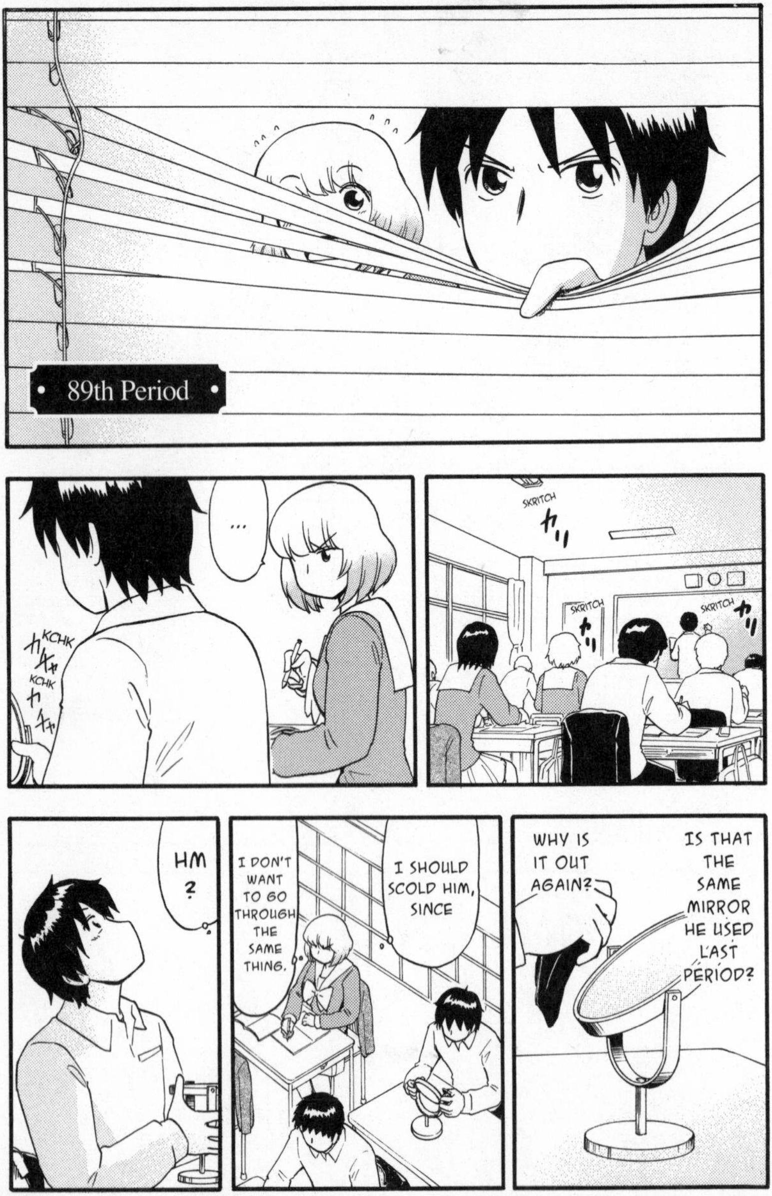
89th Period
SKRITCH
SKRITCH
SKRITCH
...
KCHK
KCHK
IS THAT THE SAME MIRROR HE USED LAST PERIOD?
WHY IS IT OUT AGAIN?
I SHOULD SCOLD HIM, SINCE
I DON'T WANT TO GO THROUGH THE SAME THING.
HM?

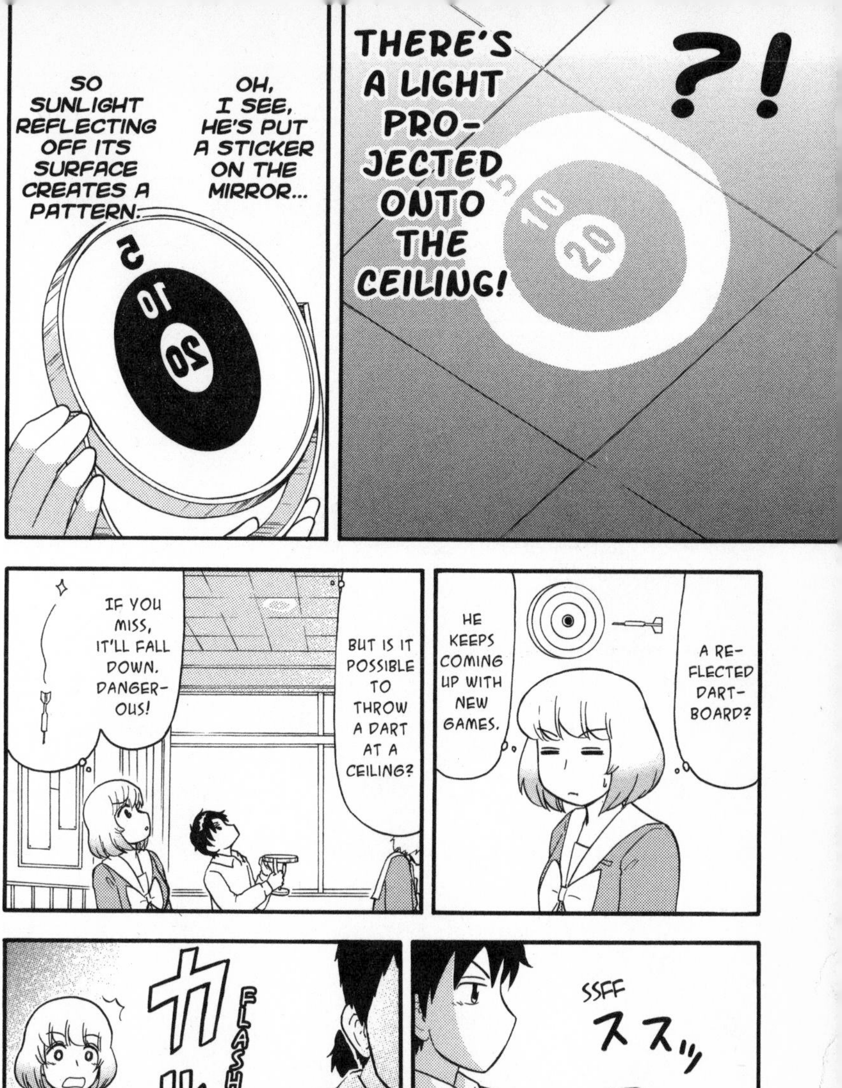
?!
THERE'S A LIGHT PRO-JECTED ONTO THE CEILING!
OH, I SEE, HE'S PUT A STICKER ON THE MIRROR...
SO SUNLIGHT REFLECTING OFF ITS SURFACE CREATES A PATTERN.
A RE-FLECTED DART-BOARD?
HE KEEPS COMING UP WITH NEW GAMES.
BUT IS IT POSSIBLE TO THROW A DART AT A CEILING?
IF YOU MISS, IT'LL FALL DOWN. DANGER-OUS!
SSFF
ススッ
カッ
FLASH

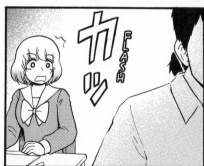

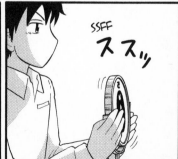

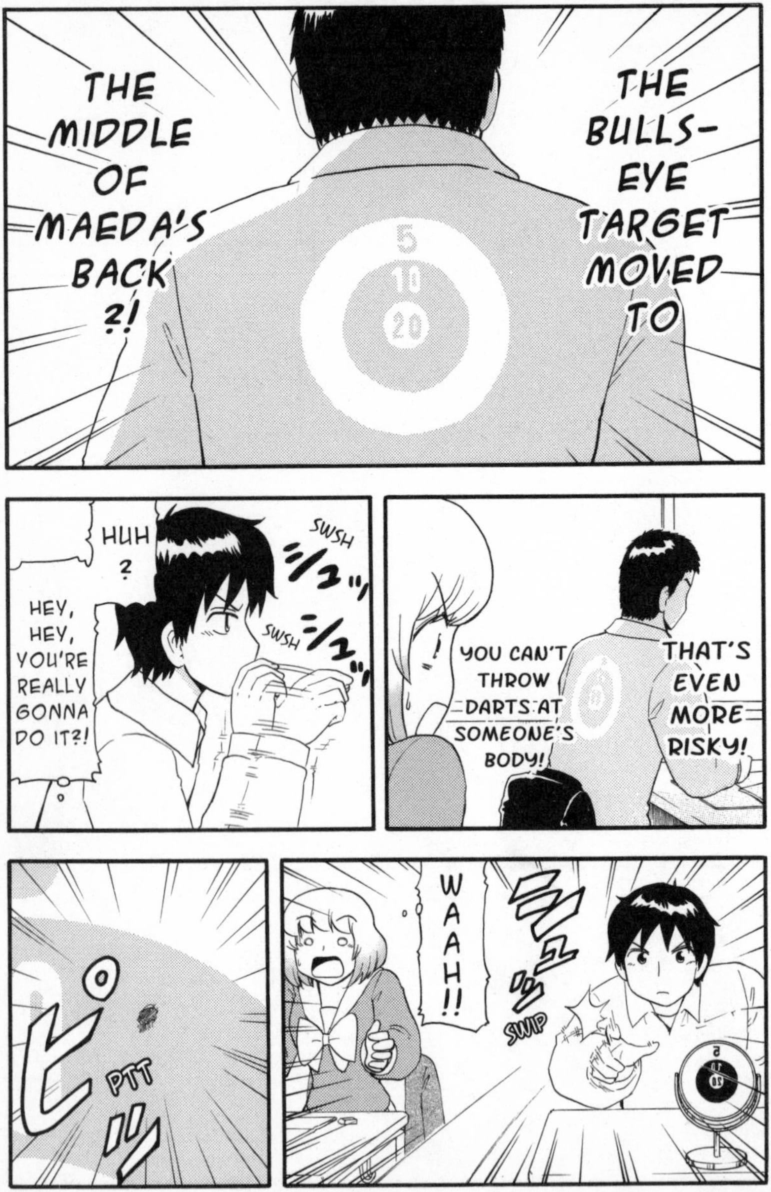
THE BULLS-EYE TARGET MOVED TO
THE MIDDLE OF MAEDA'S BACK ?!
5
10
20
THAT'S EVEN MORE RISKY!
YOU CAN'T THROW DARTS AT SOMEONE'S BODY!
SWSH
HUH ?
SWSH
HEY, HEY, YOU'RE REALLY GONNA DO IT?!
SWIP
WAAH!!
PTT

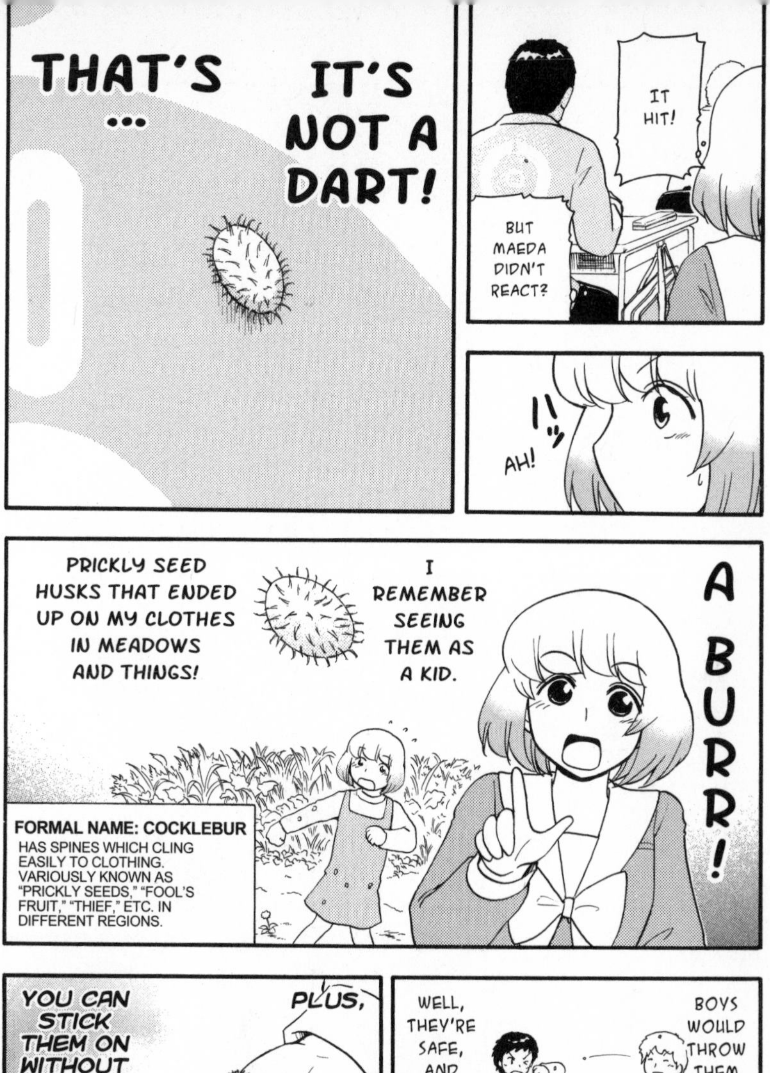
IT HIT!
BUT MAEDA DIDN'T REACT?
ハッ
AH!
IT'S NOT A DART!
THAT'S ...
A BURR!
I REMEMBER SEEING THEM AS A KID.
PRICKLY SEED HUSKS THAT ENDED UP ON MY CLOTHES IN MEADOWS AND THINGS!
FORMAL NAME: COCKLEBUR
HAS SPINES WHICH CLING EASILY TO CLOTHING. VARIOUSLY KNOWN AS "PRICKLY SEEDS," "FOOL'S FRUIT," "THIEF," ETC. IN DIFFERENT REGIONS.
BOYS WOULD THROW THEM AT EACH OTHER FOR FUN.
WELL, THEY'RE SAFE, AND SUITED FOR A CLOTH TARGET.
PLUS,
YOU CAN STICK THEM ON WITHOUT GETTING NOTICED.

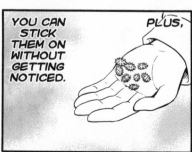

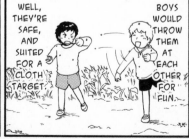

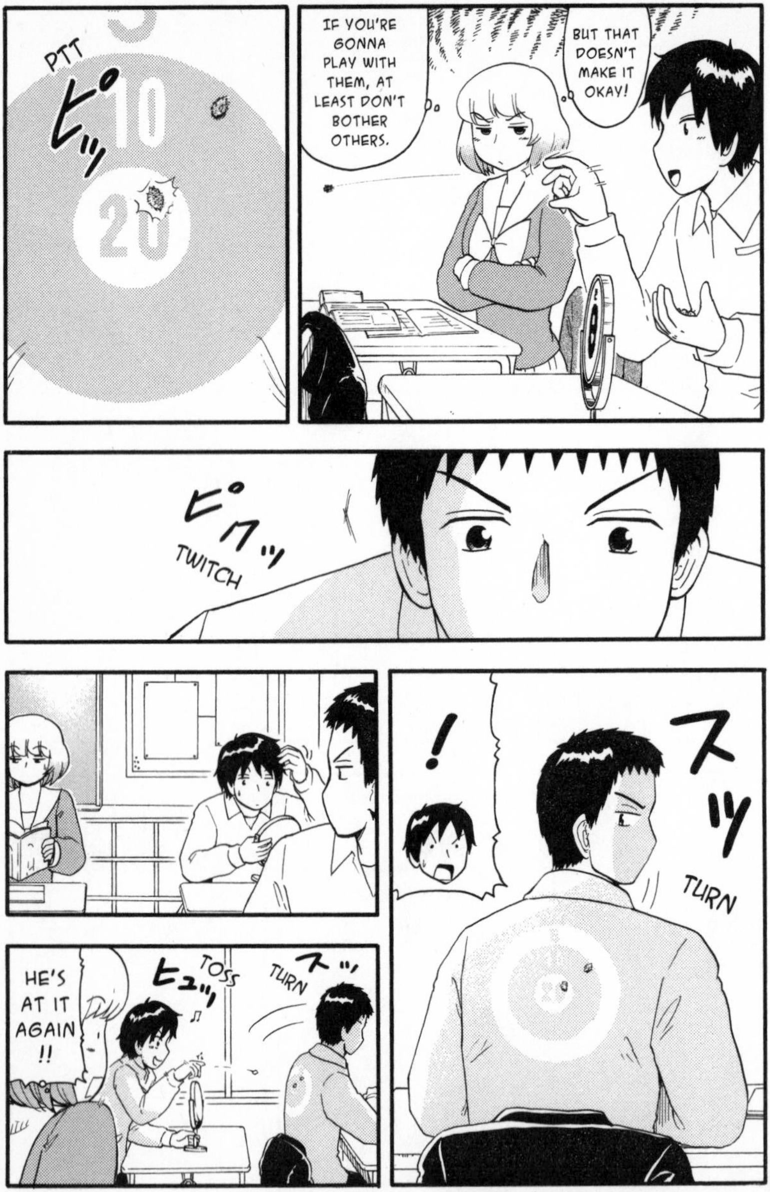
BUT THAT DOESN'T MAKE IT OKAY!
IF YOU'RE GONNA PLAY WITH THEM, AT LEAST DON'T BOTHER OTHERS.
ピッ
PTT
ピクッ
TWITCH
スッ
TURN
!
スッ
TURN
ヒュッ
TOSS
HE'S AT IT AGAIN !!

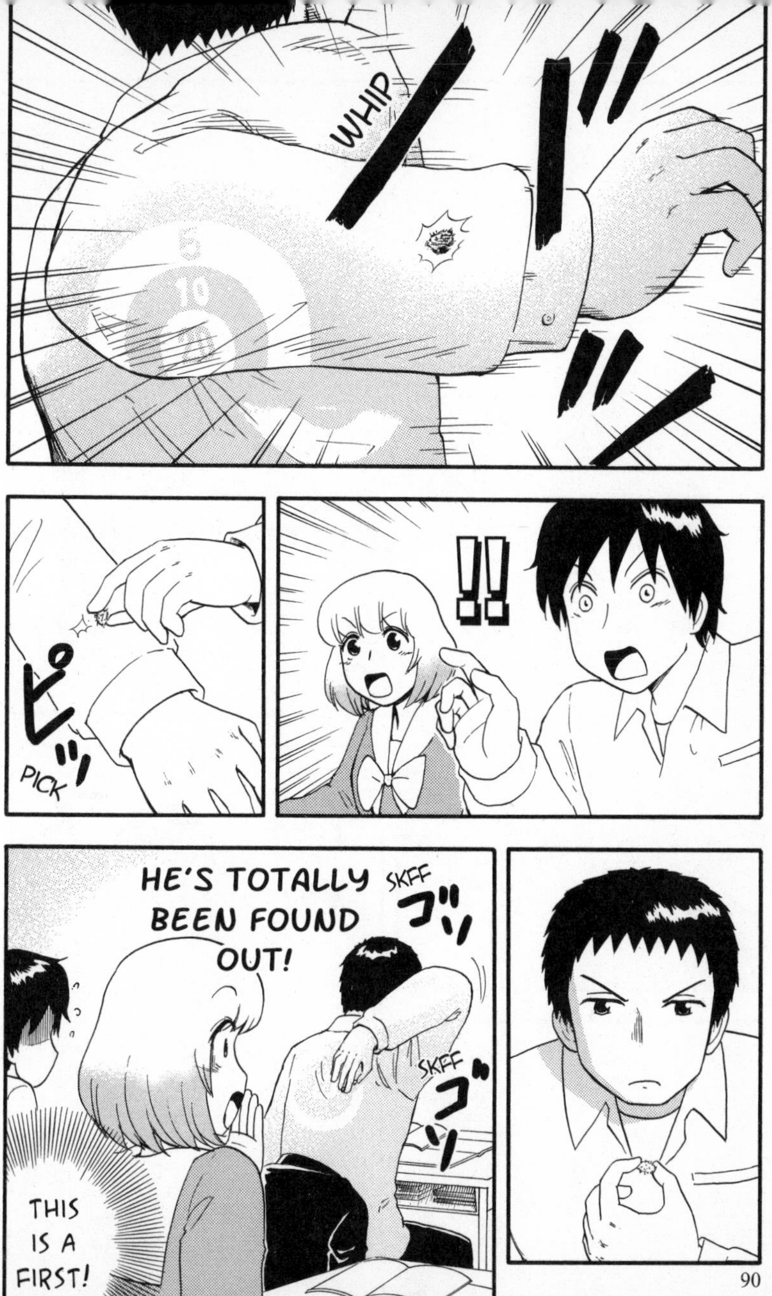
WHIP
!!
ピッ
PICK
HE'S TOTALLY BEEN FOUND OUT!
SKFF
ゴッ
SKFF
ゴッ
THIS IS A FIRST!

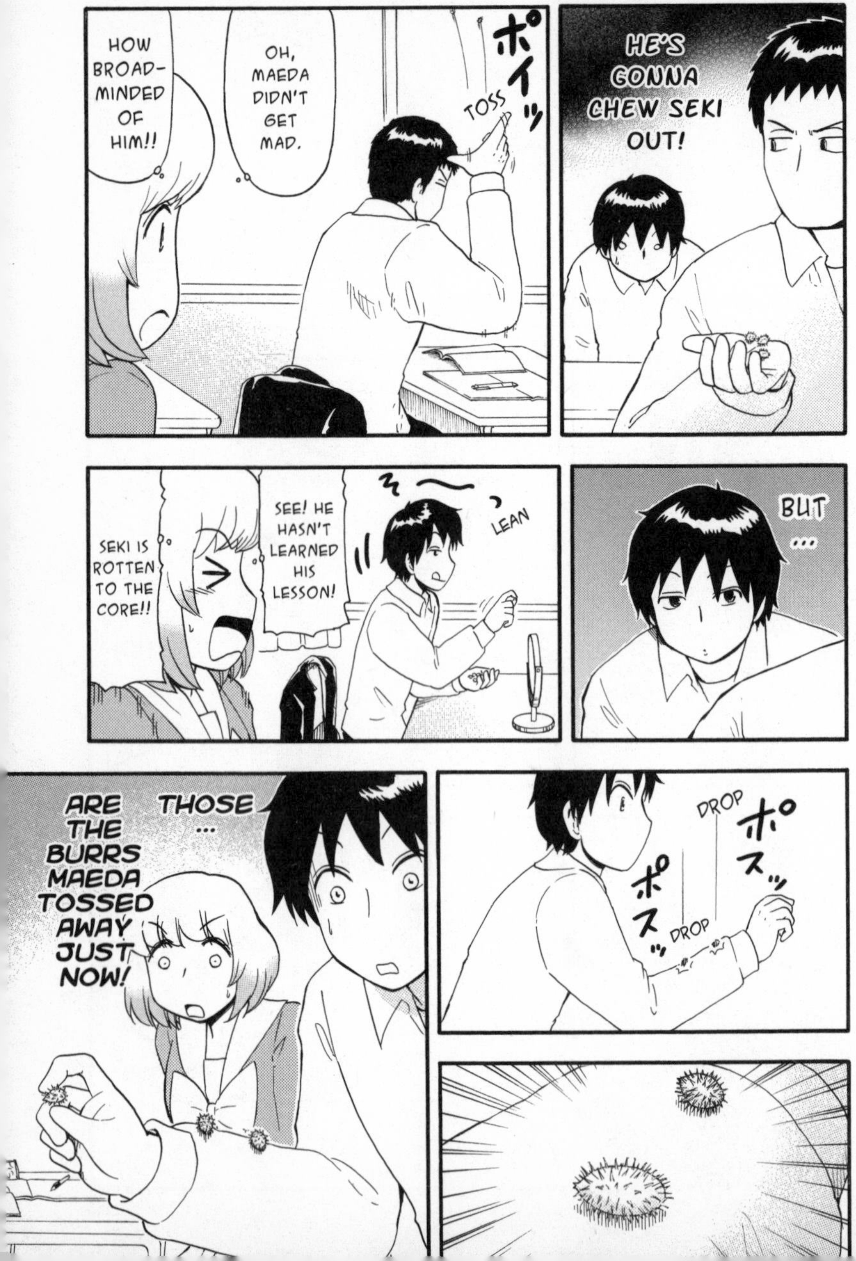
HE'S GONNA CHEW SEKI OUT!
ポイッ
TOSS
OH, MAEDA DIDN'T GET MAD.
HOW BROAD-MINDED OF HIM!!
BUT ...
LEAN
SEE! HE HASN'T LEARNED HIS LESSON!
SEKI IS ROTTEN TO THE CORE!!
ポスッ
DROP
ポスッ
DROP
ARE THOSE ... THE BURRS MAEDA TOSSED AWAY JUST NOW!

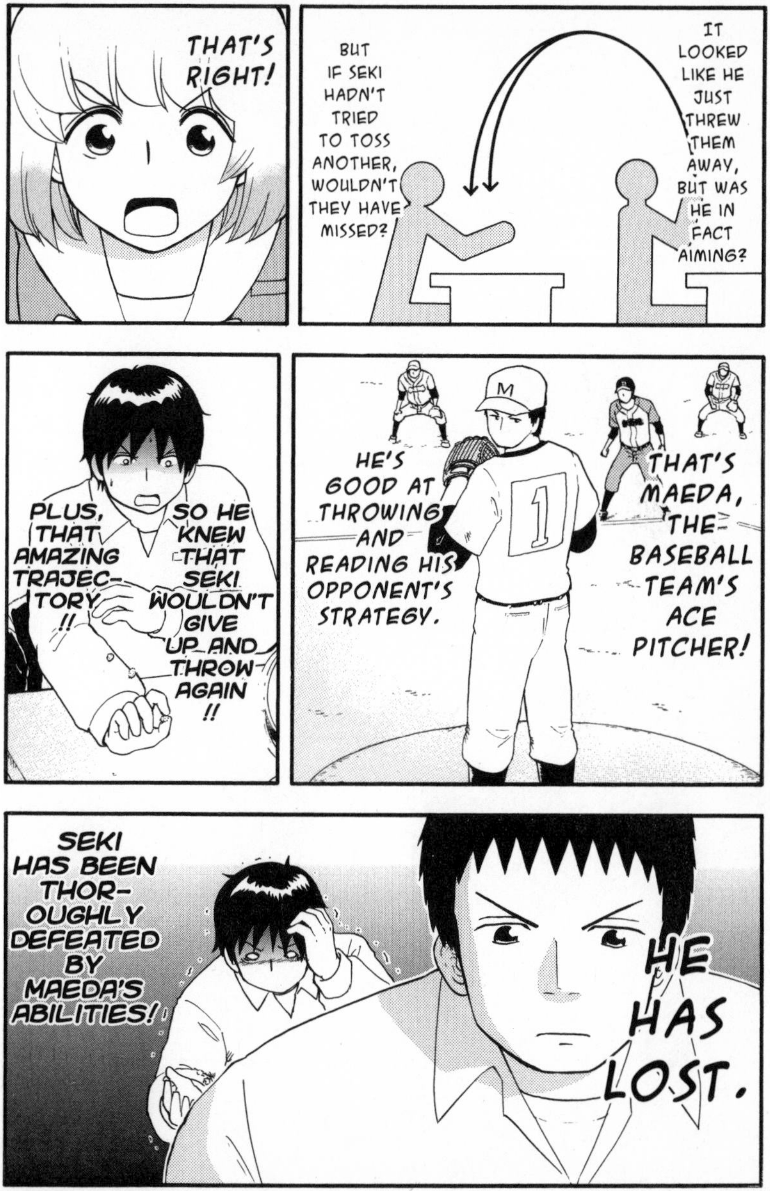
IT LOOKED LIKE HE JUST THREW THEM AWAY, BUT WAS HE IN FACT AIMING?
BUT IF SEKI HADN'T TRIED TO TOSS ANOTHER, WOULDN'T THEY HAVE MISSED?
THAT'S RIGHT!
THAT'S MAEDA, THE BASEBALL TEAM'S ACE PITCHER!
HE'S GOOD AT THROWING AND READING HIS OPPONENT'S STRATEGY.
SO HE KNEW THAT SEKI WOULDN'T GIVE UP AND THROW AGAIN!!
PLUS, THAT AMAZING TRAJEC-TORY!!
HE HAS LOST.
SEKI HAS BEEN THOR-OUGHLY DEFEATED BY MAEDA'S ABILITIES!

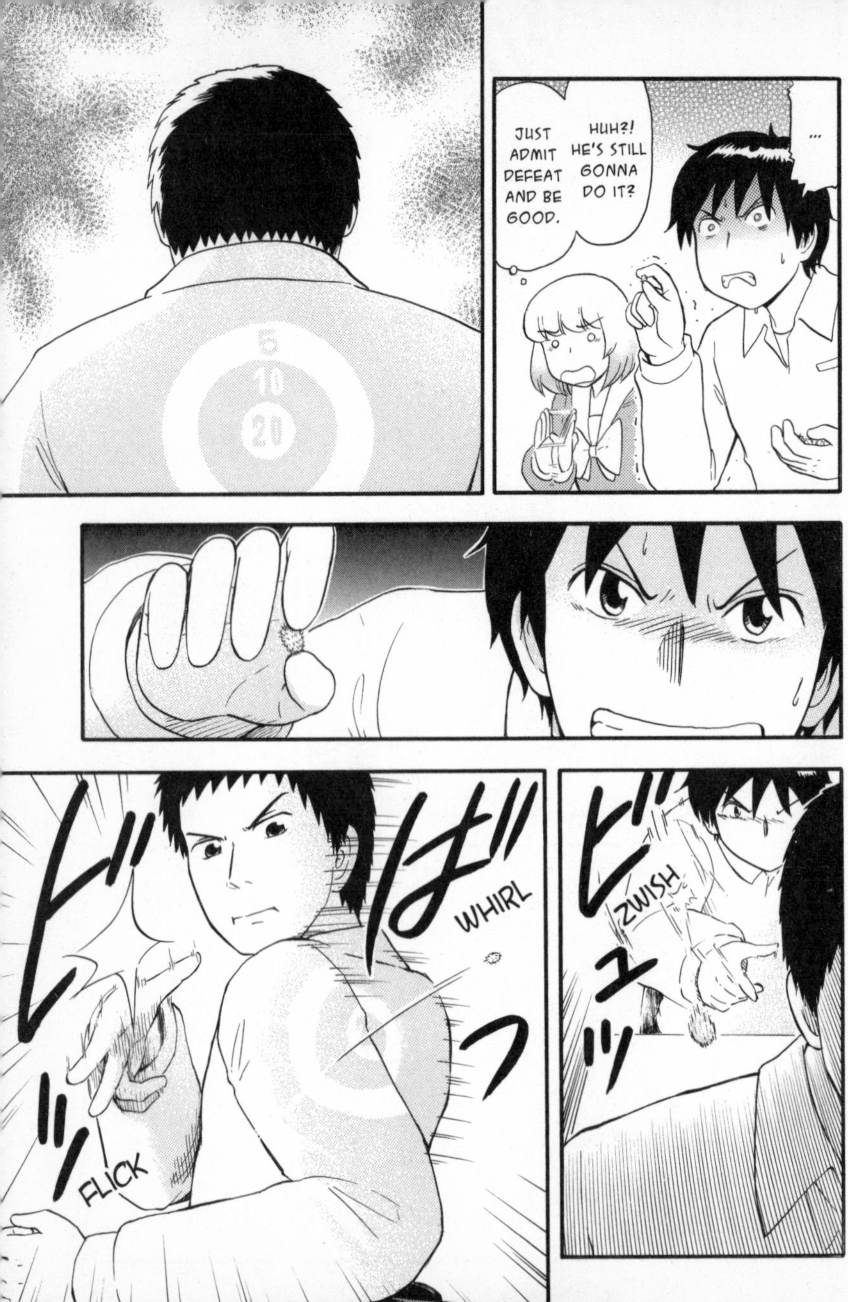
...
HUH?! HE'S STILL GONNA DO IT?
JUST ADMIT DEFEAT AND BE GOOD.
5
10
20
ビュッ
ZWISH
ばっ
WHIRL
FLICK

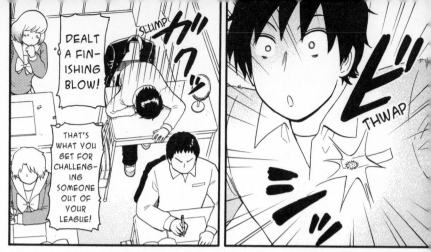

DEALT A FINISHING BLOW!

SCUMP

ガッ

プッ

THAT'S WHAT YOU GET FOR CHALLENGING SOMEONE OUT OF YOUR LEAGUE!

ド!!

THWAP

シッ!

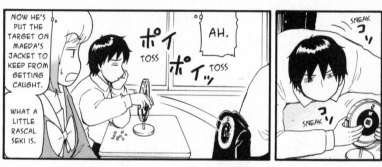

NOW HE'S PUT THE TARGET ON MAEDA'S JACKET TO KEEP FROM GETTING CAUGHT.

WHAT A LITTLE RASCAL SEKI IS.

ポイ

TOSS

AH.

ポイッ

TOSS

SNEAK

コソ

SNEAK

コソ

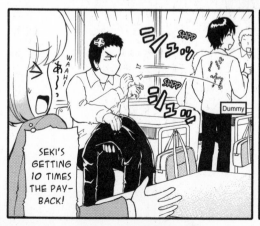

ヨッ

SHPP

ヨッ

SHPP

WAAH!

あー!

Dummy

SEKI'S GETTING 10 TIMES THE PAYBACK!

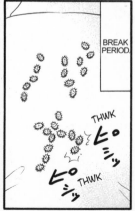

BREAK PERIOD.

THWK

ピシッ

ピシッ

THWK

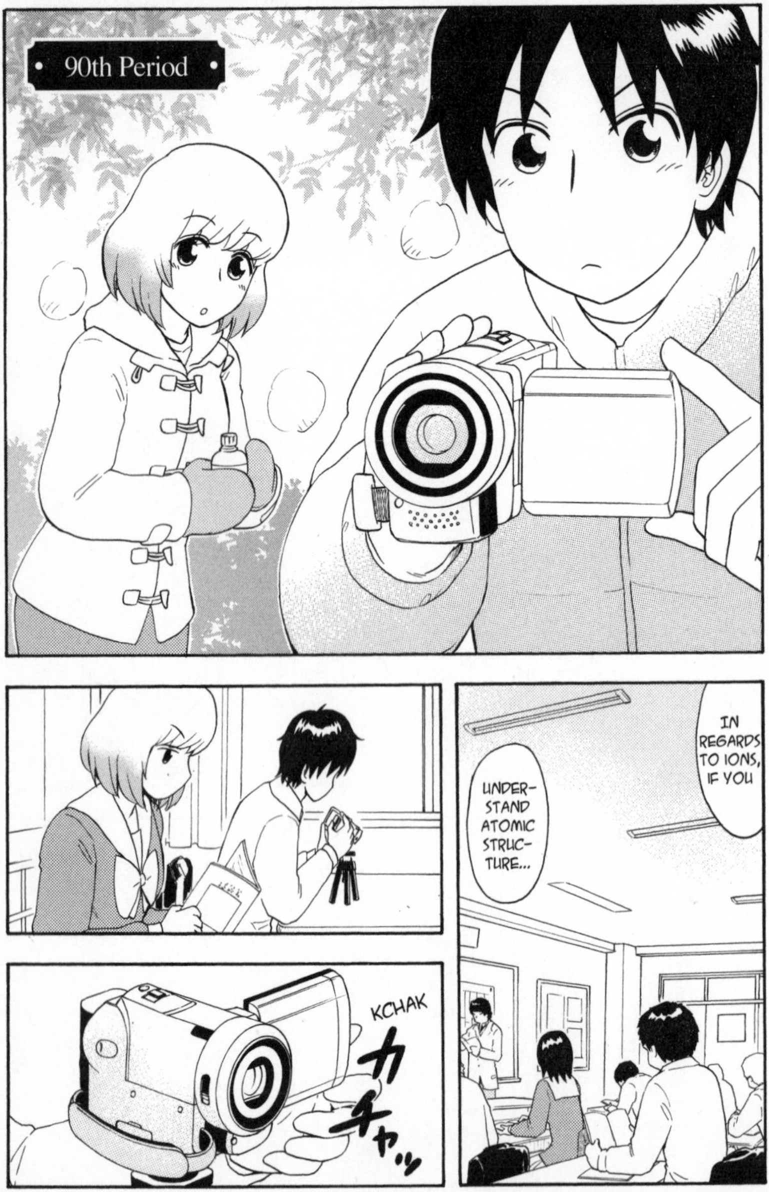
90th Period
IN REGARDS TO IONS, IF YOU
UNDER-STAND ATOMIC STRUC-TURE...
KCHAK
カチャッ

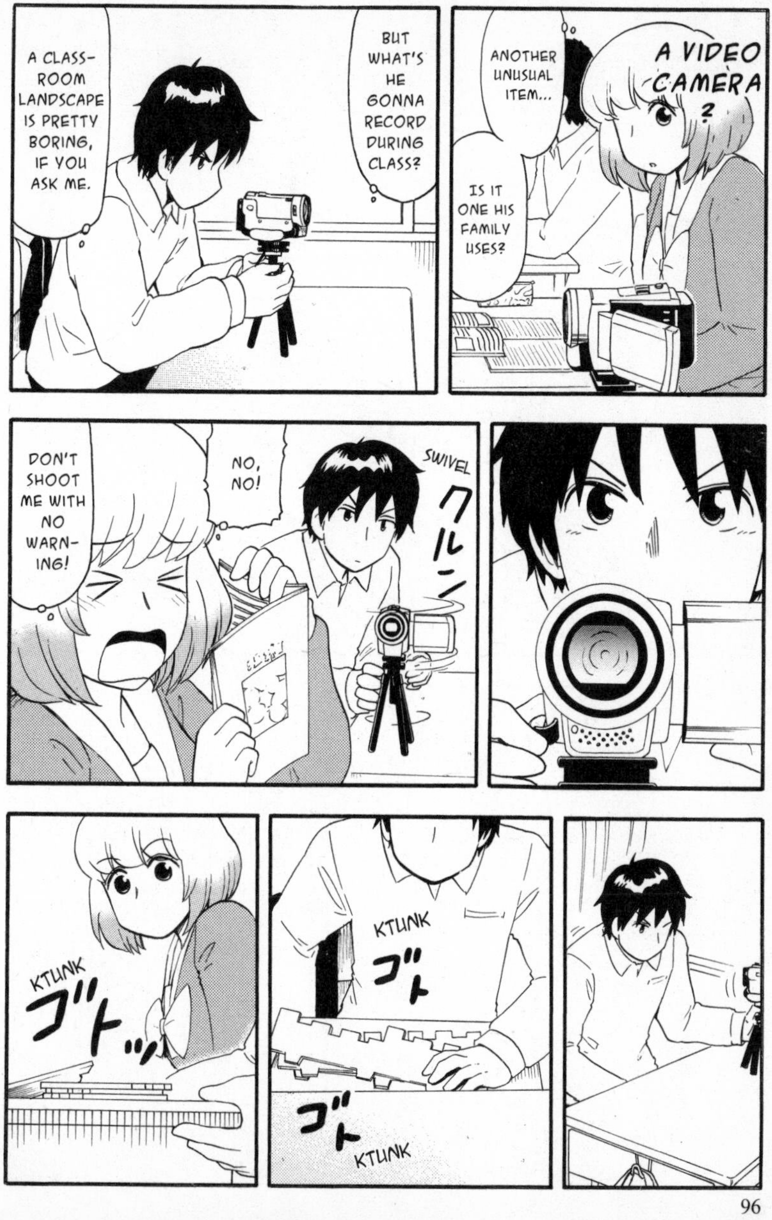
A VIDEO CAMERA?
ANOTHER UNUSUAL ITEM...
IS IT ONE HIS FAMILY USES?
BUT WHAT'S HE GONNA RECORD DURING CLASS?
A CLASS-ROOM LANDSCAPE IS PRETTY BORING, IF YOU ASK ME.
SWIVEL
クルン
NO, NO!
DON'T SHOOT ME WITH NO WARN-ING!
KTUNK
ゴト
ゴト
KTUNK
KTUNK
ゴトッ

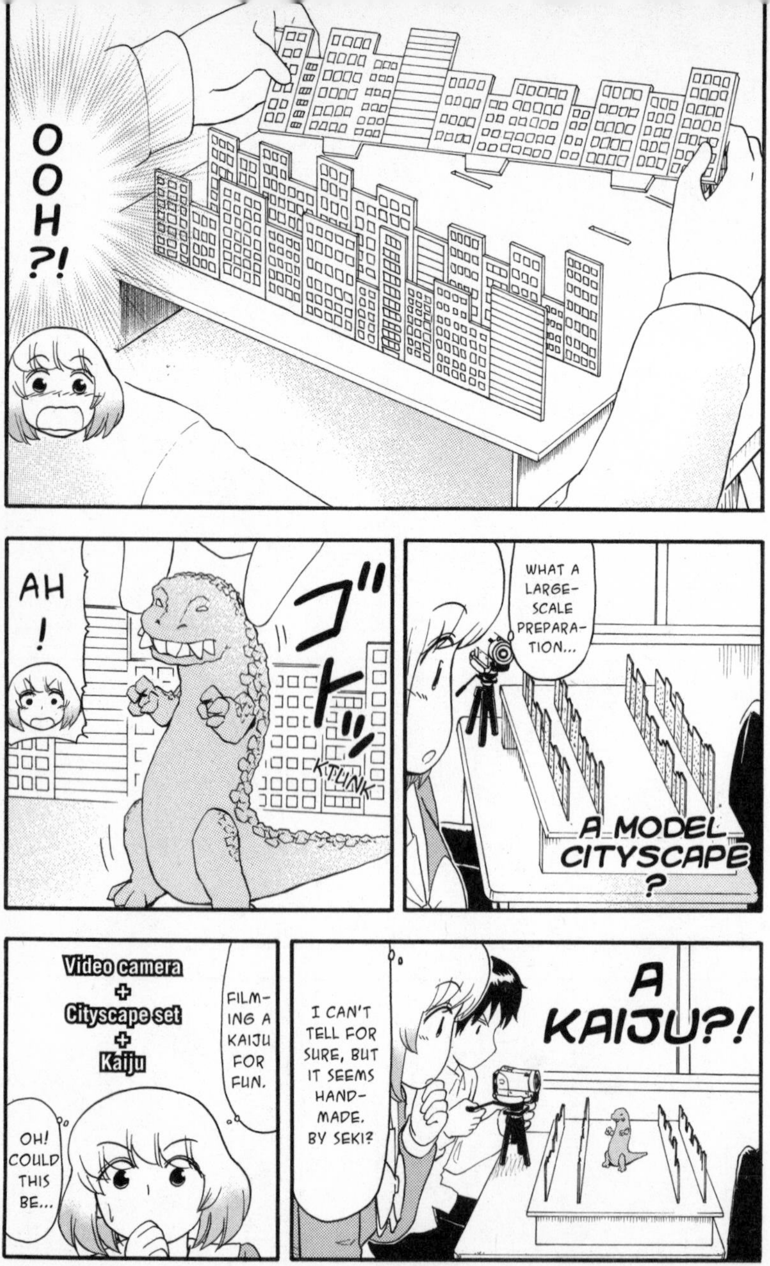
OOH?!
WHAT A LARGE-SCALE PREPARATION...
A MODEL CITYSCAPE?
AH!
ゴトッ
KTUNK
A KAIJU?!
I CAN'T TELL FOR SURE, BUT IT SEEMS HANDMADE. BY SEKI?
FILMING A KAIJU FOR FUN.
Video camera + Cityscape set + Kaiju
OH! COULD THIS BE...

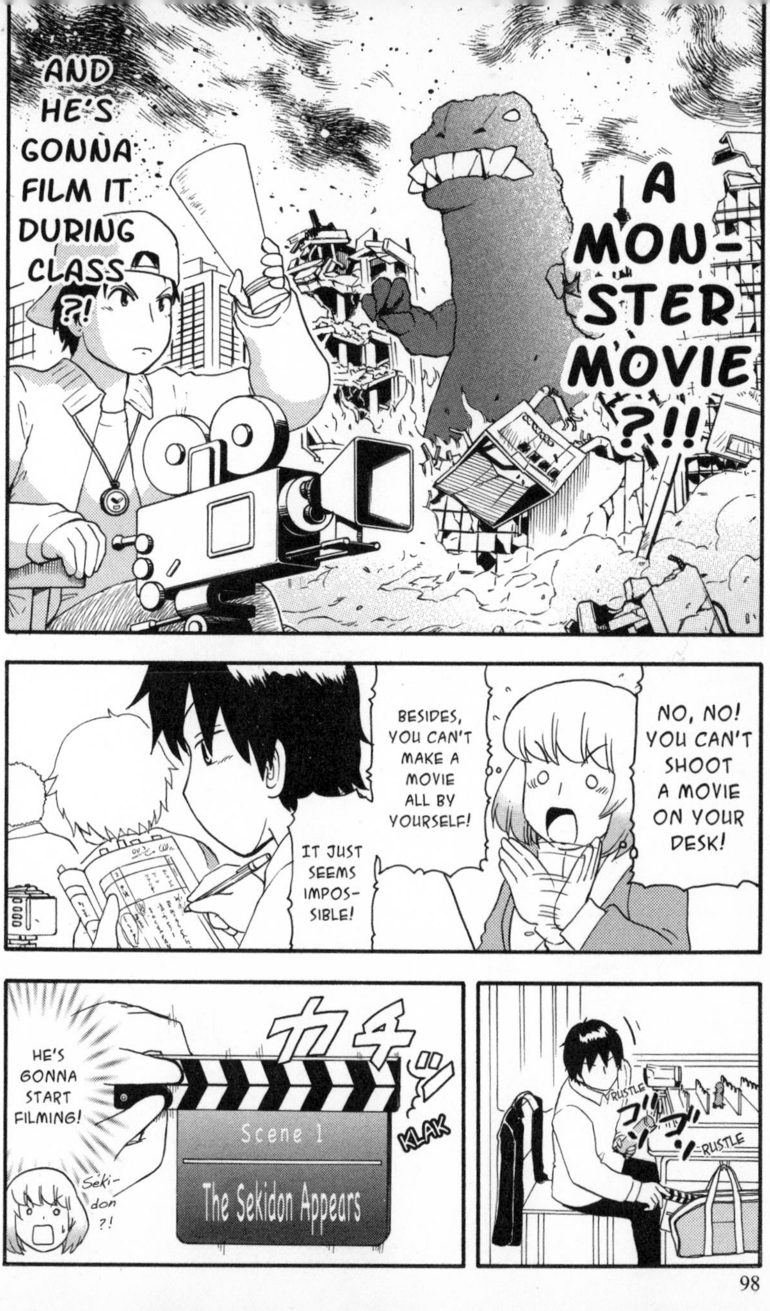
A MON-STER MOVIE ?!!
AND HE'S GONNA FILM IT DURING CLASS ?!
NO, NO! YOU CAN'T SHOOT A MOVIE ON YOUR DESK!
BESIDES, YOU CAN'T MAKE A MOVIE ALL BY YOURSELF!
IT JUST SEEMS IMPOS-SIBLE!
RUSTLE
RUSTLE
カチッ
KLAK
Scene 1
The Sekidon Appears
HE'S GONNA START FILMING!
Seki-don ?!

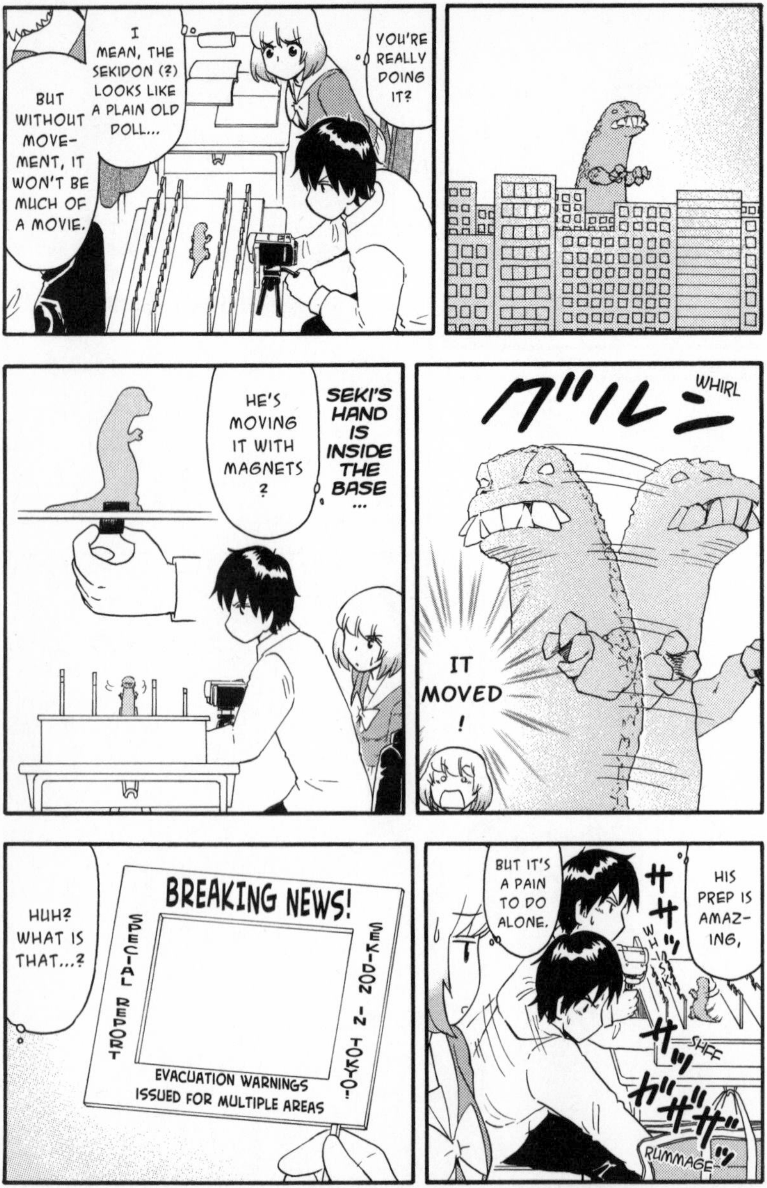
YOU'RE REALLY DOING IT?
I MEAN, THE SEKIDON (?) LOOKS LIKE A PLAIN OLD DOLL...
BUT WITHOUT MOVEMENT, IT WON'T BE MUCH OF A MOVIE.
WHIRL
IT MOVED!
SEKI'S HAND IS INSIDE THE BASE...
HE'S MOVING IT WITH MAGNETS?
HIS PREP IS AMAZING,
BUT IT'S A PAIN TO DO ALONE.
WHISK
SHFF
RUMMAGE
BREAKING NEWS!
SEKIDON IN TOKYO!
SPECIAL REPORT
EVACUATION WARNINGS ISSUED FOR MULTIPLE AREAS
HUH? WHAT IS THAT...?

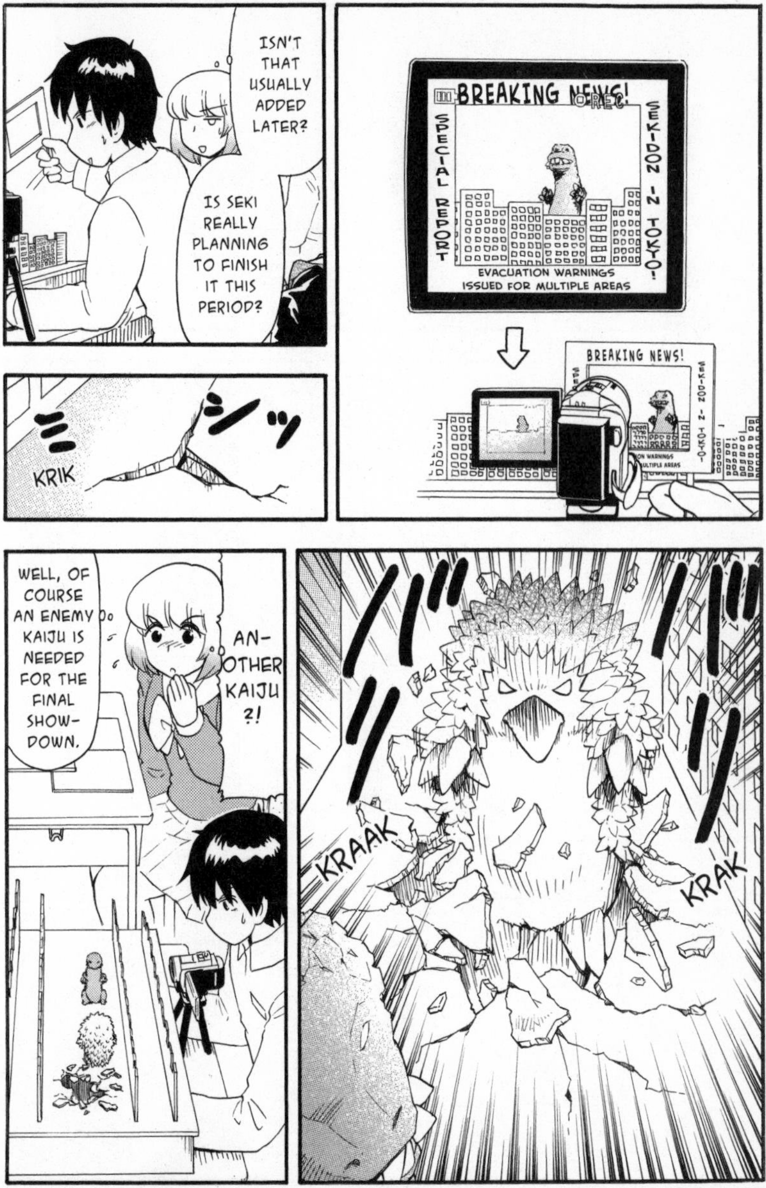
BREAKING NEWS!
REC
SPECIAL REPORT
SEKIDON IN TOKYO!
EVACUATION WARNINGS ISSUED FOR MULTIPLE AREAS
BREAKING NEWS!
SEKIDON IN TOKYO!
ISN'T THAT USUALLY ADDED LATER?
IS SEKI REALLY PLANNING TO FINISH IT THIS PERIOD?
KRIK
KRAAK
KRAK
AN-OTHER KAIJU ?!
WELL, OF COURSE AN ENEMY KAIJU IS NEEDED FOR THE FINAL SHOW-DOWN.

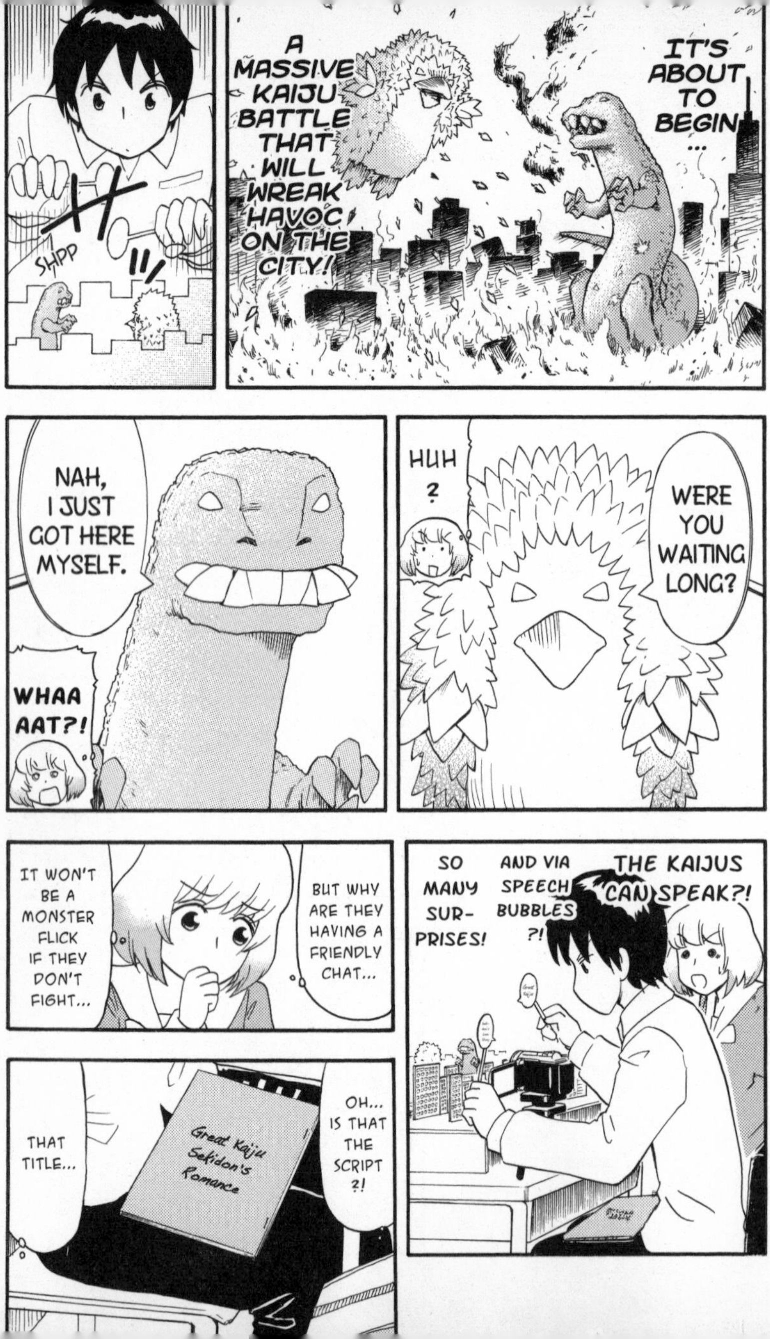

IT'S ABOUT TO BEGIN...
A MASSIVE KAIJU BATTLE THAT WILL WREAK HAVOC ON THE CITY!
SHPP
WERE YOU WAITING LONG?
HUH?
NAH, I JUST GOT HERE MYSELF.
WHAA AAT?!
THE KAIJUS CAN SPEAK?!
AND VIA SPEECH BUBBLES?!
SO MANY SURPRISES!
BUT WHY ARE THEY HAVING A FRIENDLY CHAT...
IT WON'T BE A MONSTER FLICK IF THEY DON'T FIGHT...
OH... IS THAT THE SCRIPT?!
Great Kaiju Sekidon's Romance
THAT TITLE...

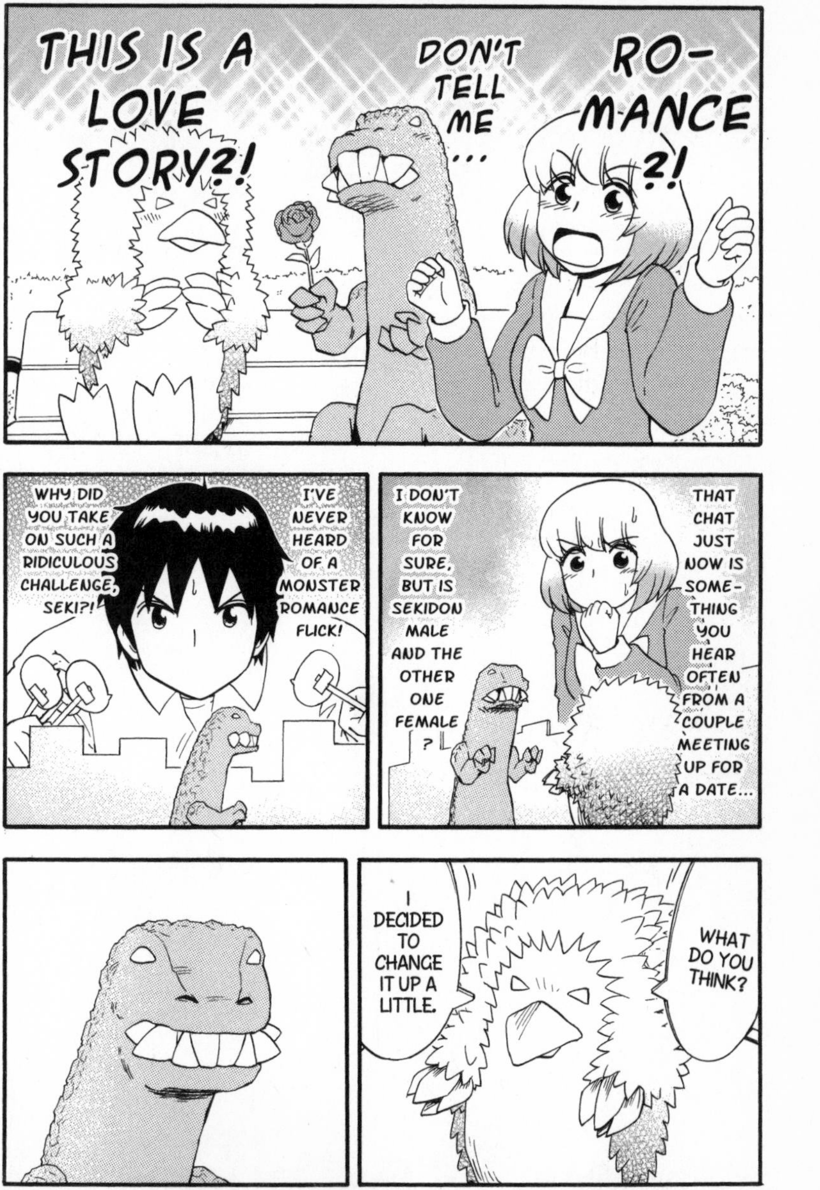
RO-MANCE?!
DON'T TELL ME...
THIS IS A LOVE STORY?!
THAT CHAT JUST NOW IS SOMETHING YOU HEAR OFTEN FROM A COUPLE MEETING UP FOR A DATE...
I DON'T KNOW FOR SURE, BUT IS SEKIDON MALE AND THE OTHER ONE FEMALE?
I'VE NEVER HEARD OF A MONSTER ROMANCE FLICK!
WHY DID YOU TAKE ON SUCH A RIDICULOUS CHALLENGE, SEKI?!
I DECIDED TO CHANGE IT UP A LITTLE.
WHAT DO YOU THINK?

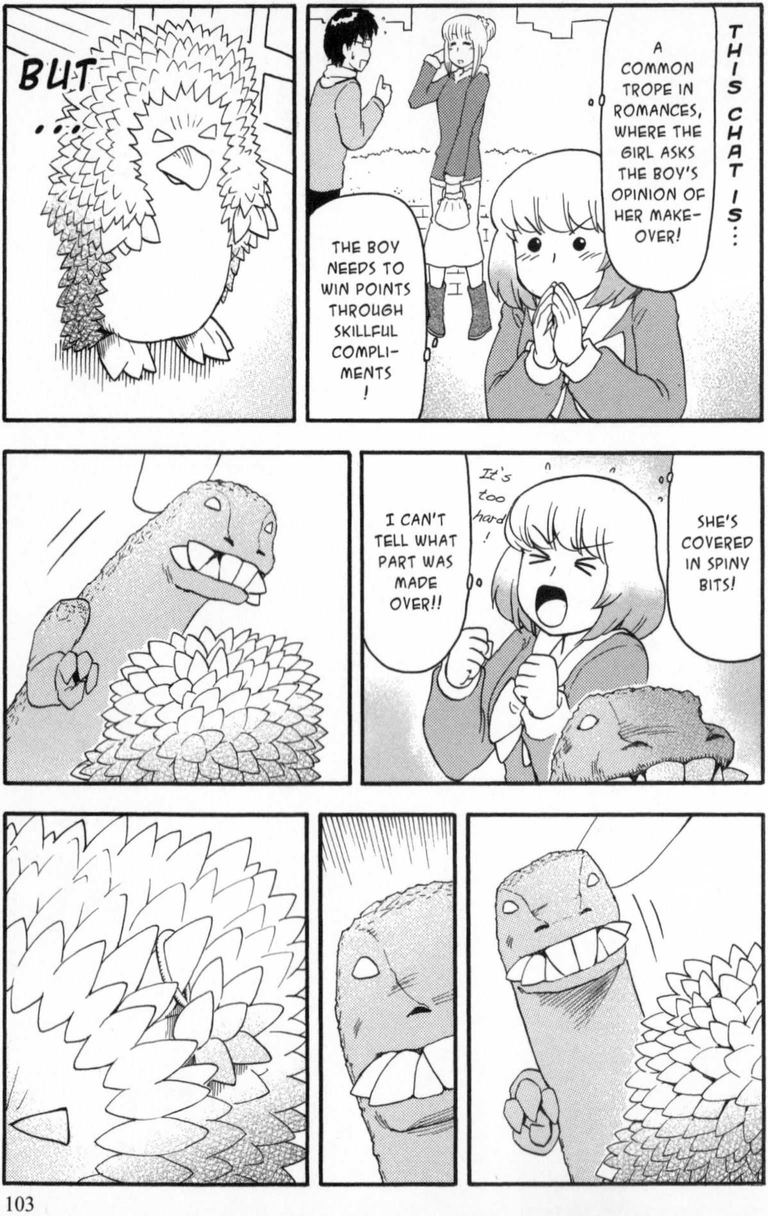
THIS CHAT IS...
A COMMON TROPE IN ROMANCES, WHERE THE GIRL ASKS THE BOY'S OPINION OF HER MAKE-OVER!
THE BOY NEEDS TO WIN POINTS THROUGH SKILLFUL COMPLI-MENTS!
BUT...
SHE'S COVERED IN SPINY BITS!
It's too hard!
I CAN'T TELL WHAT PART WAS MADE OVER!!

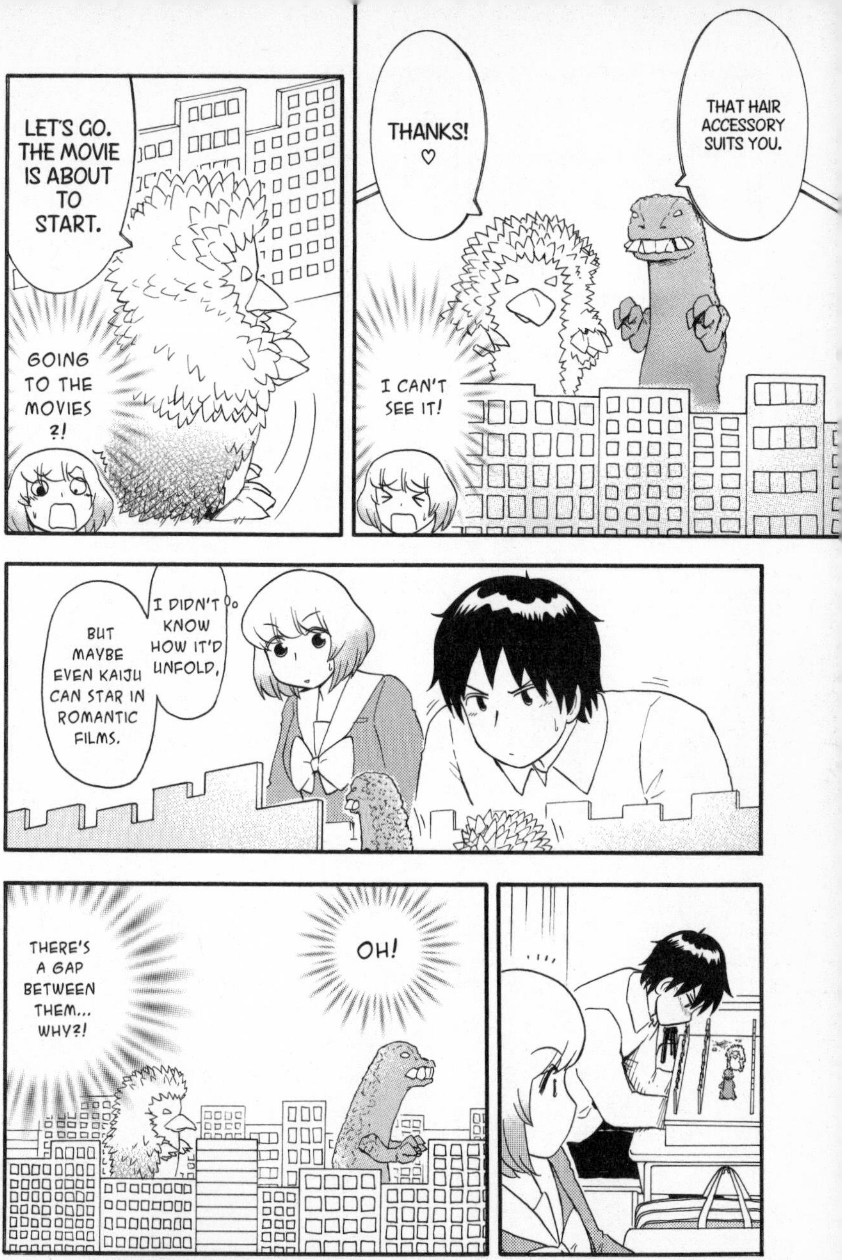
THAT HAIR ACCESSORY SUITS YOU.
THANKS! ♡
I CAN'T SEE IT!
LET'S GO. THE MOVIE IS ABOUT TO START.
GOING TO THE MOVIES?!
I DIDN'T KNOW HOW IT'D UNFOLD,
BUT MAYBE EVEN KAIJU CAN STAR IN ROMANTIC FILMS.
...
OH!
THERE'S A GAP BETWEEN THEM... WHY?!

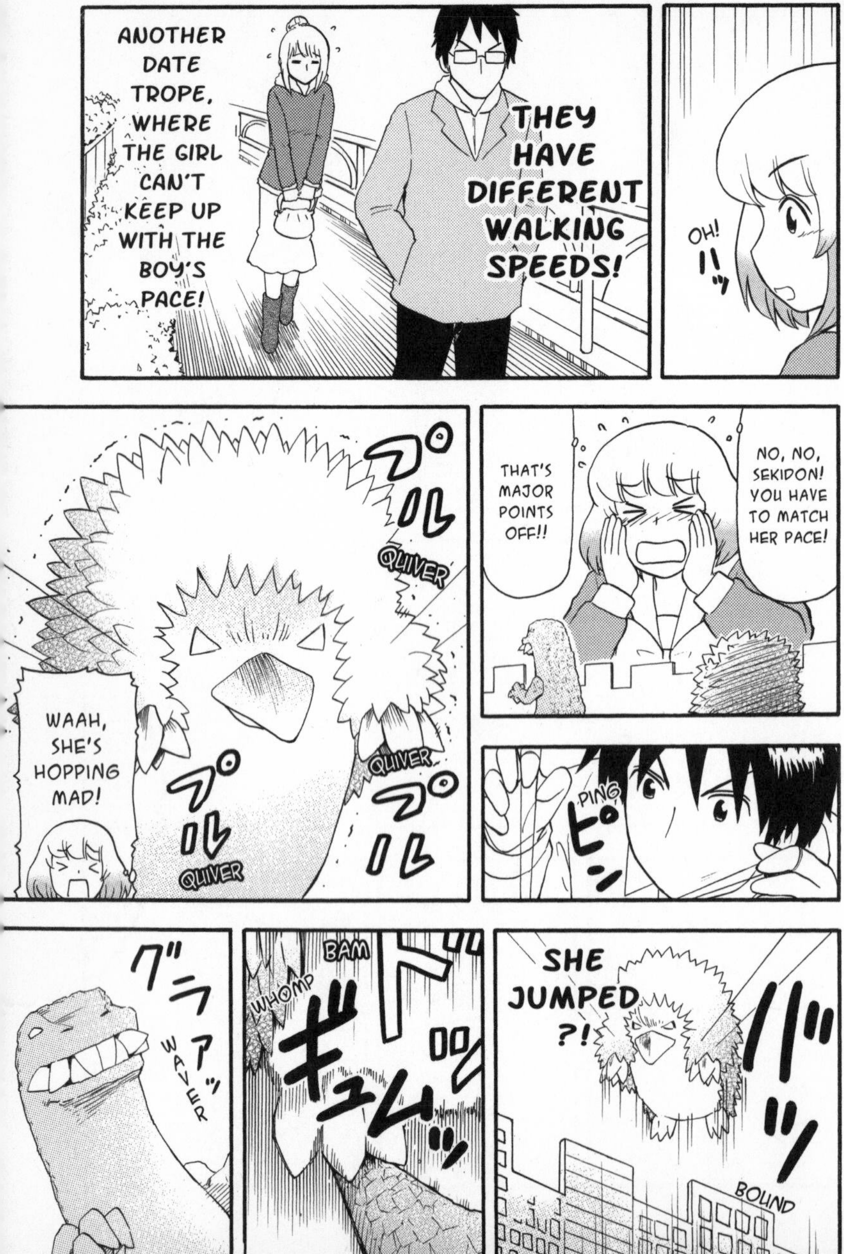

OH!
ハッ
THEY HAVE DIFFERENT WALKING SPEEDS!
ANOTHER DATE TROPE, WHERE THE GIRL CAN'T KEEP UP WITH THE BOY'S PACE!
NO, NO, SEKIDON! YOU HAVE TO MATCH HER PACE!
THAT'S MAJOR POINTS OFF!!
PING
ピン
プル
QUIVER
QUIVER
プル
プル
QUIVER
WAAH, SHE'S HOPPING MAD!
バッ
SHE JUMPED?!
BOUND
ドッ
BAM
ギュムッ
WHOMP
グラァッ
WAVER

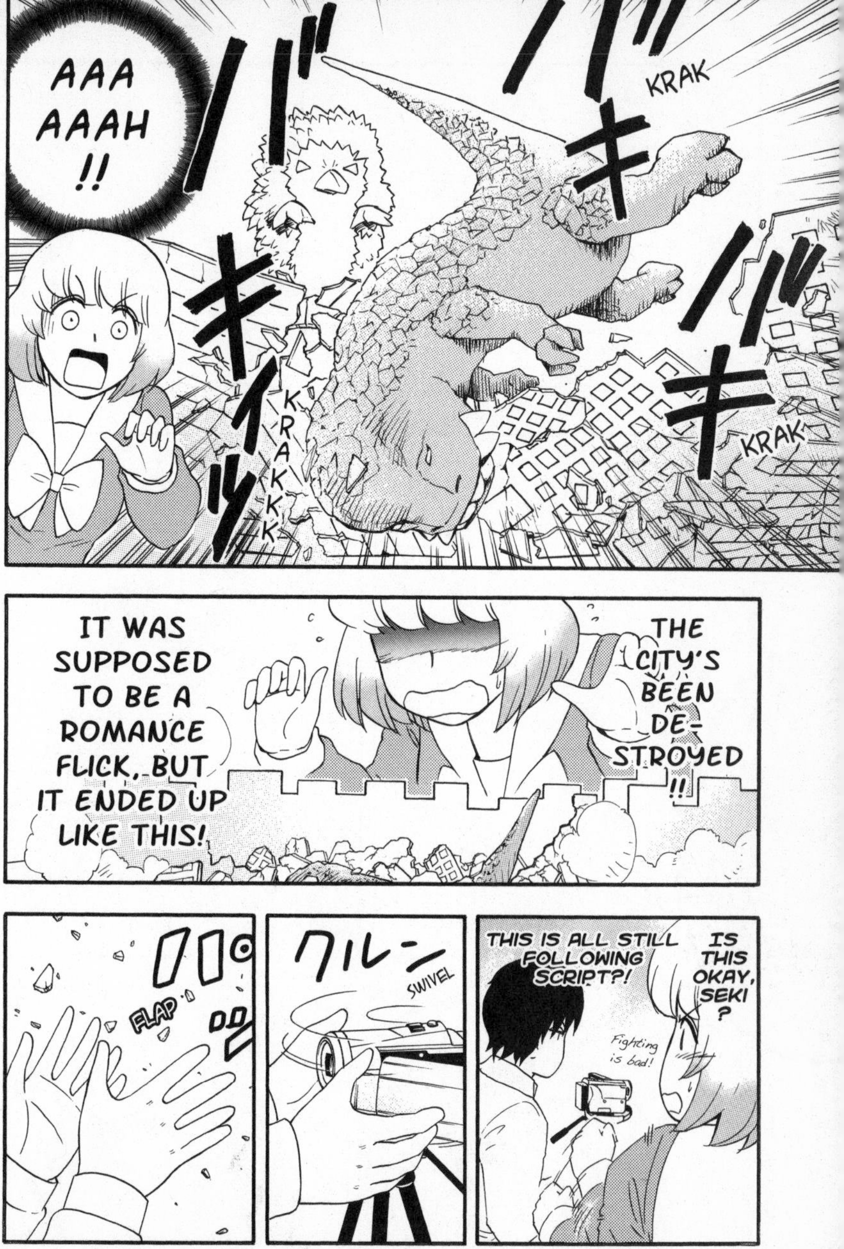
バキ
KRAK
バキ
KRAK
バキイッ
KRAKKKK
AAA AAAH!!
THE CITY'S BEEN DE-STROYED!!
IT WAS SUPPOSED TO BE A ROMANCE FLICK, BUT IT ENDED UP LIKE THIS!
IS THIS OKAY, SEKI?
THIS IS ALL STILL FOLLOWING SCRIPT?!
Fighting is bad!
クルーン
SWIVEL
FLAP

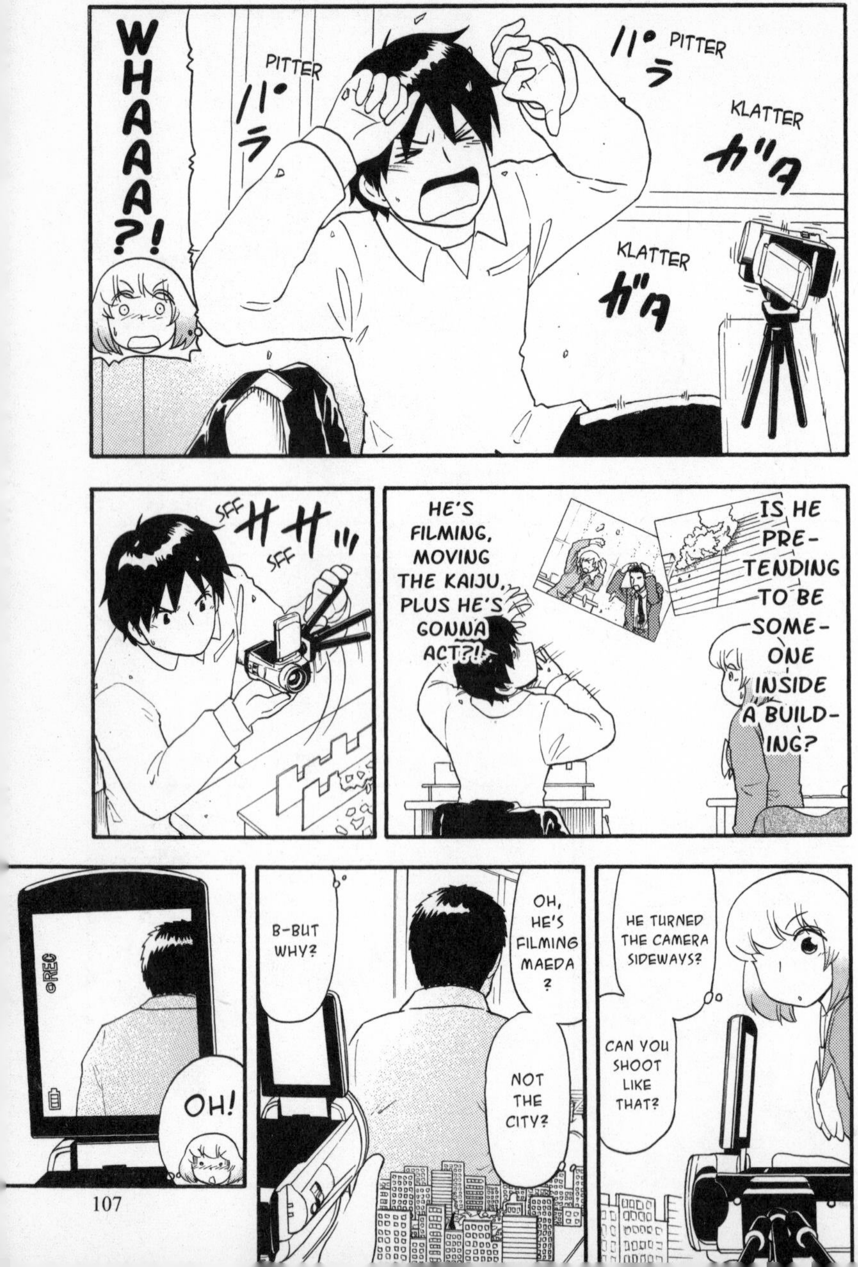
パラ PITTER
KLATTER ガタ
KLATTER ガタ
PITTER パラ
WHAAAA?!
IS HE PRE-TENDING TO BE SOME-ONE INSIDE A BUILD-ING?
HE'S FILMING, MOVING THE KAIJU, PLUS HE'S GONNA ACT?!
SFF ササッ SFF
HE TURNED THE CAMERA SIDEWAYS?
CAN YOU SHOOT LIKE THAT?
OH, HE'S FILMING MAEDA?
NOT THE CITY?
B-BUT WHY?
REC
OH!

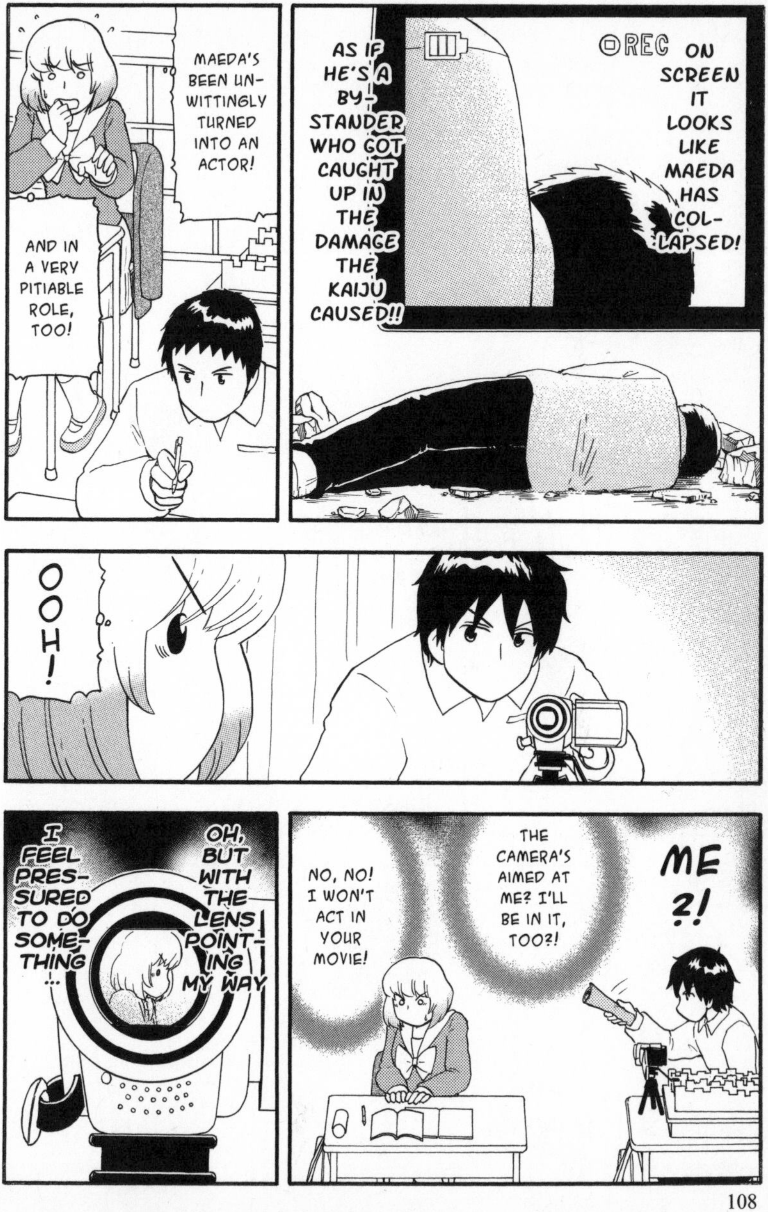
REC
ON SCREEN IT LOOKS LIKE MAEDA HAS COLLAPSED!
AS IF HE'S A BYSTANDER WHO GOT CAUGHT UP IN THE DAMAGE THE KAIJU CAUSED!!
MAEDA'S BEEN UNWITTINGLY TURNED INTO AN ACTOR!
AND IN A VERY PITIABLE ROLE, TOO!
OOH!
ME ?!
THE CAMERA'S AIMED AT ME? I'LL BE IN IT, TOO?!
NO, NO! I WON'T ACT IN YOUR MOVIE!
OH, BUT WITH THE LENS POINTING MY WAY
I FEEL PRESSURED TO DO SOMETHING...

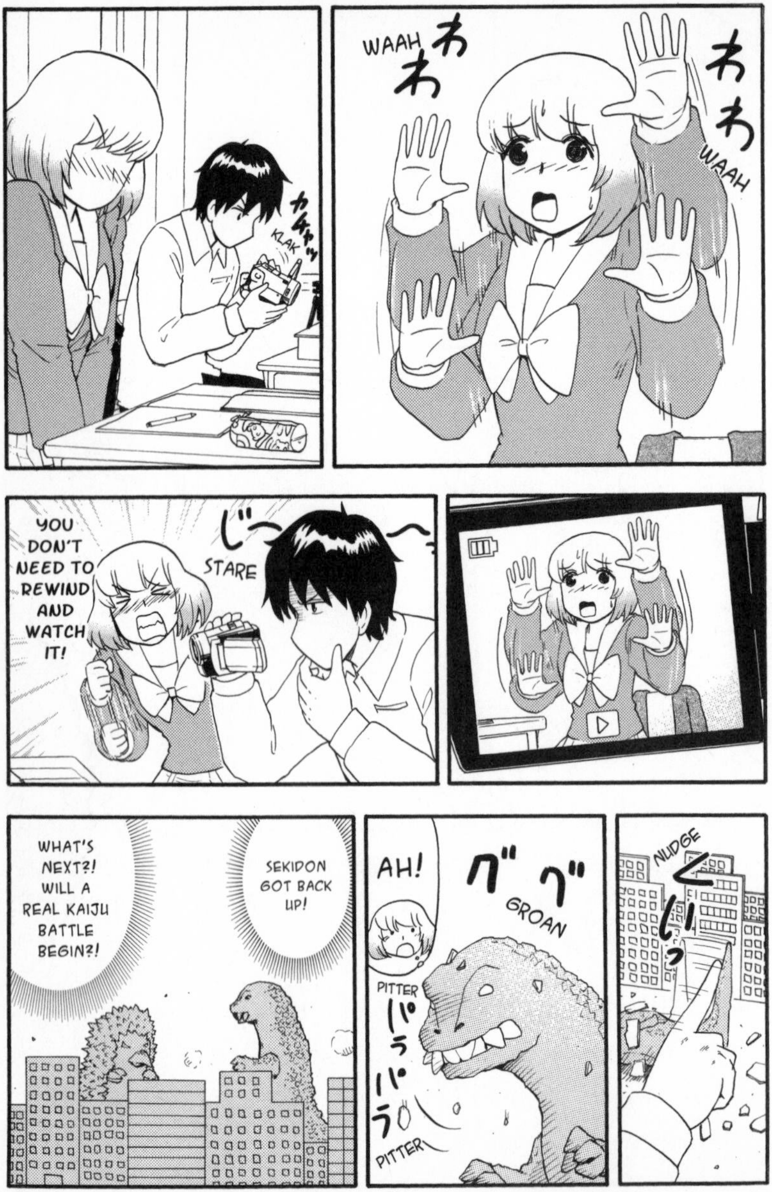

WAAH
わ
わ
わ
わ
WAAH
KLAK
STARE
じ〜
YOU DON'T NEED TO REWIND AND WATCH IT!
NUDGE
ぐいっ
AH!
グ グ
GROAN
PITTER
パラパラ
PITTER
SEKIDON GOT BACK UP!
WHAT'S NEXT?! WILL A REAL KAIJU BATTLE BEGIN?!

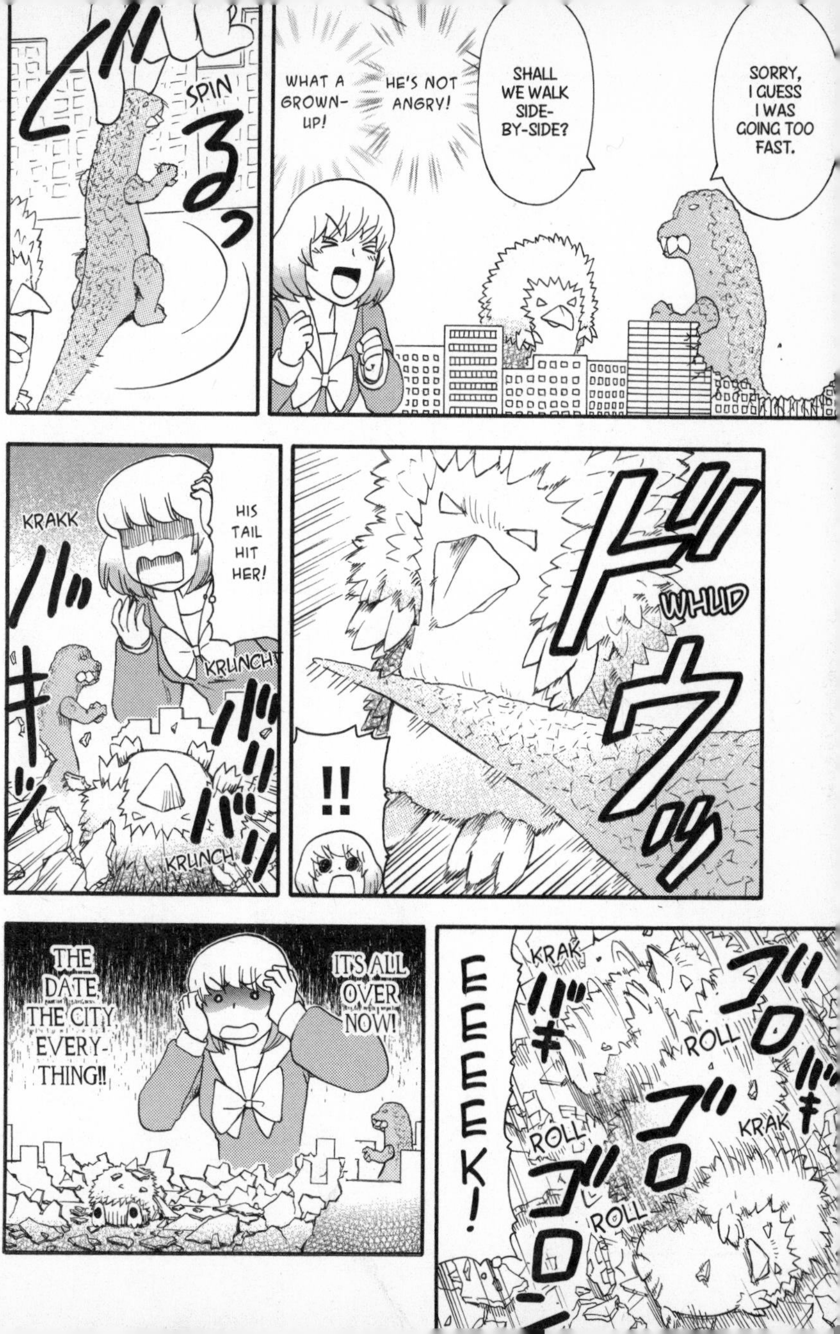
SORRY, I GUESS I WAS GOING TOO FAST.
SHALL WE WALK SIDE-BY-SIDE?
HE'S NOT ANGRY!
WHAT A GROWN-UP!
SPIN
WHUD
!!
HIS TAIL HIT HER!
KRAKK
KRUNCH
KRUNCH
EEEEEK!
KRAK
ROLL
KRAK
ROLL
ROLL
IT'S ALL OVER NOW!
THE DATE, THE CITY, EVERY-THING!!

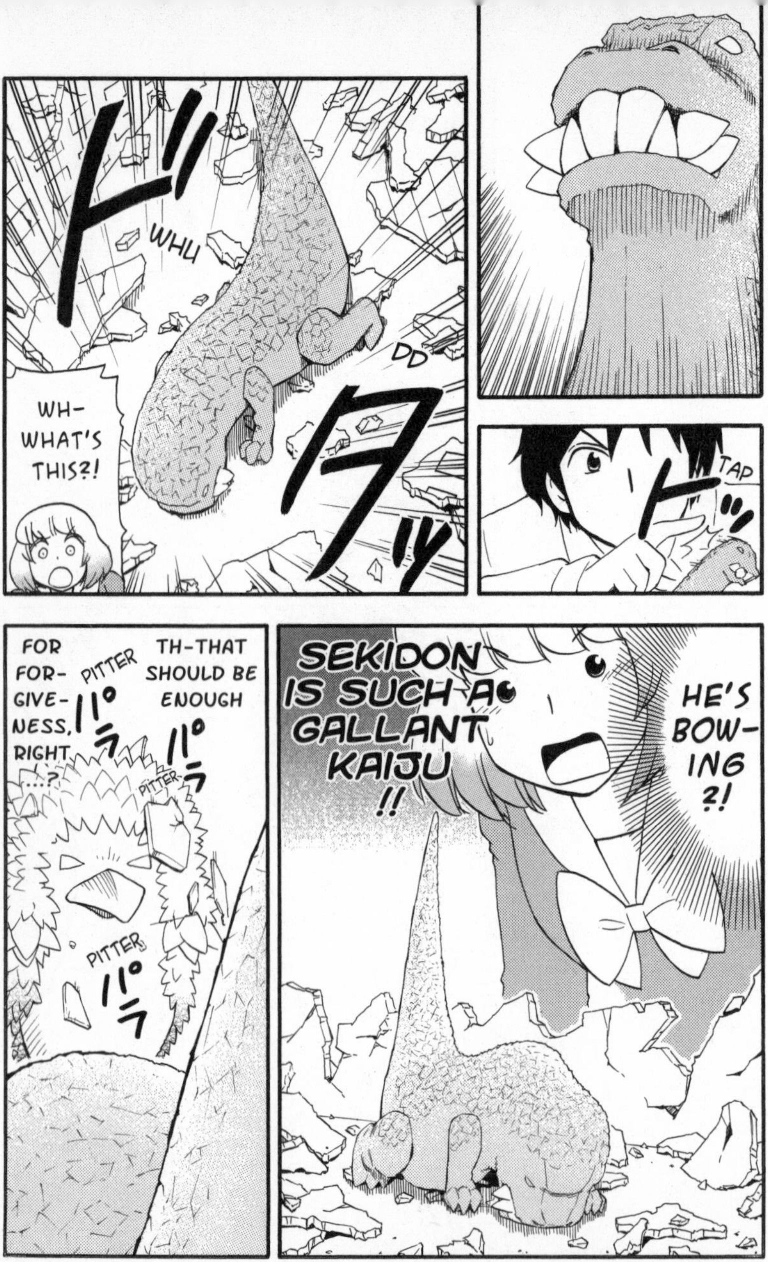
TAP
WHU
DD
WH- WHAT'S THIS?!
HE'S BOW-ING?!
SEKIDON IS SUCH A GALLANT KAIJU!!
TH-THAT SHOULD BE ENOUGH
FOR FOR-GIVE-NESS, RIGHT.....?
PITTER
PITTER
PITTER

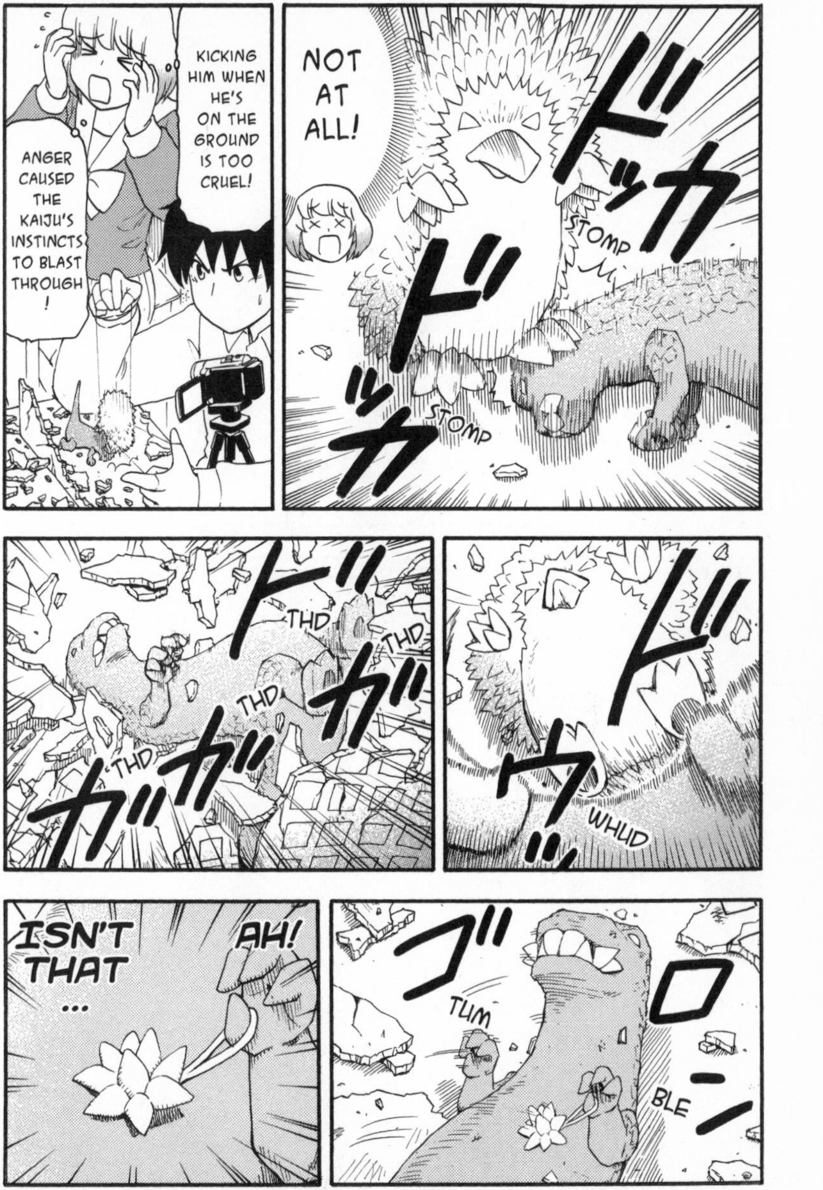
NOT AT ALL!
ドッカ
STOMP
ドッカ
STOMP
KICKING HIM WHEN HE'S ON THE GROUND IS TOO CRUEL!
ANGER CAUSED THE KAIJU'S INSTINCTS TO BLAST THROUGH!
ドウッ
WHUD
ドガガガ
THD
THD
THD
THD
ゴローン
TUM
BLE
AH!
ISN'T THAT...

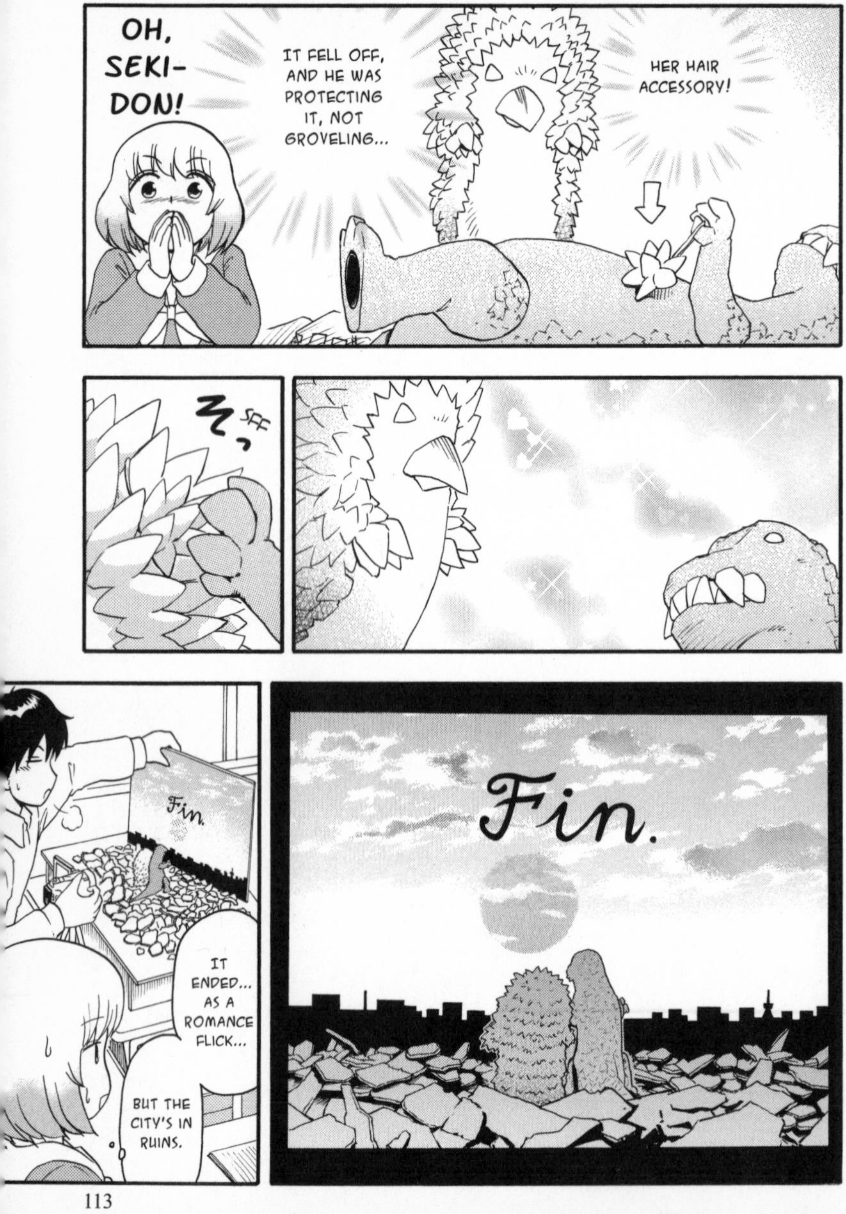
HER HAIR ACCESSORY!
IT FELL OFF, AND HE WAS PROTECTING IT, NOT GROVELING...
OH, SEKI-DON!
SFF
Fin.
Fin.
IT ENDED... AS A ROMANCE FLICK...
BUT THE CITY'S IN RUINS.

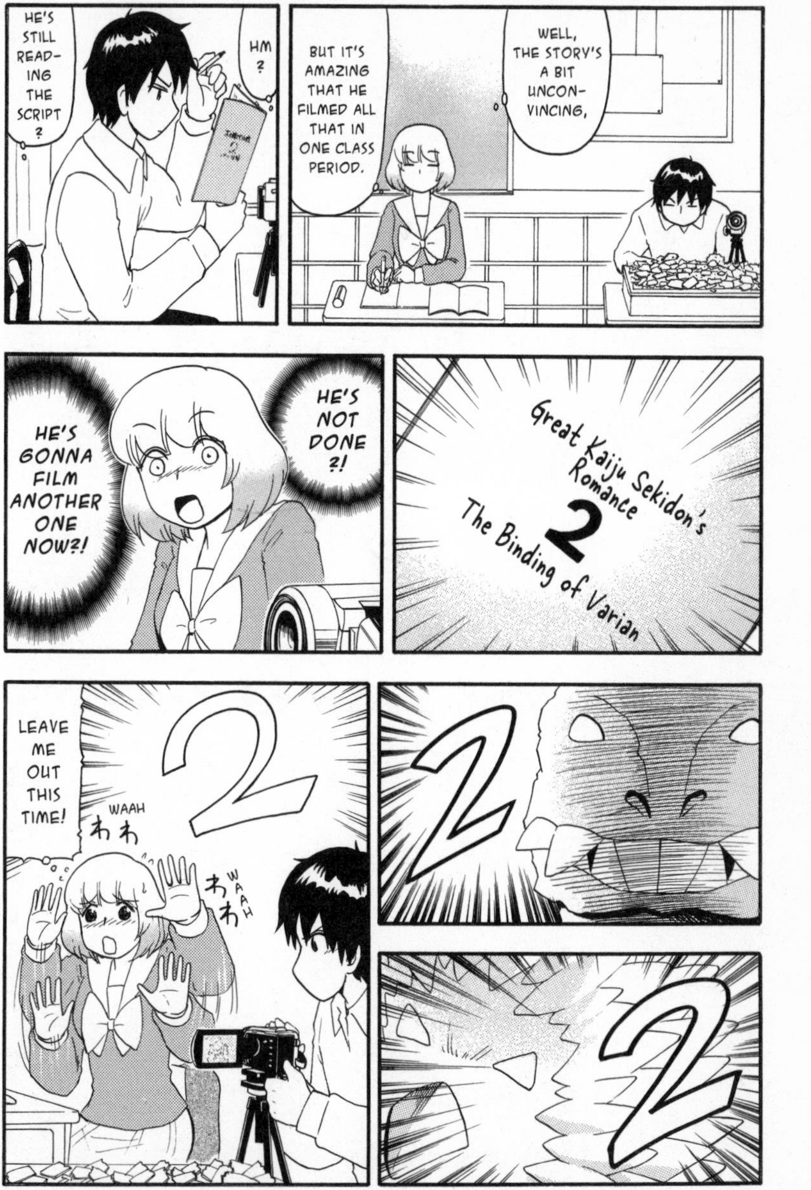
WELL, THE STORY'S A BIT UNCON-VINCING,
BUT IT'S AMAZING THAT HE FILMED ALL THAT IN ONE CLASS PERIOD.
HM?
HE'S STILL READ-ING THE SCRIPT?
Great Kaiju Sekidon's Romance
2
The Binding of Varian
HE'S NOT DONE?!
HE'S GONNA FILM ANOTHER ONE NOW?!
2
2
2
LEAVE ME OUT THIS TIME!
わわ
WAAH
わわ
WAAH

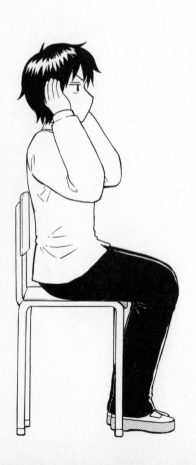

My Neighbor Seki

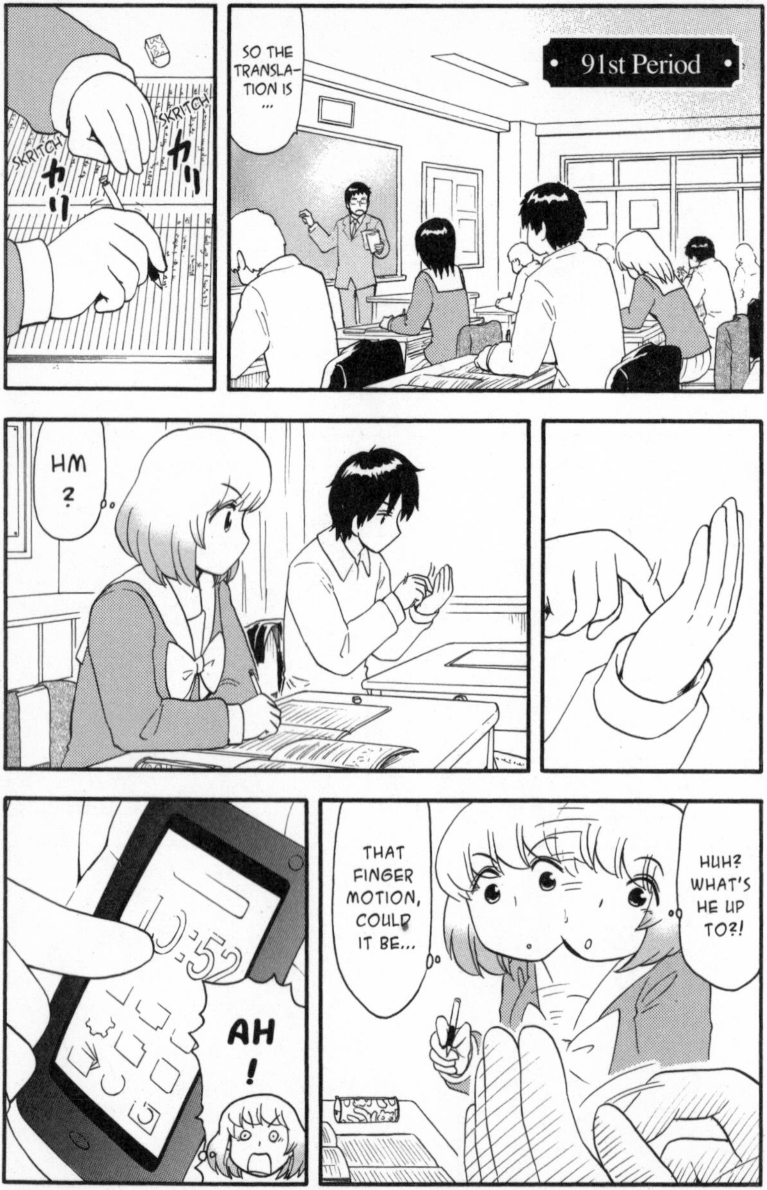
• 91st Period •
SO THE TRANSLATION IS ...
SKRITCH
カリ
SKRITCH
カリ
HM?
HUH? WHAT'S HE UP TO?!
THAT FINGER MOTION, COULD IT BE...
AH!

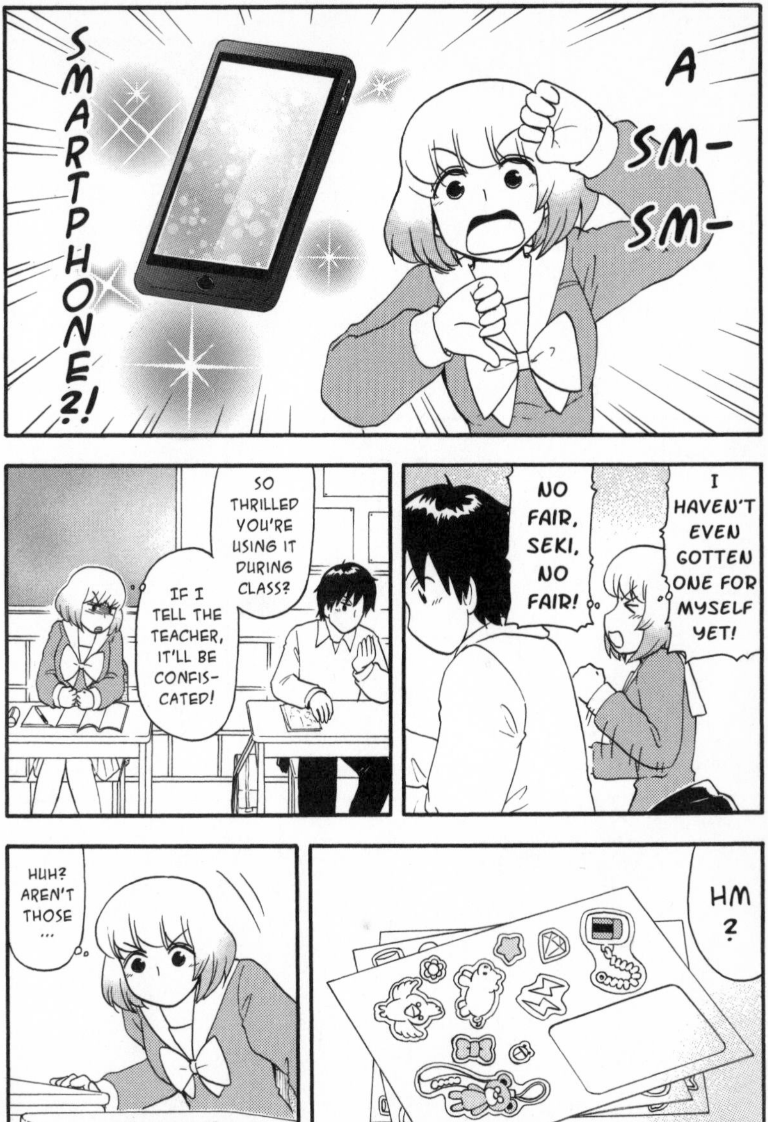
A SM-SM-
SMARTPHONE?!
I HAVEN'T EVEN GOTTEN ONE FOR MYSELF YET!
NO FAIR, SEKI, NO FAIR!
SO THRILLED YOU'RE USING IT DURING CLASS?
IF I TELL THE TEACHER, IT'LL BE CONFISCATED!
HM?
HUH? AREN'T THOSE ...

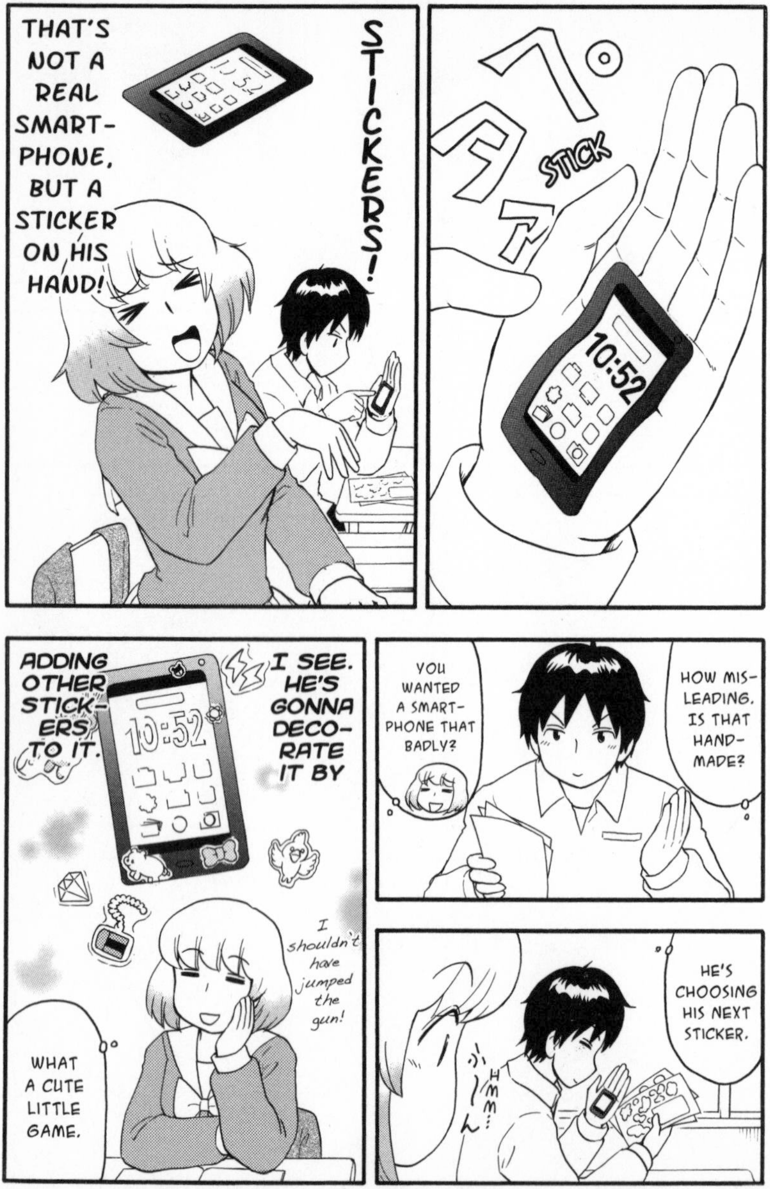
ペタ
STICK
STICKERS!
THAT'S NOT A REAL SMART-PHONE, BUT A STICKER ON HIS HAND!
HOW MIS-LEADING. IS THAT HAND-MADE?
YOU WANTED A SMART-PHONE THAT BADLY?
HE'S CHOOSING HIS NEXT STICKER.
ふ～ん
HMM...
I SEE. HE'S GONNA DECO-RATE IT BY
ADDING OTHER STICK-ERS TO IT.
I shouldn't have jumped the gun!
WHAT A CUTE LITTLE GAME.

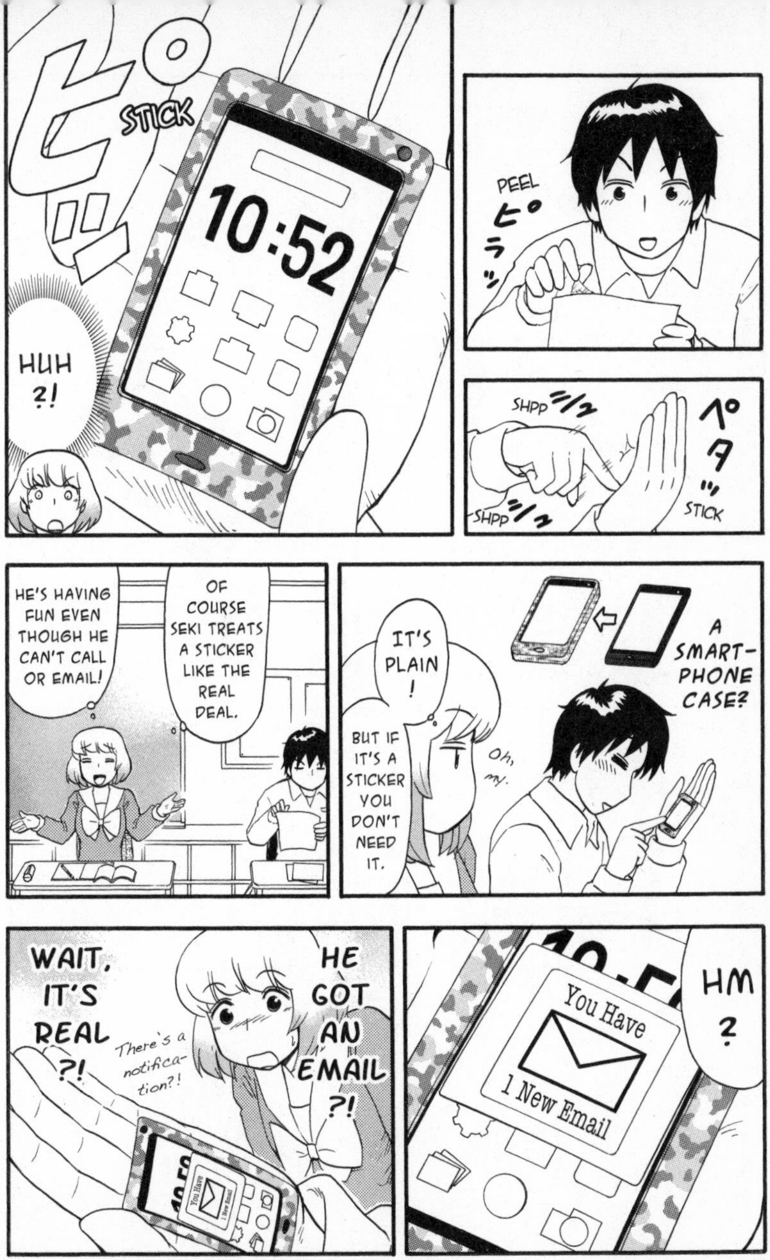
PEEL
SHPP
STICK
SHPP
STICK
HUH ?!
A SMART-PHONE CASE?
Oh, my.
IT'S PLAIN !
BUT IF IT'S A STICKER YOU DON'T NEED IT.
OF COURSE SEKI TREATS A STICKER LIKE THE REAL DEAL.
HE'S HAVING FUN EVEN THOUGH HE CAN'T CALL OR EMAIL!
HM ?
You Have 1 New Email
HE GOT AN EMAIL ?!
There's a notification?!
WAIT, IT'S REAL ?!

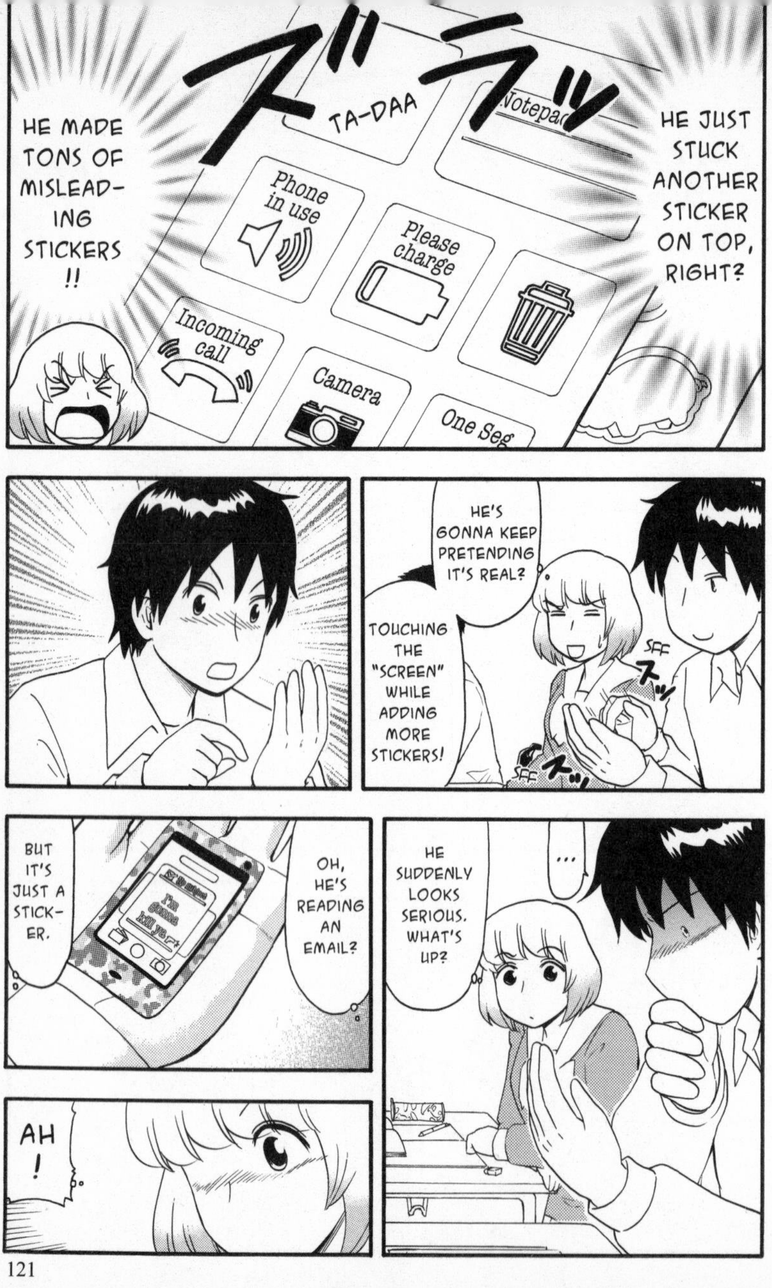
ズラッ
TA-DAA
HE JUST STUCK ANOTHER STICKER ON TOP, RIGHT?
HE MADE TONS OF MISLEAD-ING STICKERS !!
Phone in use
Please charge
Incoming call
Camera
One Seg
HE'S GONNA KEEP PRETENDING IT'S REAL?
TOUCHING THE "SCREEN" WHILE ADDING MORE STICKERS!
SFF
SFF
...
HE SUDDENLY LOOKS SERIOUS. WHAT'S UP?
OH, HE'S READING AN EMAIL?
BUT IT'S JUST A STICK-ER.
I'm gonna kill ya
AH !

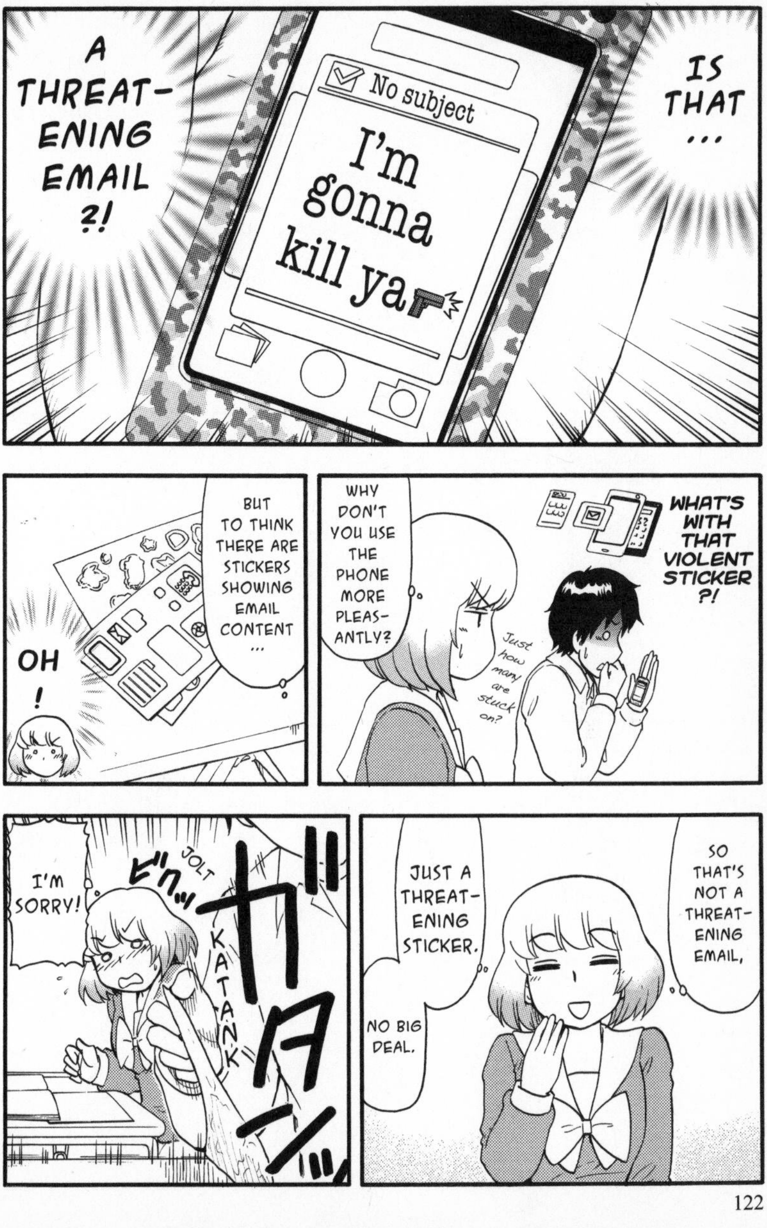

IS THAT ...
No subject
I'm gonna kill ya
A THREAT-ENING EMAIL ?!
WHAT'S WITH THAT VIOLENT STICKER ?!
WHY DON'T YOU USE THE PHONE MORE PLEAS-ANTLY?
Just how many are stuck on?
BUT TO THINK THERE ARE STICKERS SHOWING EMAIL CONTENT ...
OH !
SO THAT'S NOT A THREAT-ENING EMAIL,
JUST A THREAT-ENING STICKER.
NO BIG DEAL.
ビクッ
JOLT
ガタンッ
KATANK
I'M SORRY!

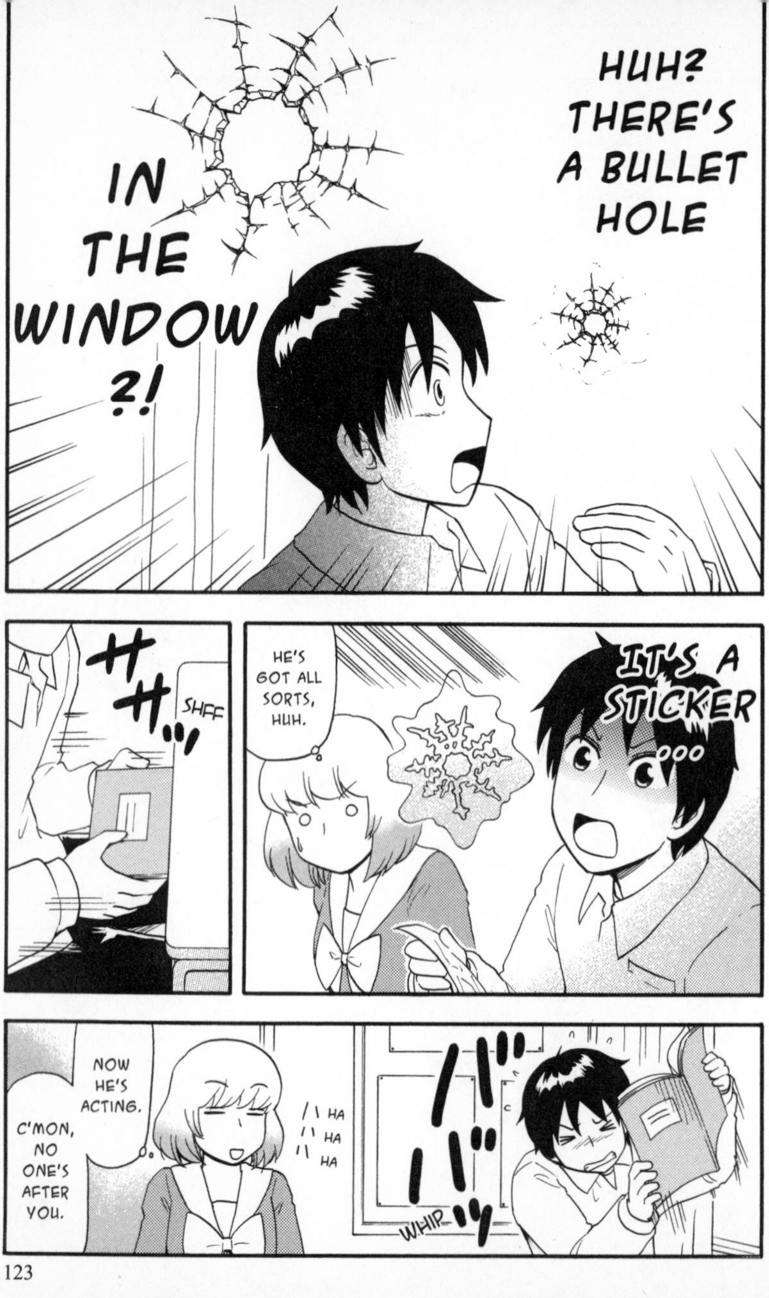
HUH? THERE'S A BULLET HOLE
IN THE WINDOW ?!
IT'S A STICKER...
HE'S GOT ALL SORTS, HUH.
SHFF
WHIP
HA HA HA
NOW HE'S ACTING.
C'MON, NO ONE'S AFTER YOU.

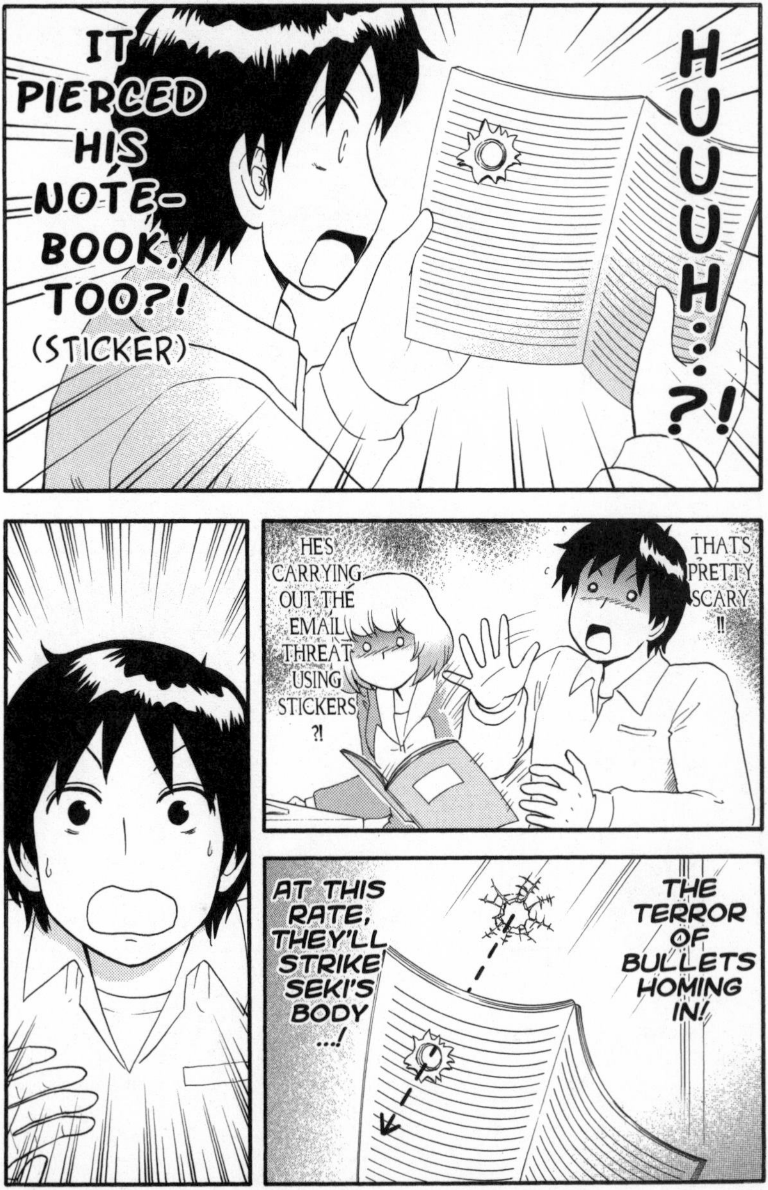
HUUUH...?!
IT PIERCED HIS NOTEBOOK, TOO?!
(STICKER)
THAT'S PRETTY SCARY!!
HE'S CARRYING OUT THE EMAIL THREAT USING STICKERS?!
THE TERROR OF BULLETS HOMING IN!
AT THIS RATE, THEY'LL STRIKE SEKI'S BODY...!

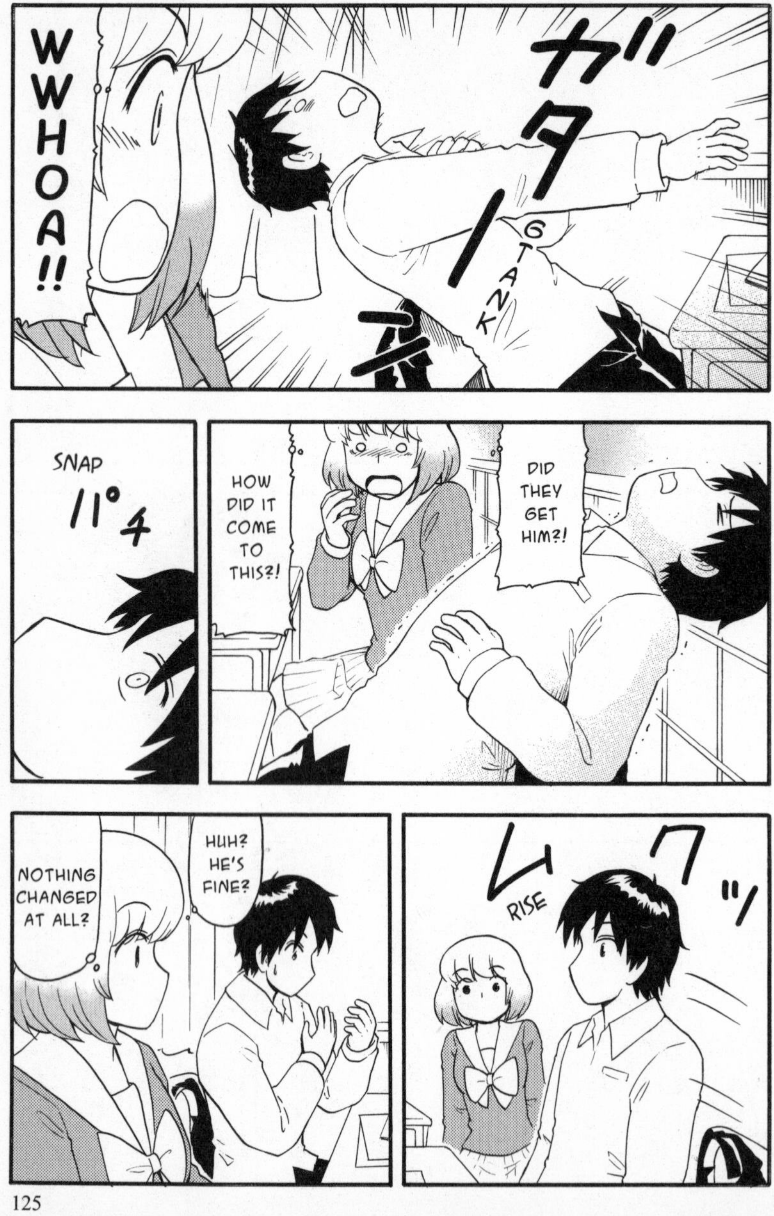
ガターン
GTANK
WWHOA!!
DID THEY GET HIM?!
HOW DID IT COME TO THIS?!
SNAP
パチ
ムクッ
RISE
HUH? HE'S FINE?
NOTHING CHANGED AT ALL?

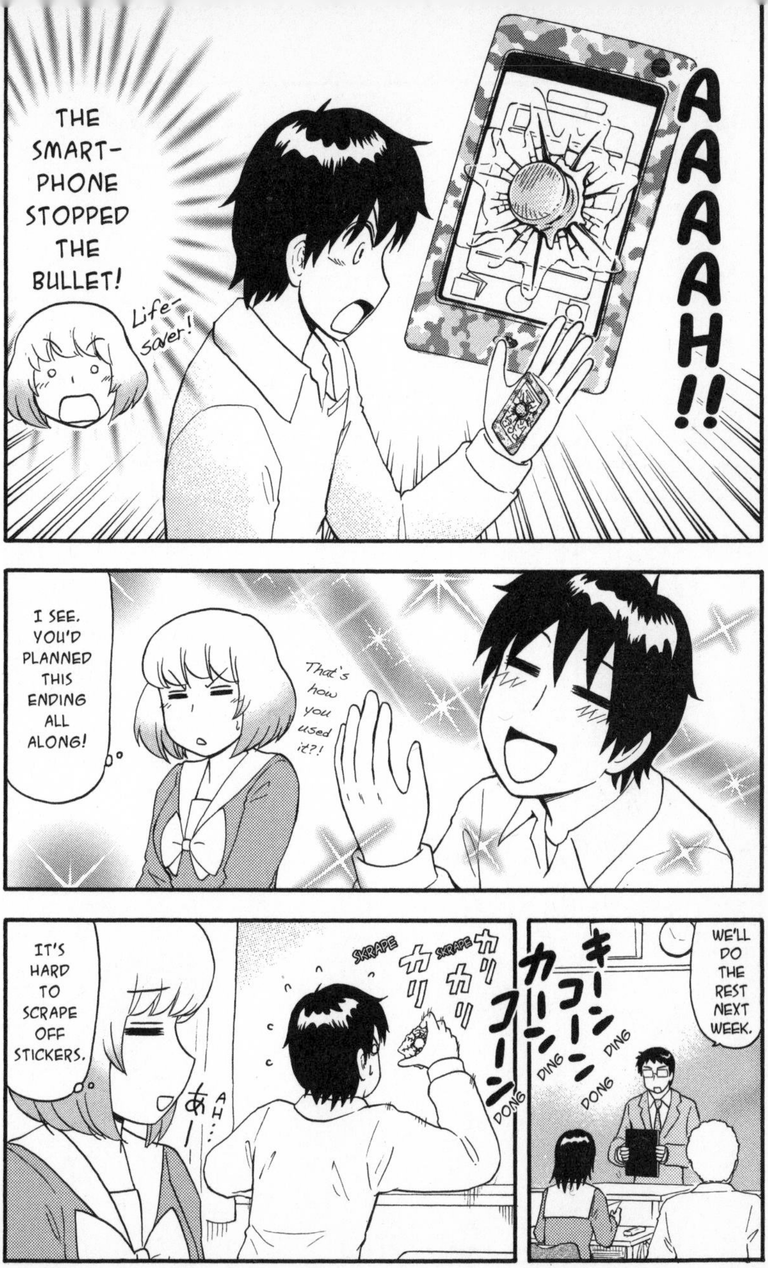
AAAAAH!!
THE SMARTPHONE STOPPED THE BULLET!
Life-saver!
That's how you used it?!
I SEE. YOU'D PLANNED THIS ENDING ALL ALONG!
WE'LL DO THE REST NEXT WEEK.
キーンコーン
カーンコーン
DING DING DONG DONG
カリカリ
SKRAPE SKRAPE
あー
AH...
IT'S HARD TO SCRAPE OFF STICKERS.

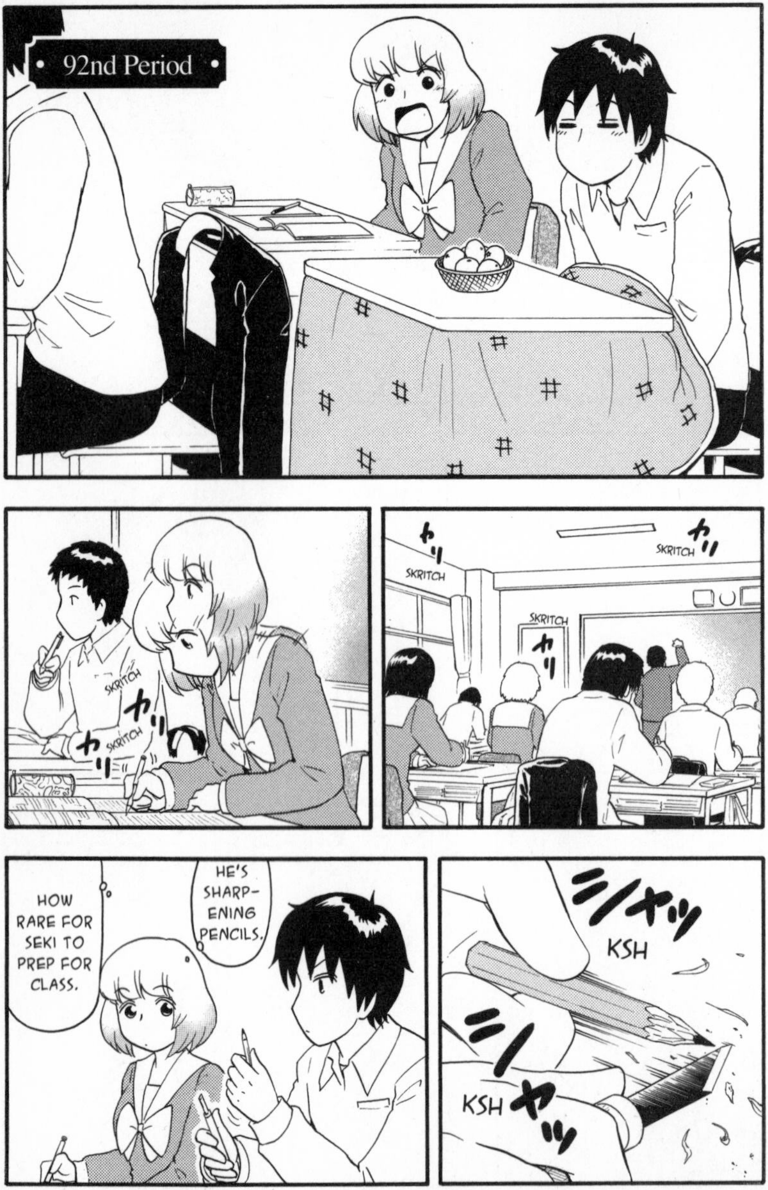
• 92nd Period •
ヤリ
SKRITCH
ヤリ
SKRITCH
SKRITCH
ヤリ
SKRITCH
ヤリ
SKRITCH
ヤリ
シャッ
KSH
シャッ
KSH
HE'S SHARPENING PENCILS.
HOW RARE FOR SEKI TO PREP FOR CLASS.

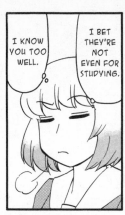

BUT YOU DON'T NEED THAT MANY, DO YOU?
CLASS WILL END BEFORE YOU FINISH SHARPENING THEM ALL!
SCATTER
I BET THEY'RE NOT EVEN FOR STUDYING.
I KNOW YOU TOO WELL.
HM?
SKRIT SKRIT SKRIT
HE'S WHITTLING THE ERASER END...
BUT WHY?
BLOW
KCHIK
SQK
SQK

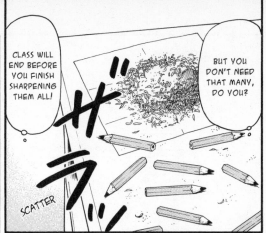

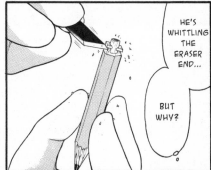

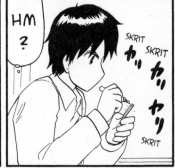

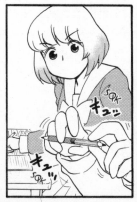

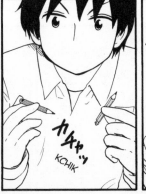

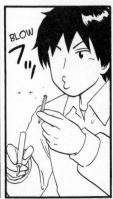

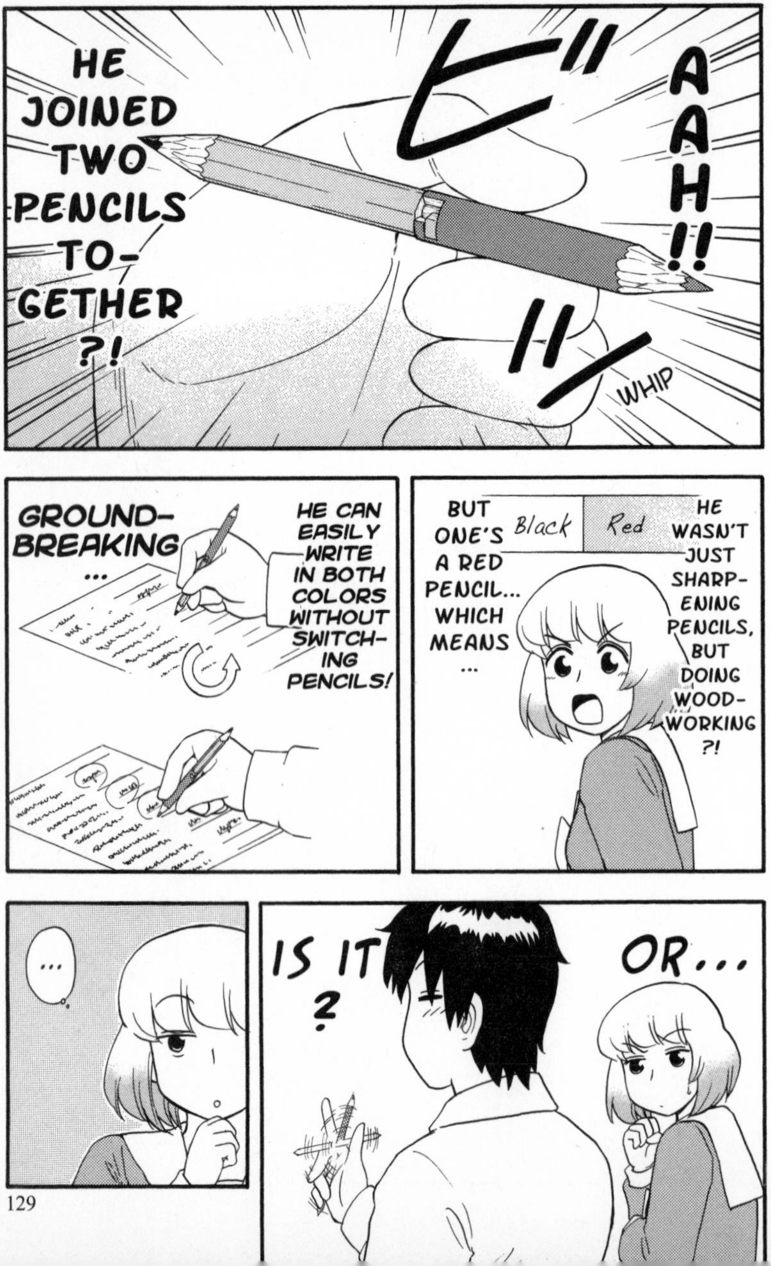
AAH!!
ビッ
WHIP
HE JOINED TWO PENCILS TOGETHER?!
HE WASN'T JUST SHARPENING PENCILS, BUT DOING WOODWORKING?!
Red
Black
BUT ONE'S A RED PENCIL... WHICH MEANS...
HE CAN EASILY WRITE IN BOTH COLORS WITHOUT SWITCHING PENCILS!
GROUNDBREAKING...
OR...
IS IT ?
...

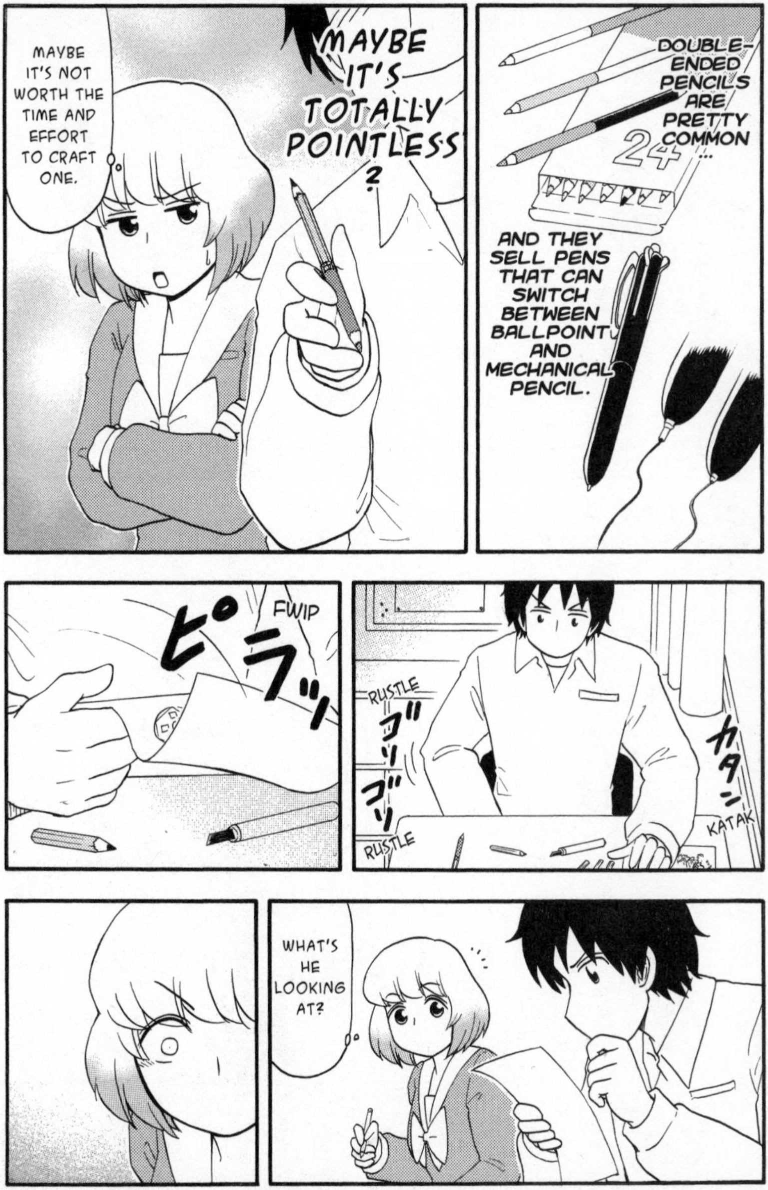
DOUBLE-ENDED PENCILS ARE PRETTY COMMON ...
AND THEY SELL PENS THAT CAN SWITCH BETWEEN BALLPOINT AND MECHANICAL PENCIL.
MAYBE IT'S TOTALLY POINTLESS?
MAYBE IT'S NOT WORTH THE TIME AND EFFORT TO CRAFT ONE.
カタン
KATAK
ゴソ
RUSTLE
ゴソ
RUSTLE
ピラッ
FWIP
WHAT'S HE LOOKING AT?

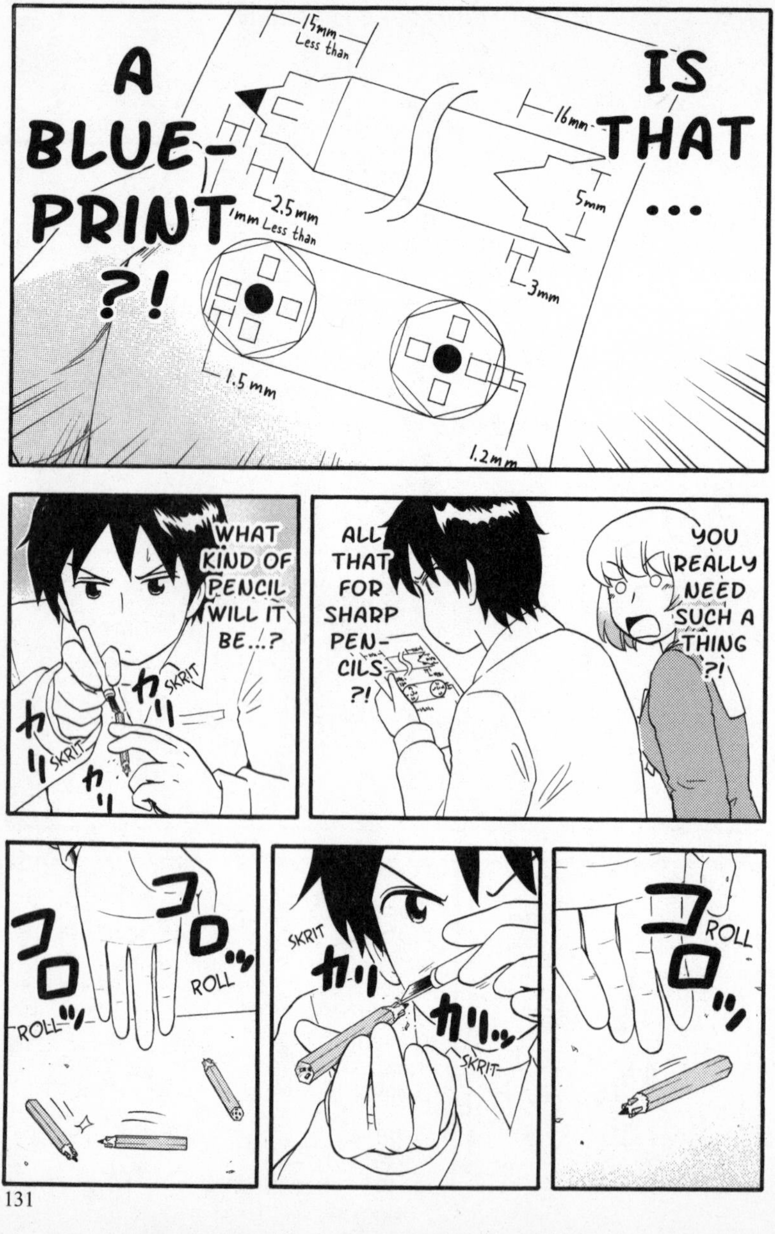
IS THAT...
A BLUE-PRINT?!
15mm Less than
16mm
5mm
3mm
2.5mm
1mm Less than
1.5mm
1.2mm
YOU REALLY NEED SUCH A THING?!
ALL THAT FOR SHARP PEN-CILS?!
WHAT KIND OF PENCIL WILL IT BE...?
カリ SKRIT
カリ SKRIT
カリ
コロッ ROLL
カリ SKRIT
カリッ SKRIT
コロ ROLL
コロッ ROLL

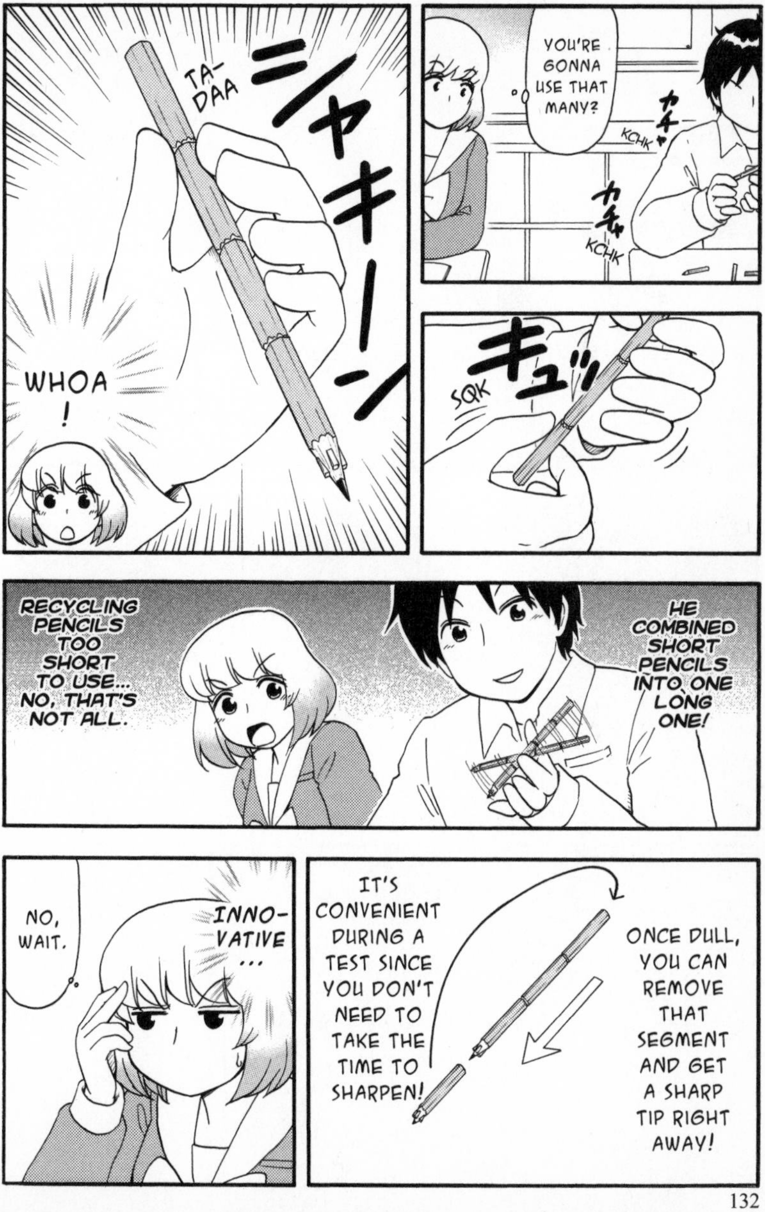
YOU'RE GONNA USE THAT MANY?
カチャ
KCHK
カチャ
KCHK
キュッ
SQK
シャキーン
TA-DAA
WHOA!
HE COMBINED SHORT PENCILS INTO ONE LONG ONE!
RECYCLING PENCILS TOO SHORT TO USE... NO, THAT'S NOT ALL.
IT'S CONVENIENT DURING A TEST SINCE YOU DON'T NEED TO TAKE THE TIME TO SHARPEN!
ONCE DULL, YOU CAN REMOVE THAT SEGMENT AND GET A SHARP TIP RIGHT AWAY!
INNOVATIVE...
NO, WAIT.

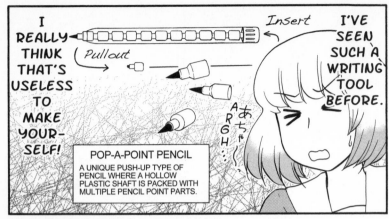

I'VE SEEN SUCH A WRITING TOOL BEFORE.
あちゃ～っ
ARGH...
Insert
Pullout
I REALLY THINK THAT'S USELESS TO MAKE YOURSELF!
POP-A-POINT PENCIL
A UNIQUE PUSH-UP TYPE OF PENCIL WHERE A HOLLOW PLASTIC SHAFT IS PACKED WITH MULTIPLE PENCIL POINT PARTS.
HM?
A DIFFERENT BLUEPRINT?
Ⓐ
Ⓑ
THERE ARE MORE NEW PENCIL TYPES?
LIKE WHAT? LET'S SEE...
A DEVICE WHERE PENCIL Ⓐ, WHITTLED DOWN ALMOST TO THE LEAD, IS INSERTED INSIDE THE HOLLOWED-OUT SHAFT OF PENCIL Ⓑ...
SO THAT Ⓐ POPS OUT WHEN PUSHED WITH A FINGER?
Ⓐ
Ⓑ
COMPLETE
YOU STILL HAVE TO SHARPEN THE TIP ONCE IT'S BLUNT...
BUT THIS WAY, YOU ONLY NEED TO WHITTLE THE LEAD, SO IT'LL GO QUICKLY...
I see.

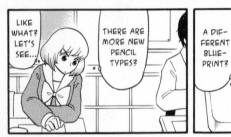

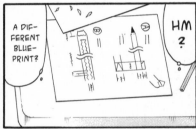

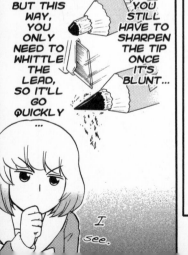

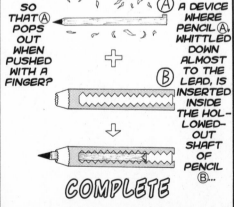

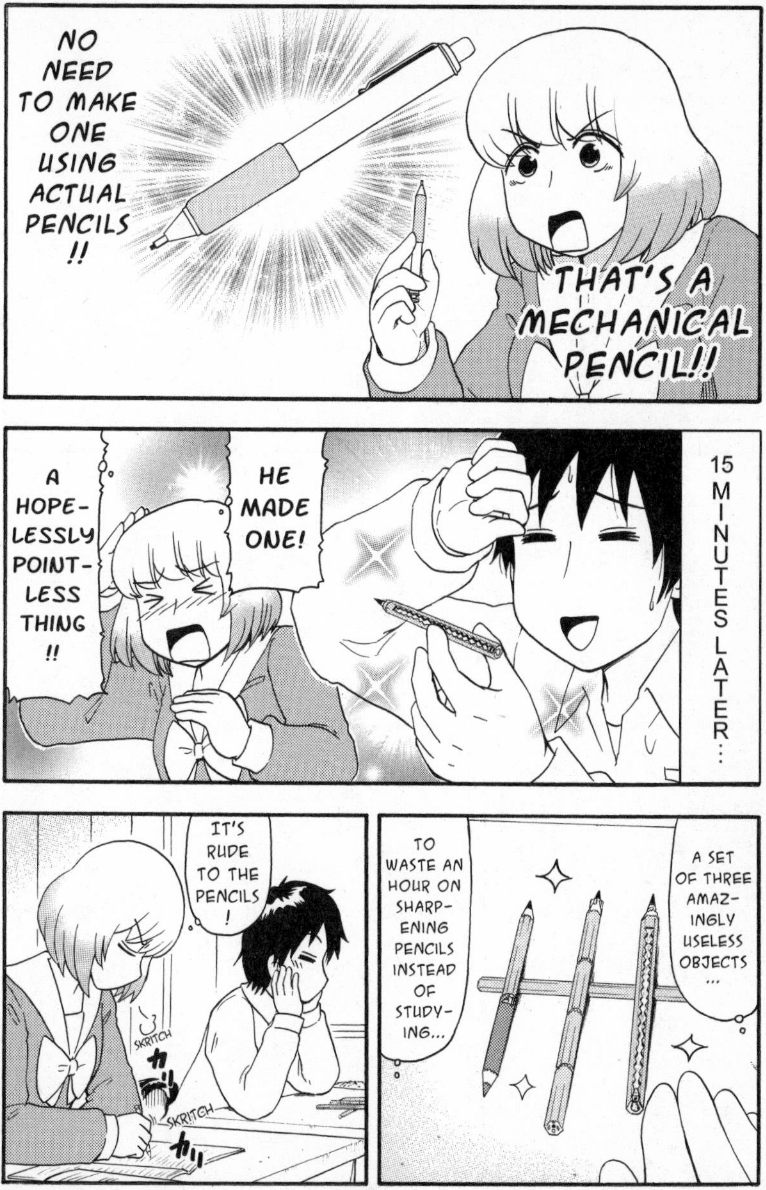
THAT'S A MECHANICAL PENCIL!!
NO NEED TO MAKE ONE USING ACTUAL PENCILS!!
15 MINUTES LATER...
HE MADE ONE!
A HOPELESSLY POINTLESS THING!!
A SET OF THREE AMAZINGLY USELESS OBJECTS...
TO WASTE AN HOUR ON SHARPENING PENCILS INSTEAD OF STUDYING...
IT'S RUDE TO THE PENCILS!
SKRITCH
SKRITCH

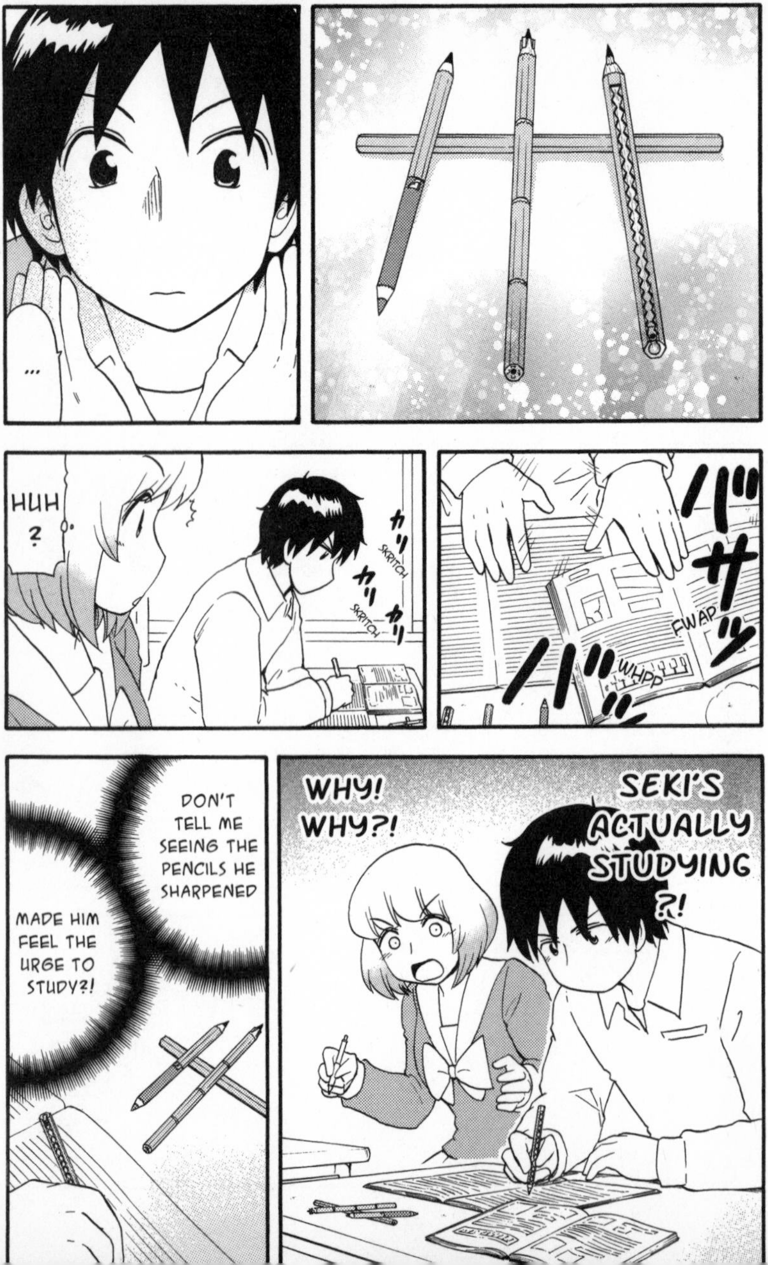
...
バサッ
FWAP
WHPP
カリ
SKRITCH
カリ カリ
SKRITCH
HUH?
SEKI'S ACTUALLY STUDYING?!
WHY! WHY?!
DON'T TELL ME SEEING THE PENCILS HE SHARPENED
MADE HIM FEEL THE URGE TO STUDY?!

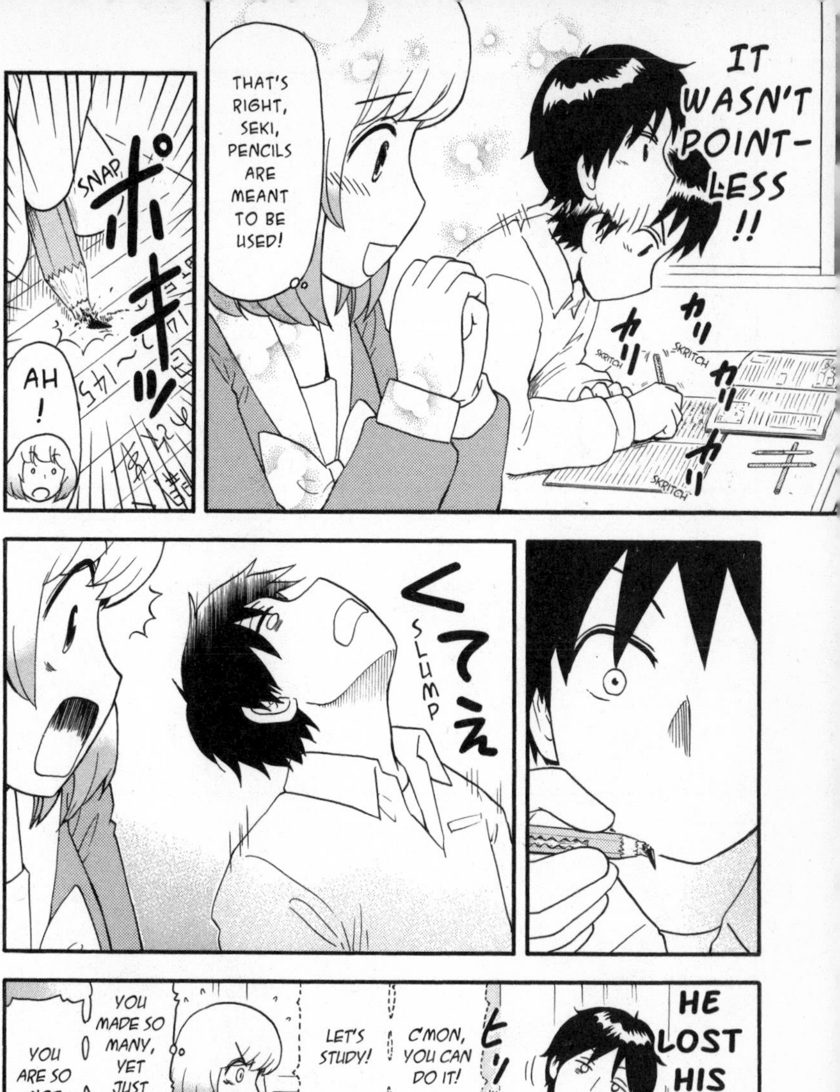
IT WASN'T POINT-LESS!!
カリ
カリ
SKRITCH
SKRITCH
カリカリ
SKRITCH
THAT'S RIGHT, SEKI, PENCILS ARE MEANT TO BE USED!
ポキッ
SNAP
AH!
くてえ
SLUMP
HE LOST HIS MO-TIVA-TION?!
ヒソ
WHISPER
C'MON, YOU CAN DO IT!
LET'S STUDY!
ヒソ
WHISPER
YOU MADE SO MANY, YET JUST ONE DOES YOU IN?
YOU ARE SO NOT CUT OUT FOR STUDY-ING!

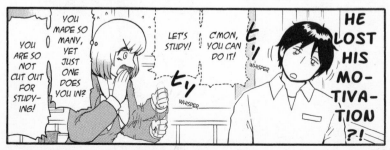

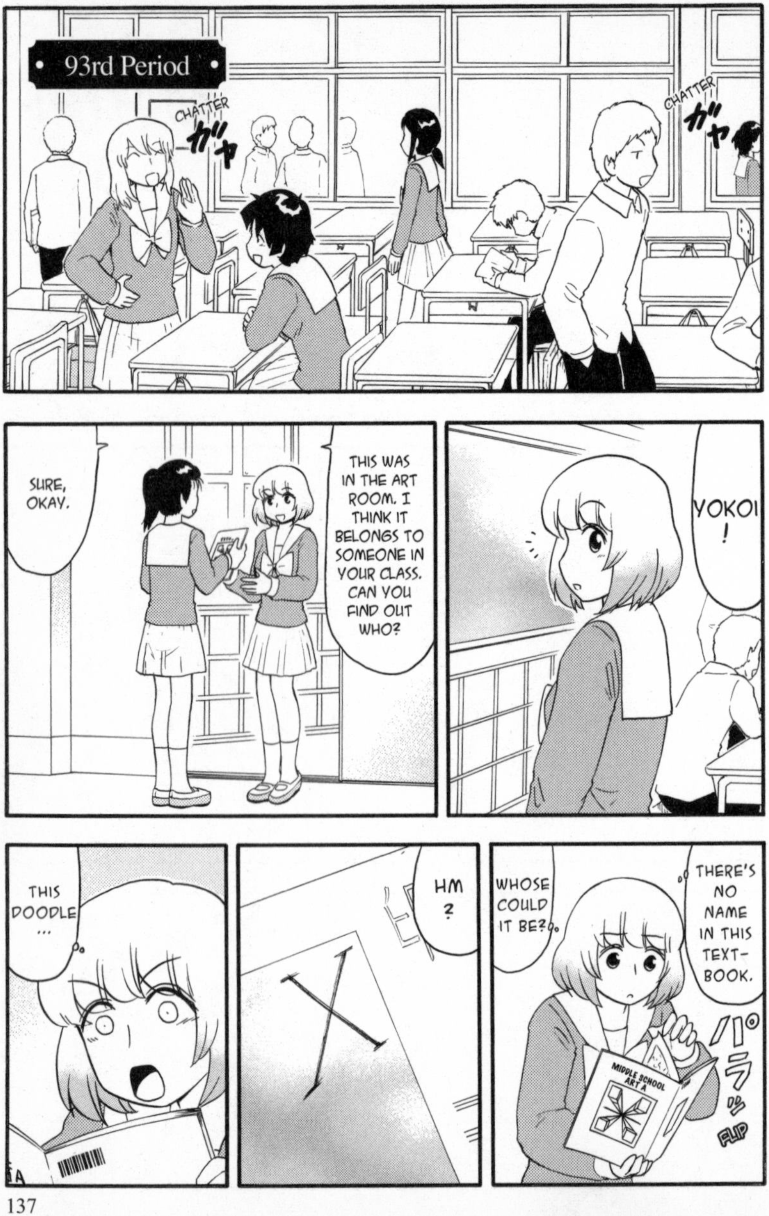
93rd Period
CHATTER
CHATTER
YOKOI!
THIS WAS IN THE ART ROOM. I THINK IT BELONGS TO SOMEONE IN YOUR CLASS. CAN YOU FIND OUT WHO?
SURE, OKAY.
THERE'S NO NAME IN THIS TEXT-BOOK.
WHOSE COULD IT BE?
MIDDLE SCHOOL ART A
FLIP
HM?
THIS DOODLE...

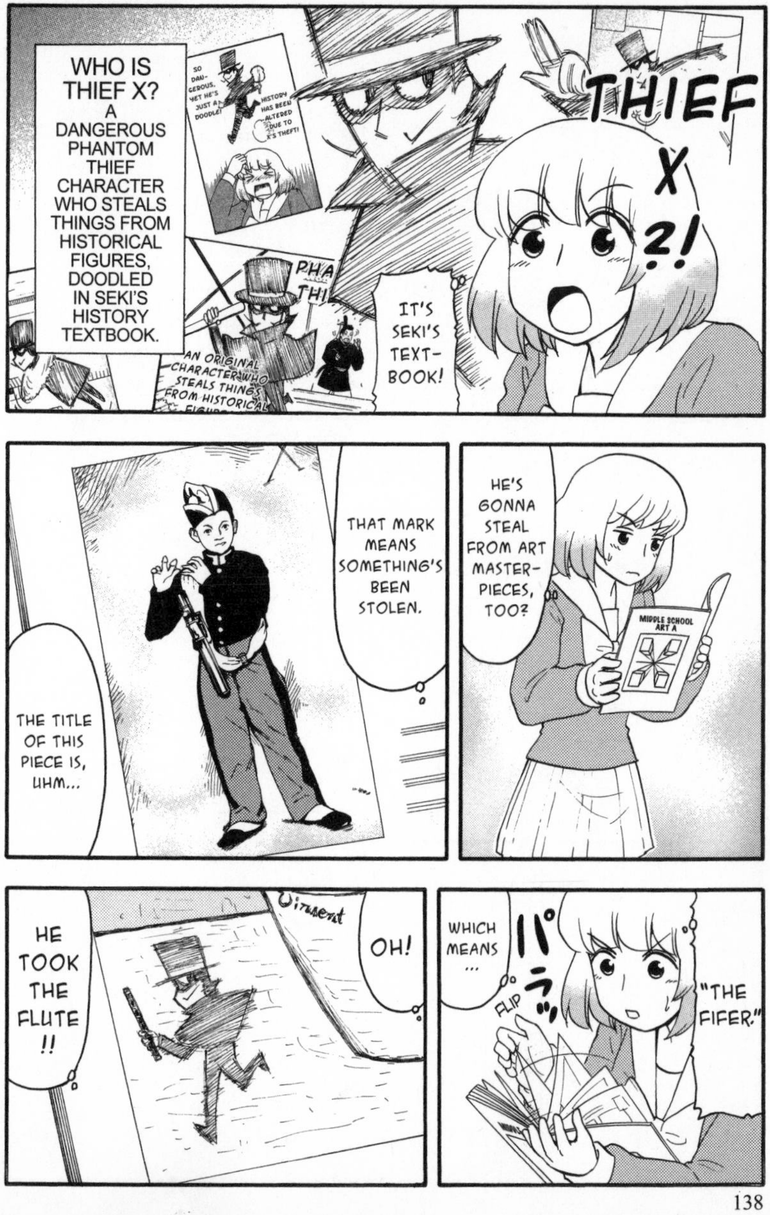
THIEF X?!
IT'S SEKI'S TEXTBOOK!
SO DANGEROUS, YET HE'S JUST A DOODLE!
HISTORY HAS BEEN ALTERED DUE TO X'S THEFT!
AN ORIGINAL CHARACTER WHO STEALS THINGS FROM HISTORICAL
WHO IS THIEF X? A DANGEROUS PHANTOM THIEF CHARACTER WHO STEALS THINGS FROM HISTORICAL FIGURES, DOODLED IN SEKI'S HISTORY TEXTBOOK.
HE'S GONNA STEAL FROM ART MASTERPIECES, TOO?
MIDDLE SCHOOL ART A
THAT MARK MEANS SOMETHING'S BEEN STOLEN.
THE TITLE OF THIS PIECE IS, UHM...
"THE FIFER."
パラッ
FLIP
WHICH MEANS ...
OH!
Vincent
HE TOOK THE FLUTE!!

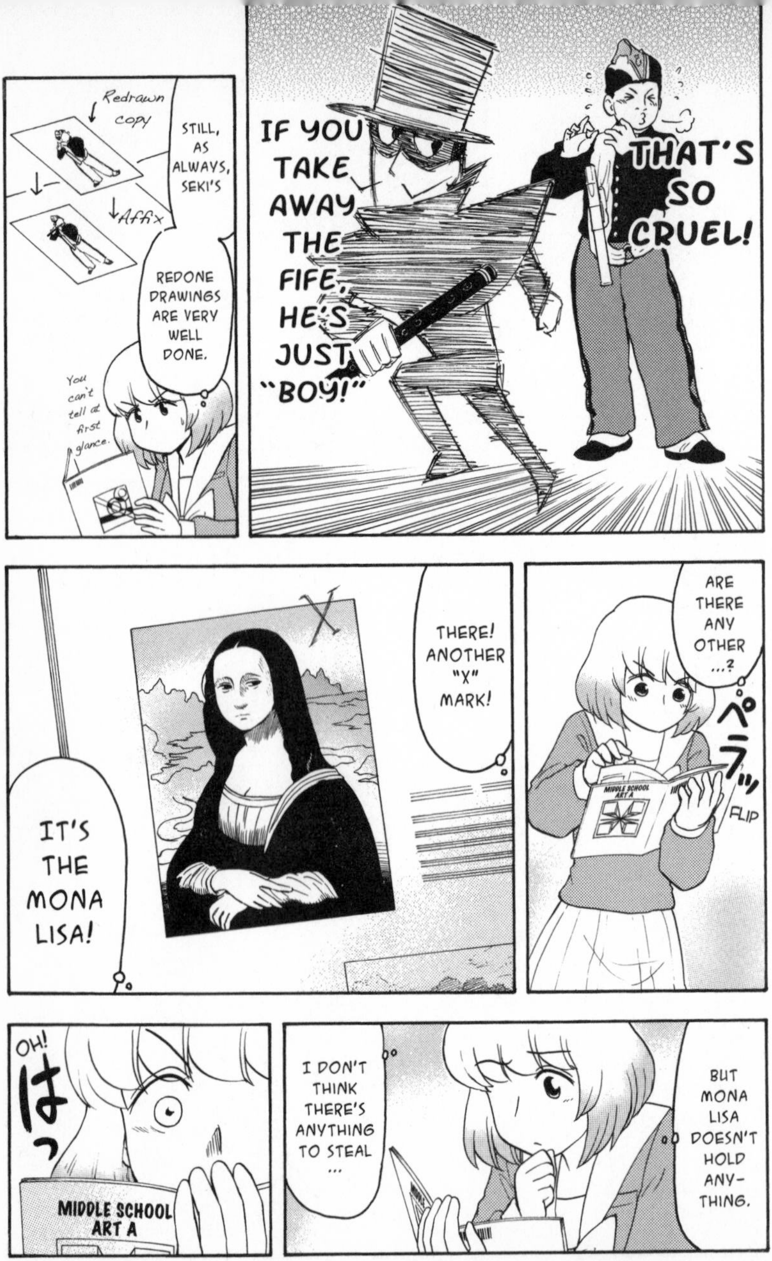
IF YOU TAKE AWAY THE FIFE, HE'S JUST "BOY!"
THAT'S SO CRUEL!
STILL, AS ALWAYS, SEKI'S
Redrawn copy
Affix
REDONE DRAWINGS ARE VERY WELL DONE.
You can't tell at first glance.
ARE THERE ANY OTHER ...?
ペラッ
FLIP
MIDDLE SCHOOL ART A
THERE! ANOTHER "X" MARK!
IT'S THE MONA LISA!
BUT MONA LISA DOESN'T HOLD ANY-THING.
I DON'T THINK THERE'S ANYTHING TO STEAL ...
OH!
はっ
MIDDLE SCHOOL ART A

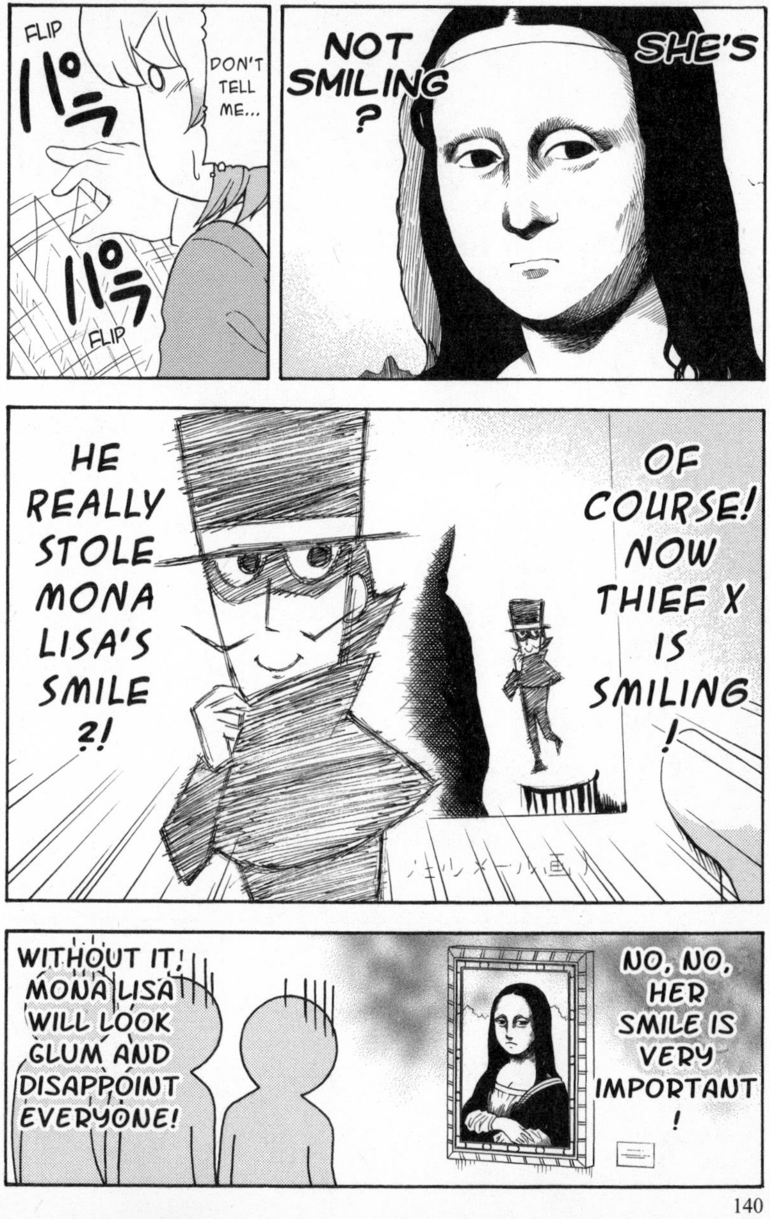
SHE'S
NOT SMILING?
DON'T TELL ME...
FLIP
パラ
パラ
FLIP
OF COURSE! NOW THIEF X IS SMILING!
HE REALLY STOLE MONA LISA'S SMILE?!
フェルメール画
NO, NO, HER SMILE IS VERY IMPORTANT!
WITHOUT IT, MONA LISA WILL LOOK GLUM AND DISAPPOINT EVERYONE!

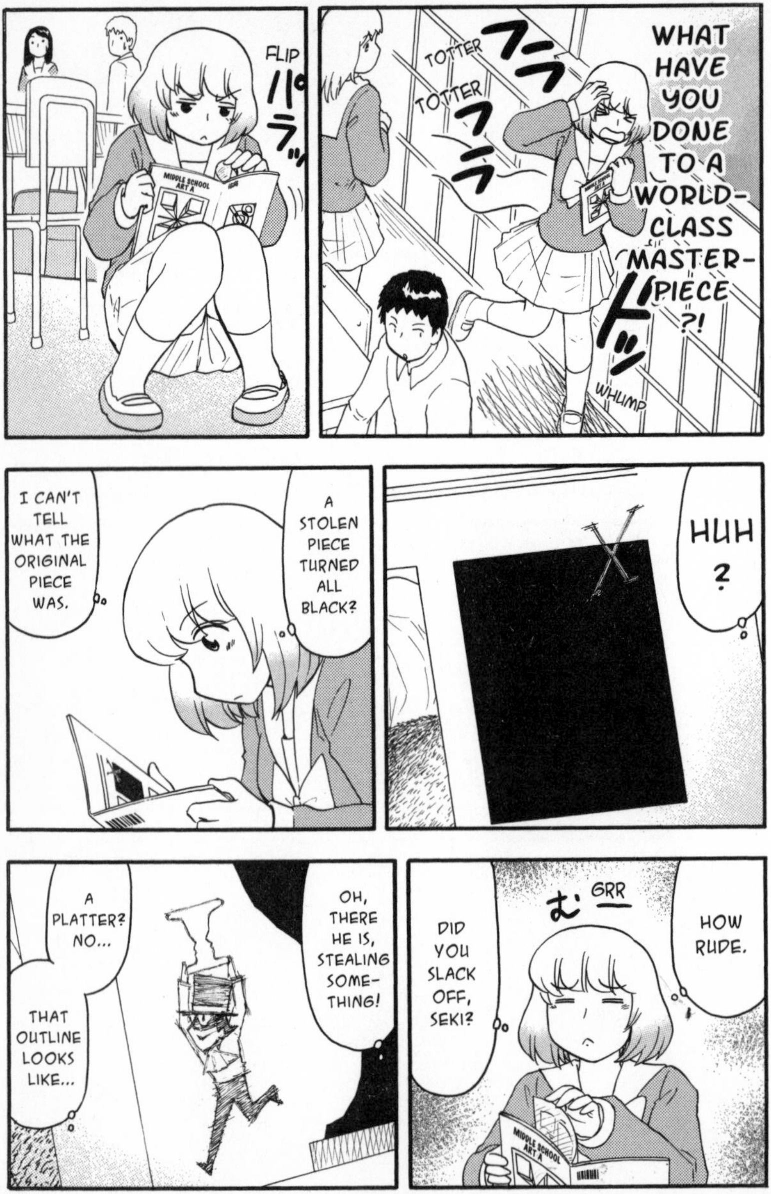
TOTTER
フラ
TOTTER
フラ
WHAT HAVE YOU DONE TO A WORLD-CLASS MASTERPIECE?!
ドッ
WHUMP
FLIP
パラッ
MIDDLE SCHOOL ART A
HUH?
A STOLEN PIECE TURNED ALL BLACK?
I CAN'T TELL WHAT THE ORIGINAL PIECE WAS.
HOW RUDE.
む
GRR
DID YOU SLACK OFF, SEKI?
MIDDLE SCHOOL ART A
OH, THERE HE IS, STEALING SOMETHING!
A PLATTER? NO...
THAT OUTLINE LOOKS LIKE...

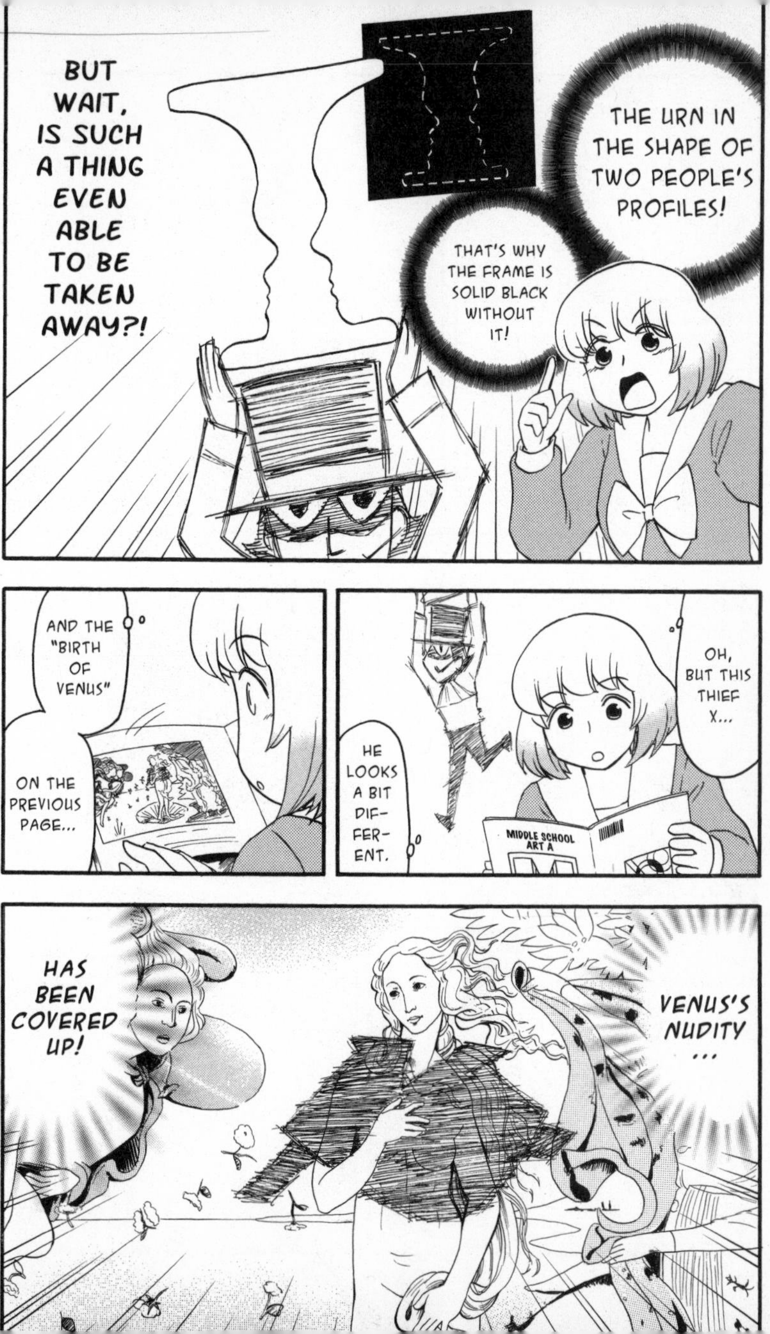
THE URN IN THE SHAPE OF TWO PEOPLE'S PROFILES!
THAT'S WHY THE FRAME IS SOLID BLACK WITHOUT IT!
BUT WAIT, IS SUCH A THING EVEN ABLE TO BE TAKEN AWAY?!
OH, BUT THIS THIEF X...
HE LOOKS A BIT DIF-FER-ENT.
MIDDLE SCHOOL ART A
AND THE "BIRTH OF VENUS"
ON THE PREVIOUS PAGE...
VENUS'S NUDITY...
HAS BEEN COVERED UP!

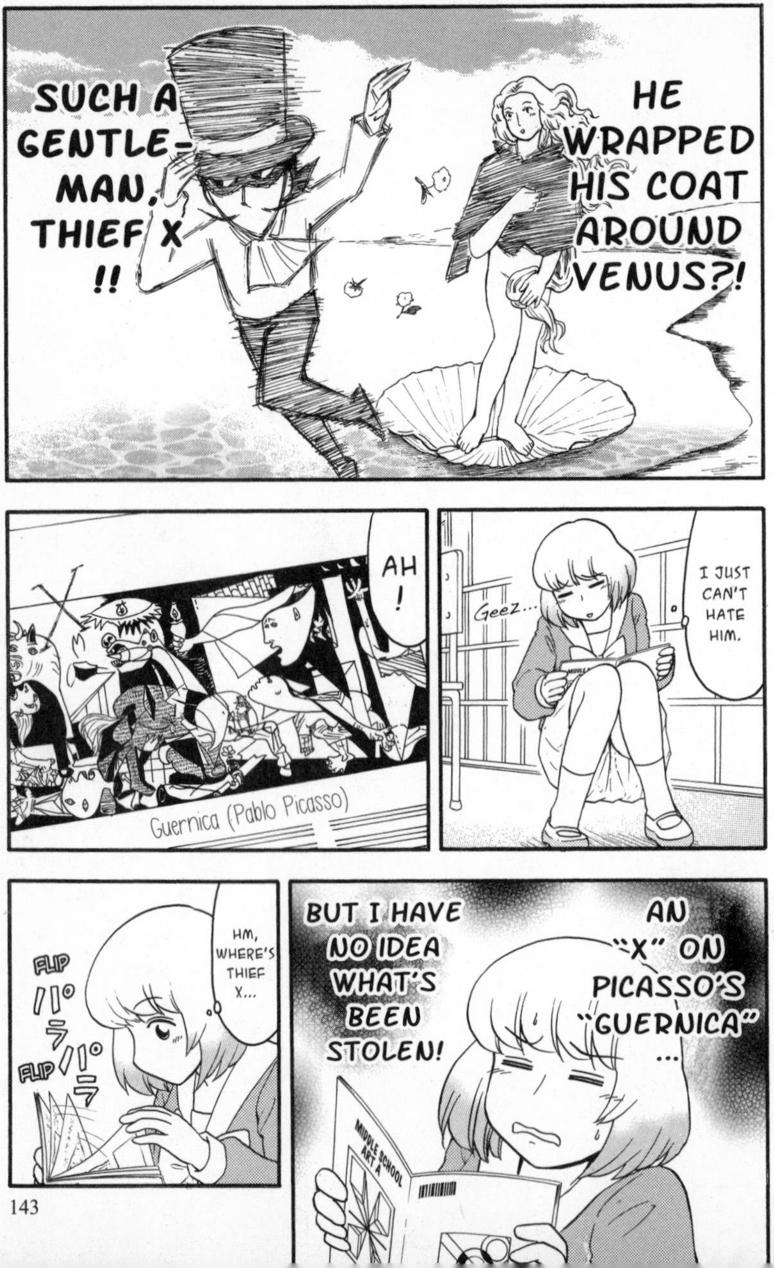
HE WRAPPED HIS COAT AROUND VENUS?!
SUCH A GENTLE-MAN, THIEF X !!
I JUST CAN'T HATE HIM.
Geez...
AH!
Guernica (Pablo Picasso)
AN "X" ON PICASSO'S "GUERNICA"...
BUT I HAVE NO IDEA WHAT'S BEEN STOLEN!
MIDDLE SCHOOL ART A
HM, WHERE'S THIEF X...
FLIP パラ
FLIP パラ

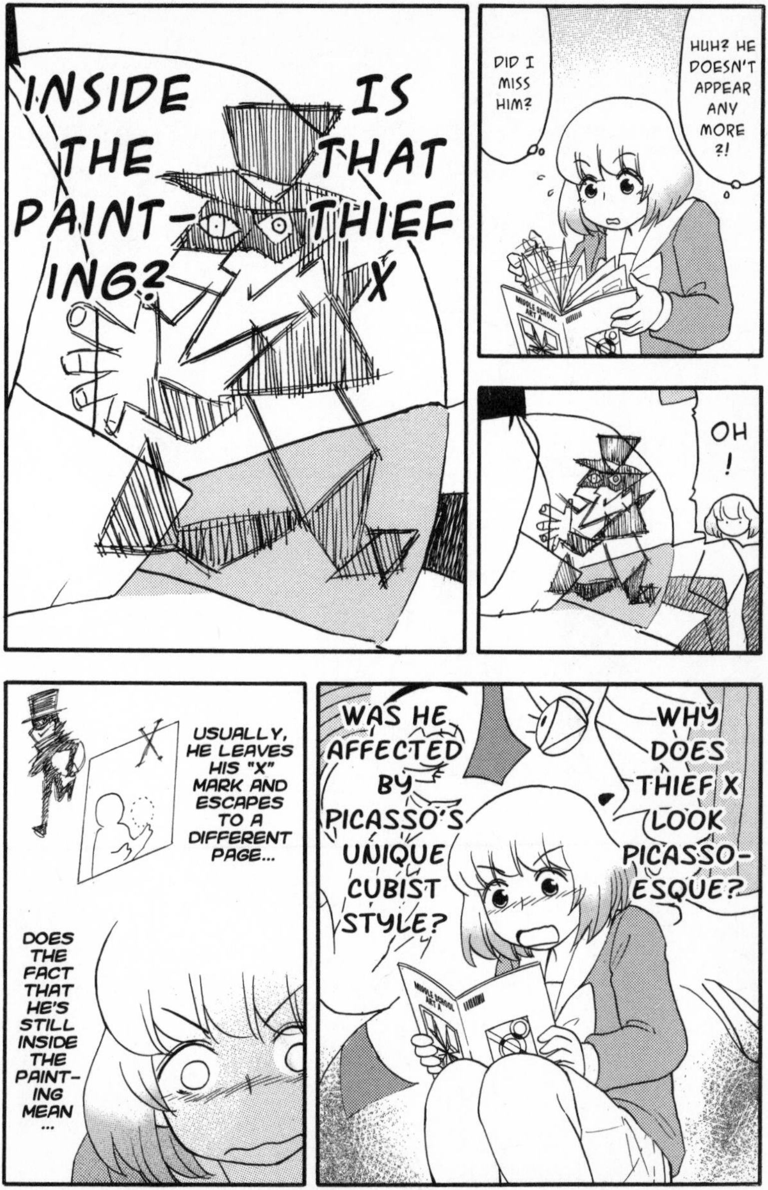
HUH? HE DOESN'T APPEAR ANY MORE ?!
DID I MISS HIM?
OH !
IS THAT THIEF X
INSIDE THE PAINT-ING?
WHY DOES THIEF X LOOK PICASSO-ESQUE?
WAS HE AFFECTED BY PICASSO'S UNIQUE CUBIST STYLE?
MIDDLE SCHOOL ART A
USUALLY, HE LEAVES HIS "X" MARK AND ESCAPES TO A DIFFERENT PAGE...
DOES THE FACT THAT HE'S STILL INSIDE THE PAINT-ING MEAN ...

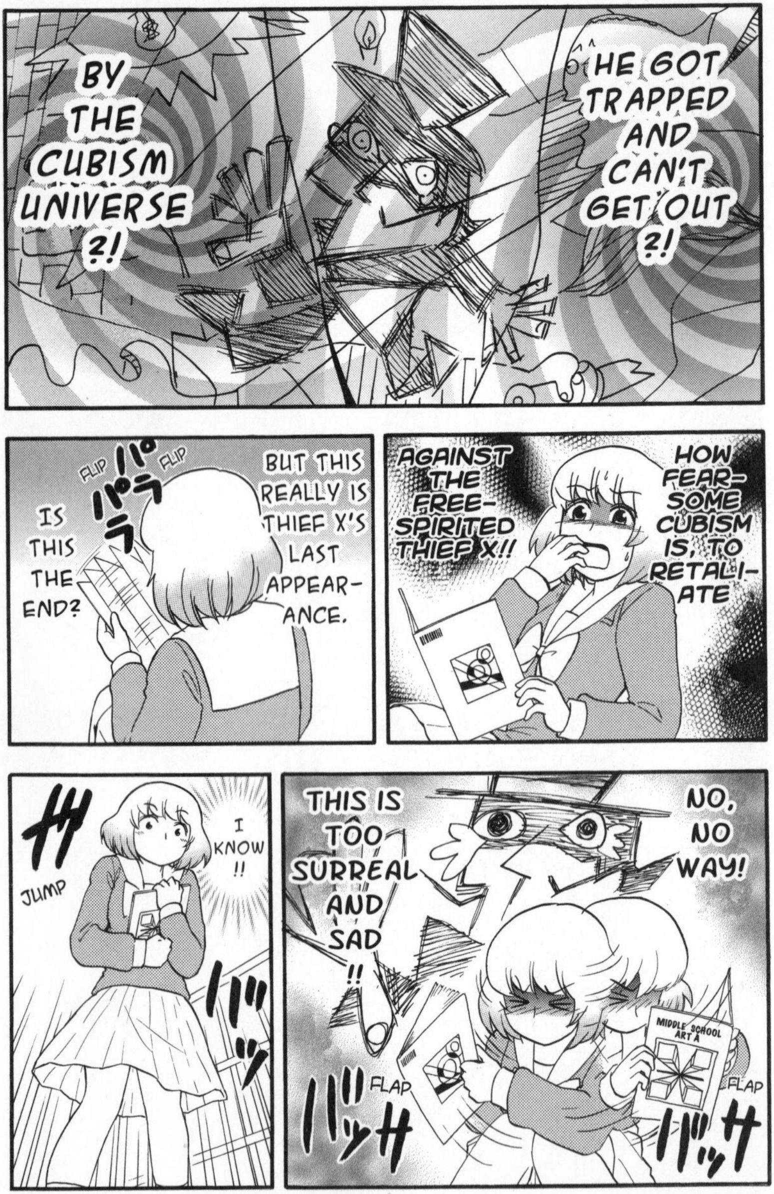
HE GOT TRAPPED AND CAN'T GET OUT ?!
BY THE CUBISM UNIVERSE ?!
HOW FEAR-SOME CUBISM IS, TO RETALI-ATE
AGAINST THE FREE-SPIRITED THIEF X!!
BUT THIS REALLY IS THIEF X'S LAST APPEAR-ANCE.
パ
FLIP
FLIP
パラ
ラ
IS THIS THE END?
NO, NO WAY!
THIS IS TOO SURREAL AND SAD !!
MIDDLE SCHOOL ART A
FLAP
バッサ
FLAP
バッサ
I KNOW !!
ザ
JUMP
バッ

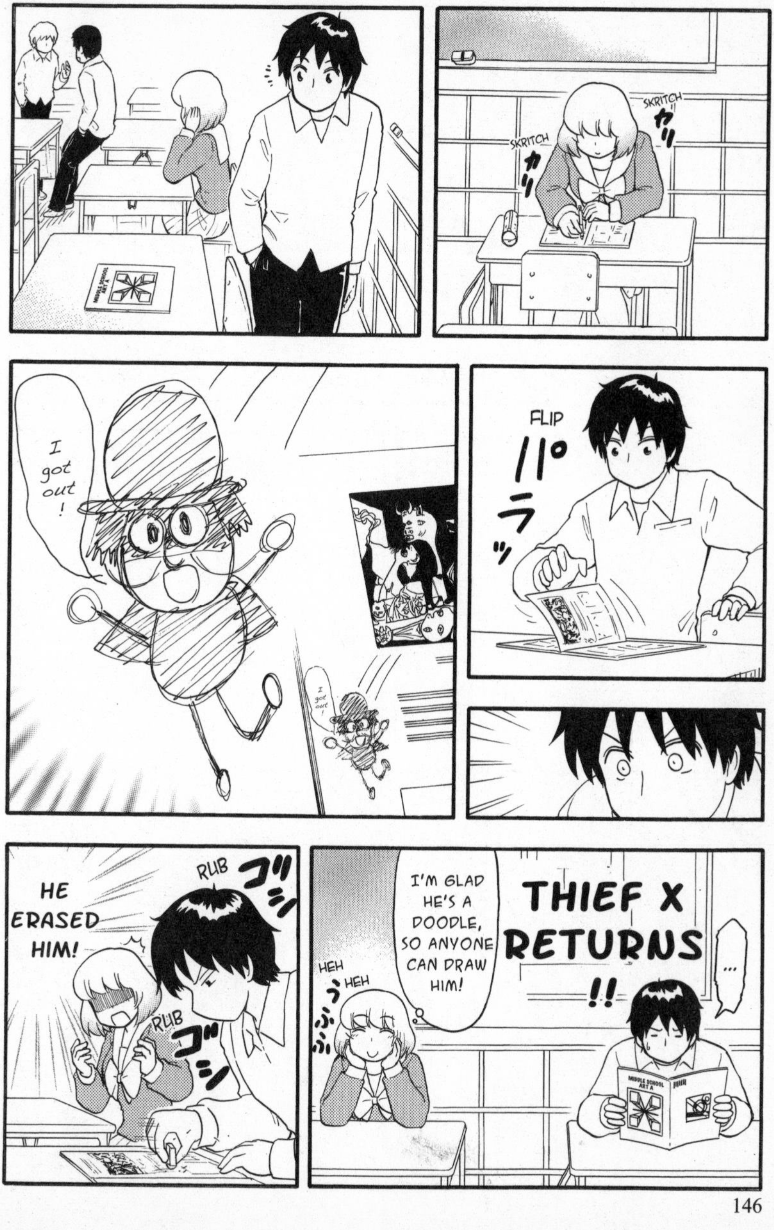
SKRITCH
カリ
SKRITCH
カリ
FLIP
パラッ
I got out!
I got out!
...
THIEF X RETURNS!!
I'M GLAD HE'S A DOODLE, SO ANYONE CAN DRAW HIM!
HEH HEH
ふふ
RUB
ゴシ
HE ERASED HIM!
RUB
ゴシ
MIDDLE SCHOOL ART A

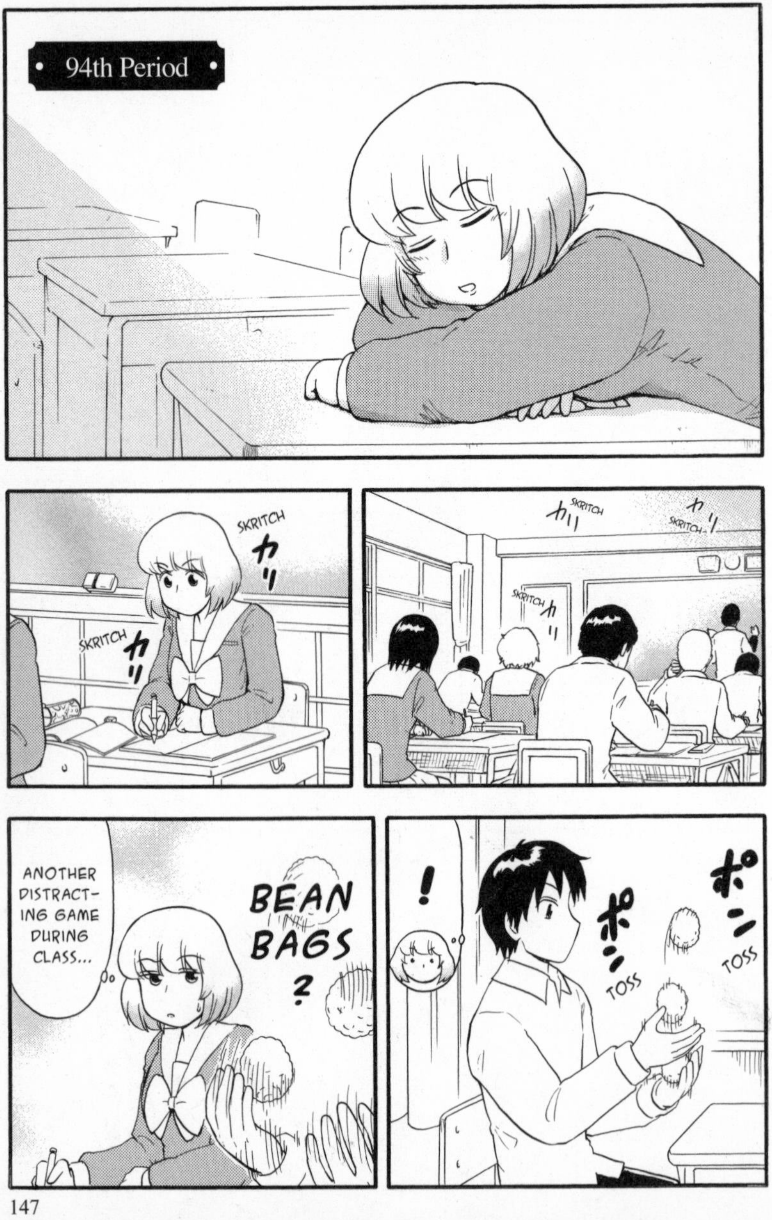

• 94th Period •
SKRITCH
カリ
SKRITCH
カリ
SKRITCH
カリ
SKRITCH
カリ
SKRITCH
カリ
!
ポン
TOSS
ポン
TOSS
ANOTHER DISTRACTING GAME DURING CLASS...
BEAN BAGS?

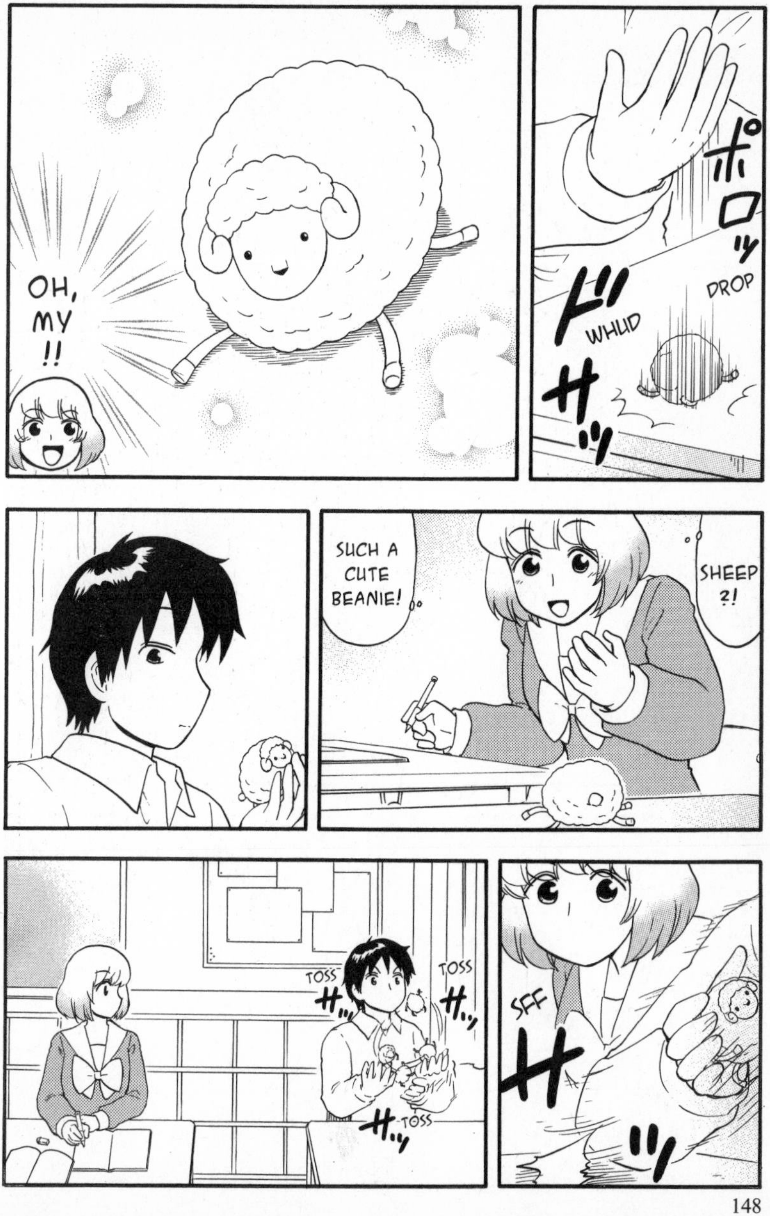

ポロッ
DROP
ドサッ
WHUD
OH, MY !!
SHEEP ?!
SUCH A CUTE BEANIE!
SFF
TOSS
TOSS
TOSS

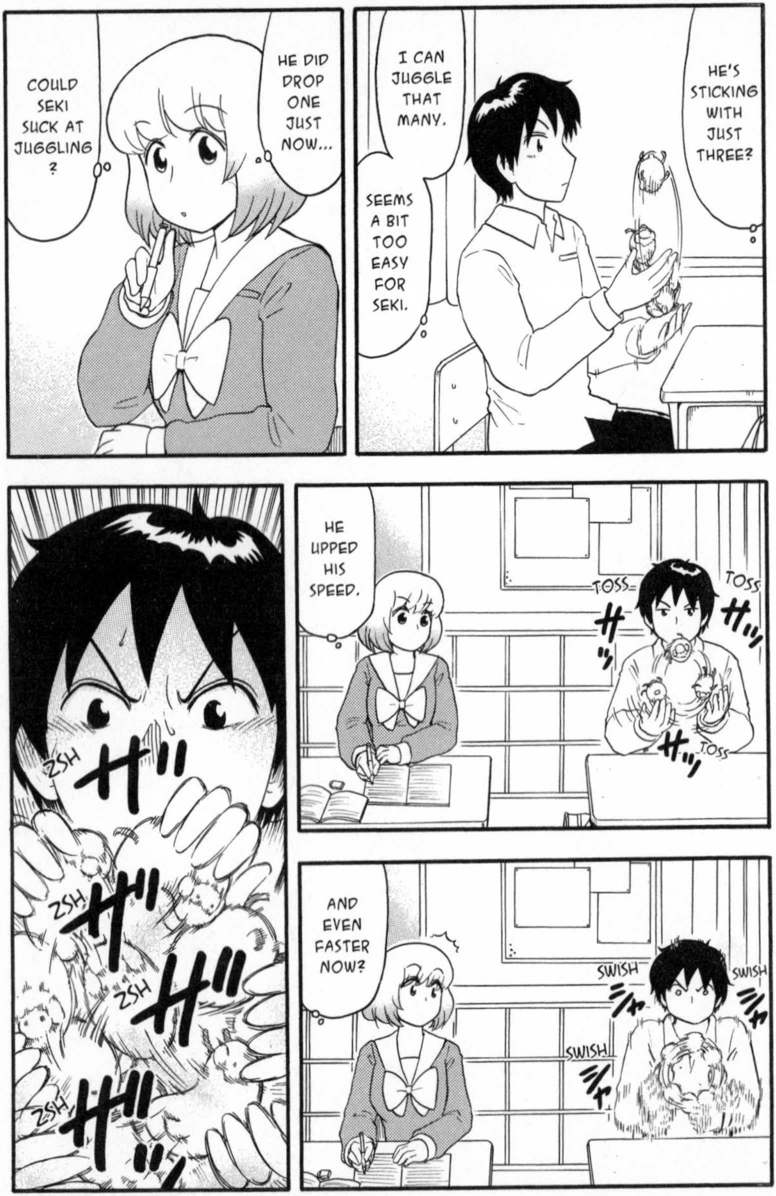
HE'S STICKING WITH JUST THREE?
I CAN JUGGLE THAT MANY.
SEEMS A BIT TOO EASY FOR SEKI.
HE DID DROP ONE JUST NOW...
COULD SEKI SUCK AT JUGGLING?
HE UPPED HIS SPEED.
TOSS
TOSS
TOSS
AND EVEN FASTER NOW?
SWISH
SWISH
SWISH
ZSH
ZSH
ZSH
ZSH

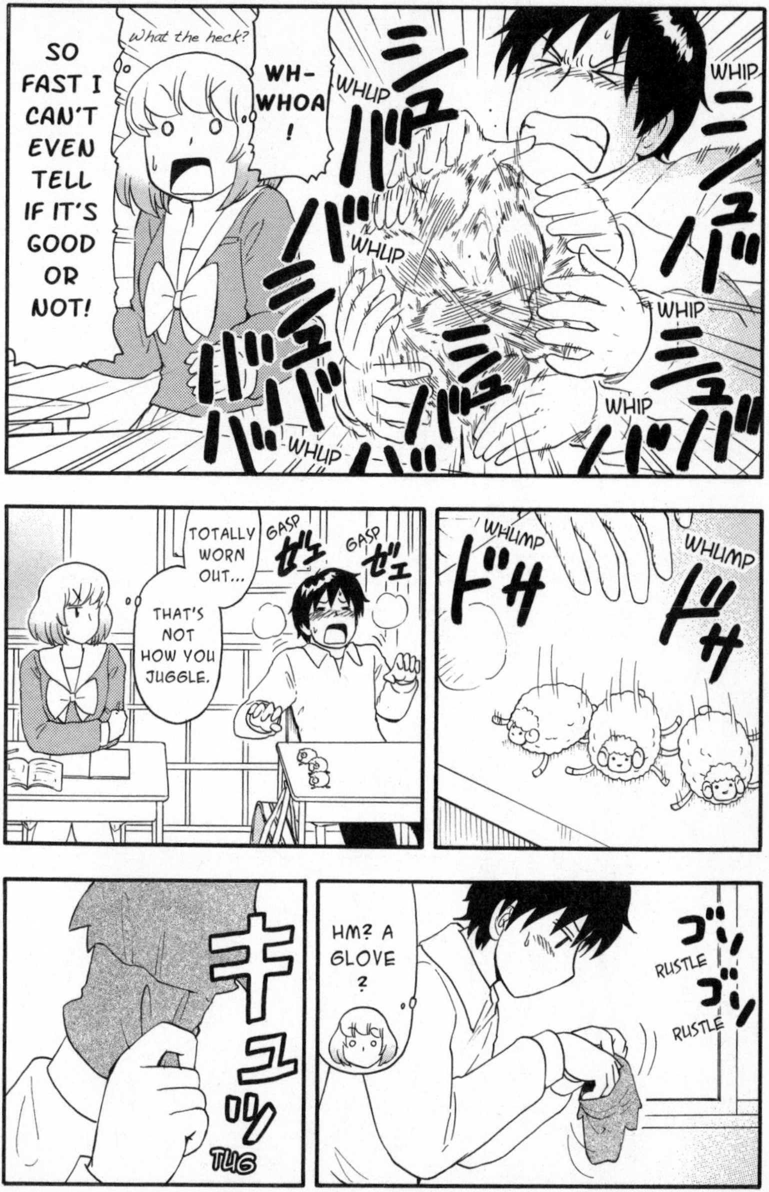
WHIP
WHUP
WH-WHOA!
What the heck?
SO FAST I CAN'T EVEN TELL IF IT'S GOOD OR NOT!
WHUP
WHIP
WHIP
WHUP
WHUMP
ドサ
WHUMP
ドサ
GASP
ゼェ
GASP
ゼェ
TOTALLY WORN OUT...
THAT'S NOT HOW YOU JUGGLE.
ゴソ
RUSTLE
ゴソ
RUSTLE
HM? A GLOVE?
キュッ
TUG

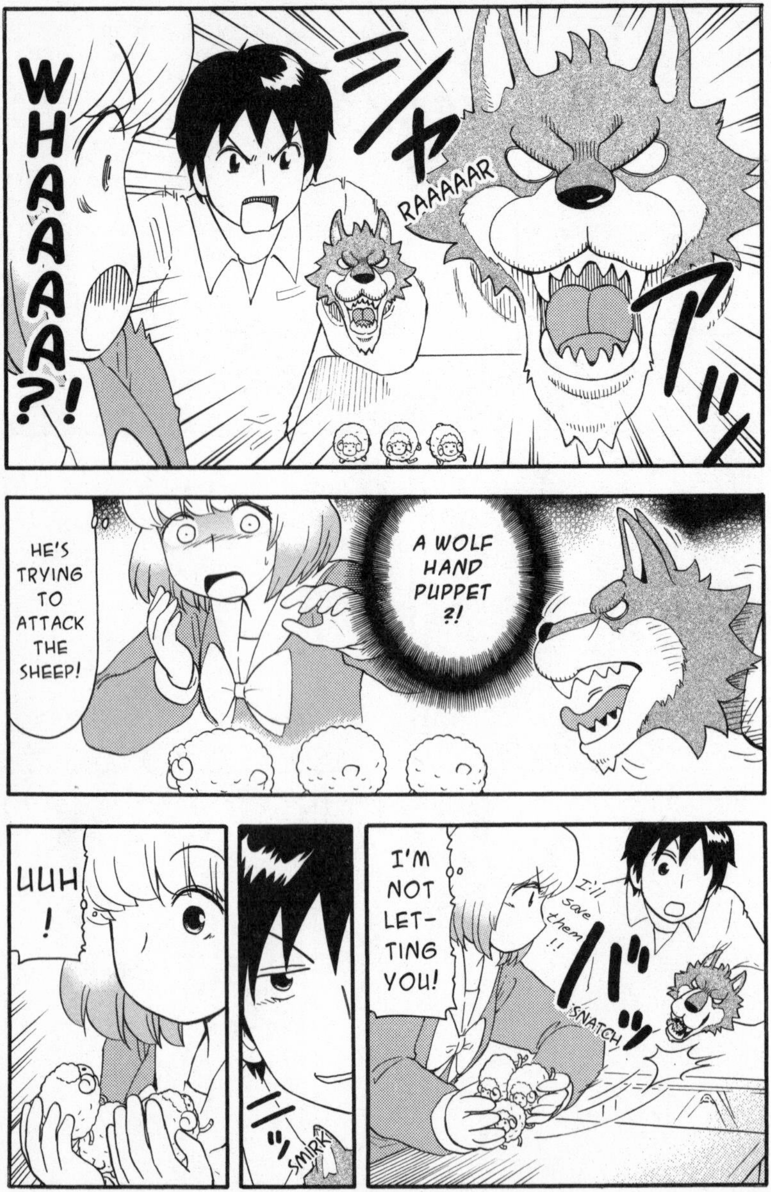

シャ
RAAAAAR
アッ
WHAAAAA?!
A WOLF HAND PUPPET?!
HE'S TRYING TO ATTACK THE SHEEP!
I'll save them!!
バッ
SNATCH
I'M NOT LET-TING YOU!
ニッ
SMIRK
UUH!

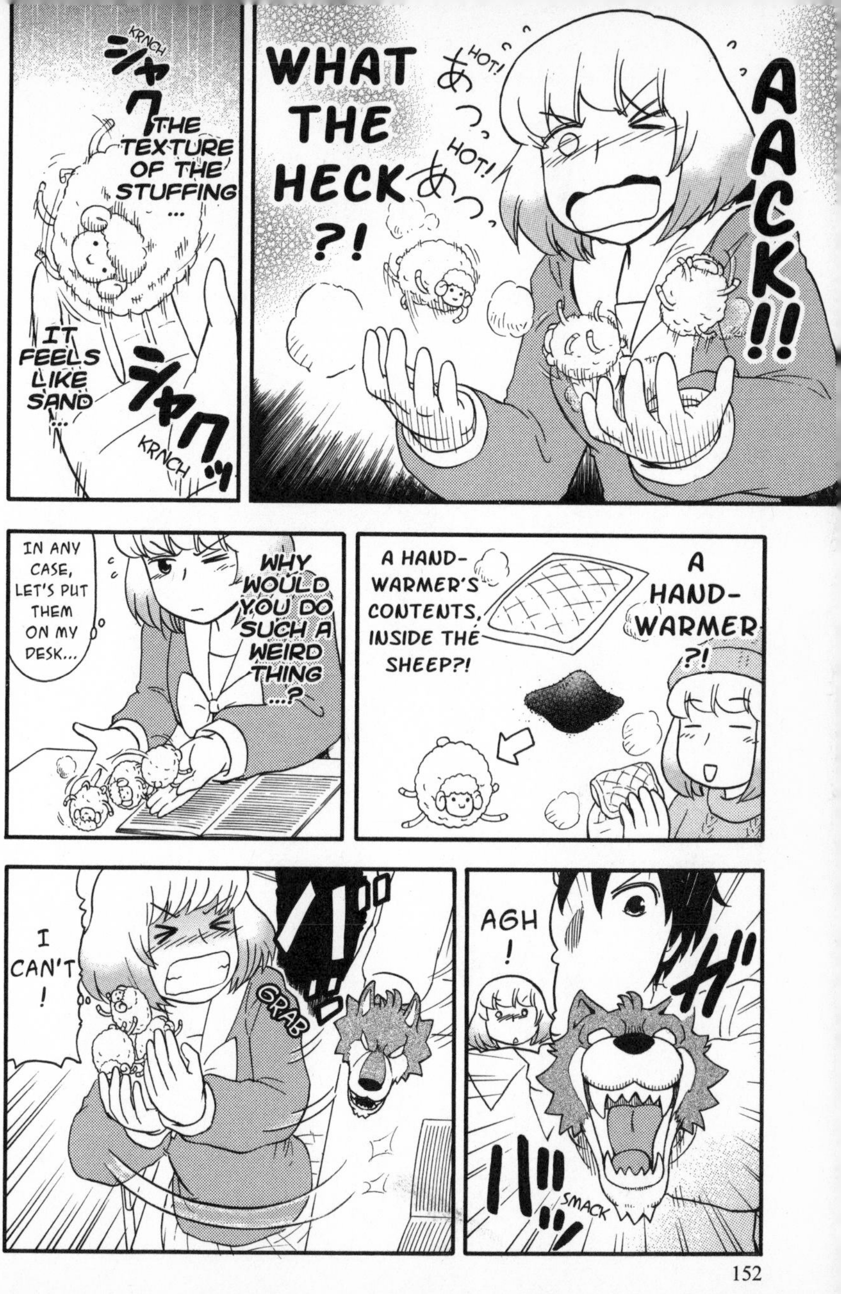
AACK!!
HOT! あっ
HOT! あっ
WHAT THE HECK ?!
KRNCH シャク
THE TEXTURE OF THE STUFFING ...
シャクッ KRNCH
IT FEELS LIKE SAND ...
A HAND-WARMER ?!
A HAND-WARMER'S CONTENTS, INSIDE THE SHEEP?!
WHY WOULD YOU DO SUCH A WEIRD THING ...?
IN ANY CASE, LET'S PUT THEM ON MY DESK...
AGH !
SMACK
GRAB
I CAN'T !

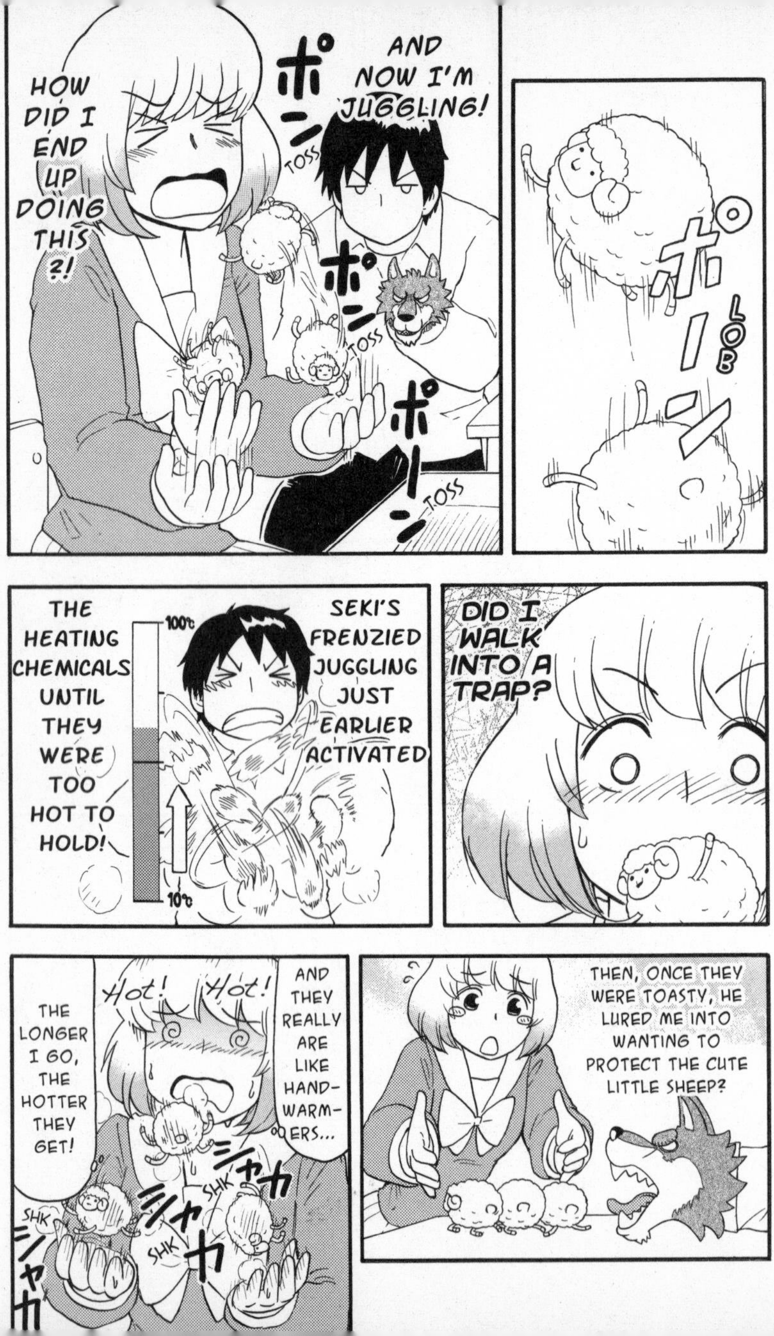
ポーン
LOB
AND NOW I'M JUGGLING!
ポン
TOSS
HOW DID I END UP DOING THIS ?!
ポン
TOSS
ポーン
TOSS
DID I WALK INTO A TRAP?
SEKI'S FRENZIED JUGGLING JUST EARLIER ACTIVATED
100°c
THE HEATING CHEMICALS UNTIL THEY WERE TOO HOT TO HOLD!
10°c
THEN, ONCE THEY WERE TOASTY, HE LURED ME INTO WANTING TO PROTECT THE CUTE LITTLE SHEEP?
AND THEY REALLY ARE LIKE HAND-WARMERS...
Hot! Hot!
THE LONGER I GO, THE HOTTER THEY GET!
シャカ
SHK
シャカ
SHK
シャカ
SHK

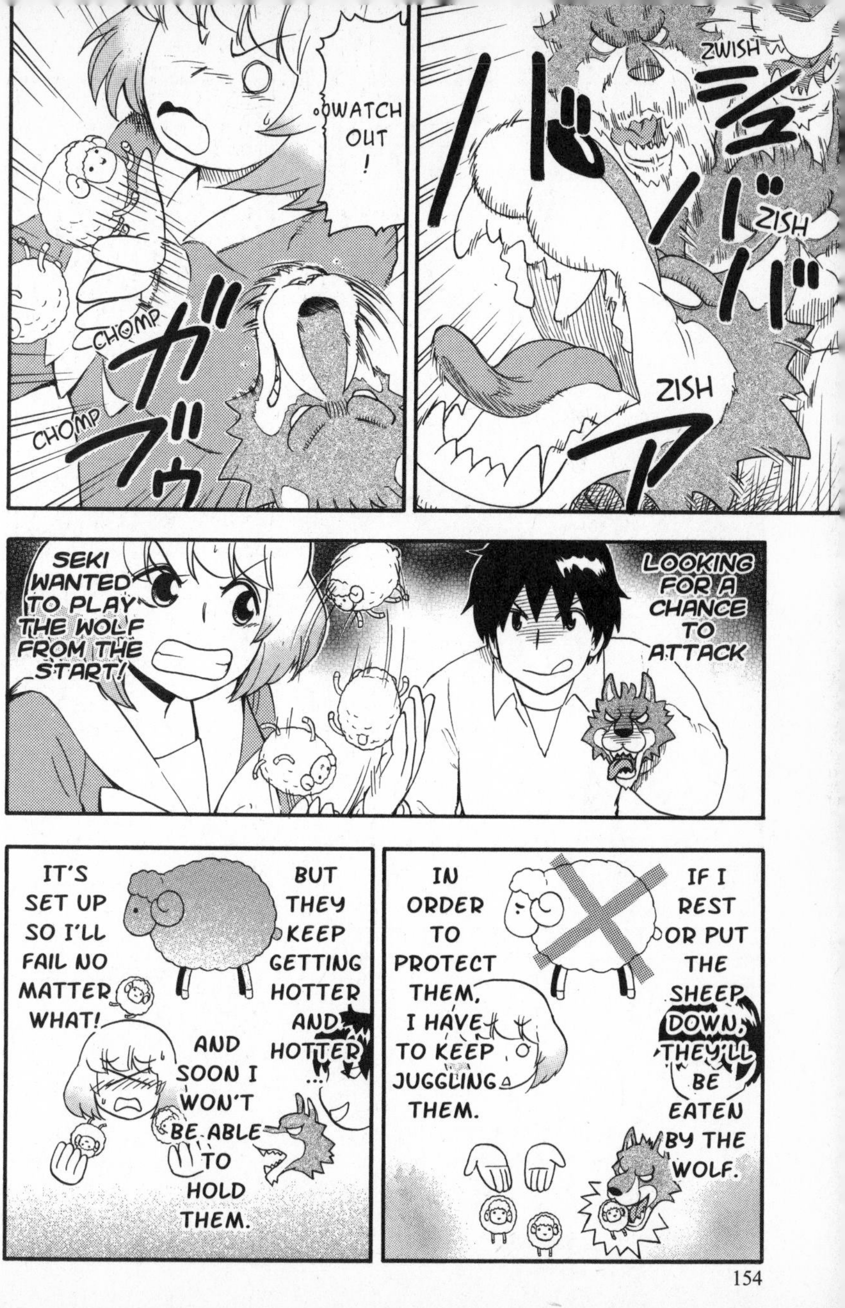
ZWISH
ZISH
ZISH
...WATCH OUT!
CHOMP
CHOMP
LOOKING FOR A CHANCE TO ATTACK
SEKI WANTED TO PLAY THE WOLF FROM THE START!
IF I REST OR PUT THE SHEEP DOWN, THEY'LL BE EATEN BY THE WOLF.
IN ORDER TO PROTECT THEM, I HAVE TO KEEP JUGGLING THEM.
BUT THEY KEEP GETTING HOTTER AND HOTTER...
IT'S SET UP SO I'LL FAIL NO MATTER WHAT!
AND SOON I WON'T BE ABLE TO HOLD THEM.

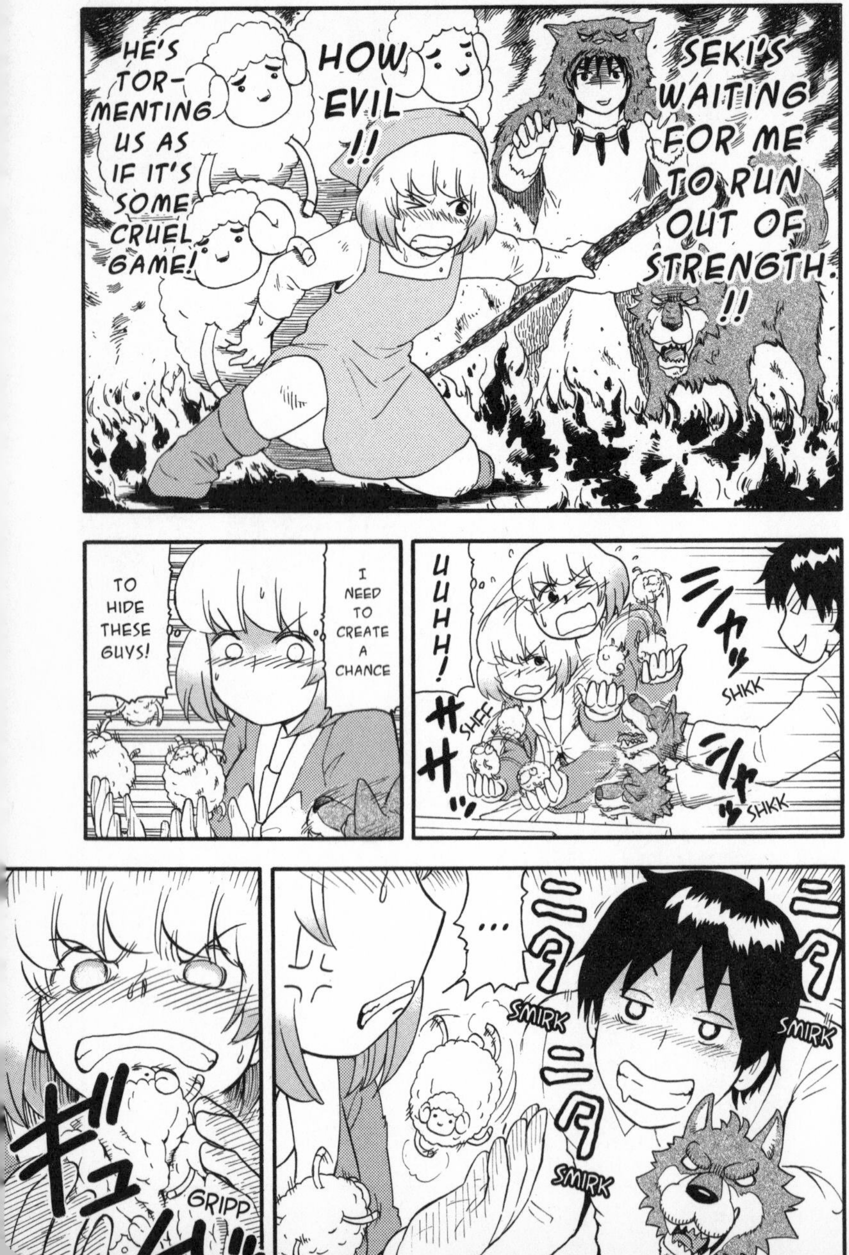
SEKI'S WAITING FOR ME TO RUN OUT OF STRENGTH.!!
HOW EVIL!!
HE'S TOR-MENTING US AS IF IT'S SOME CRUEL GAME!
SHKK
SHKK
UUHHH!
SHFF
I NEED TO CREATE A CHANCE
TO HIDE THESE GUYS!
SMIRK
SMIRK
...
SMIRK
GRIPP

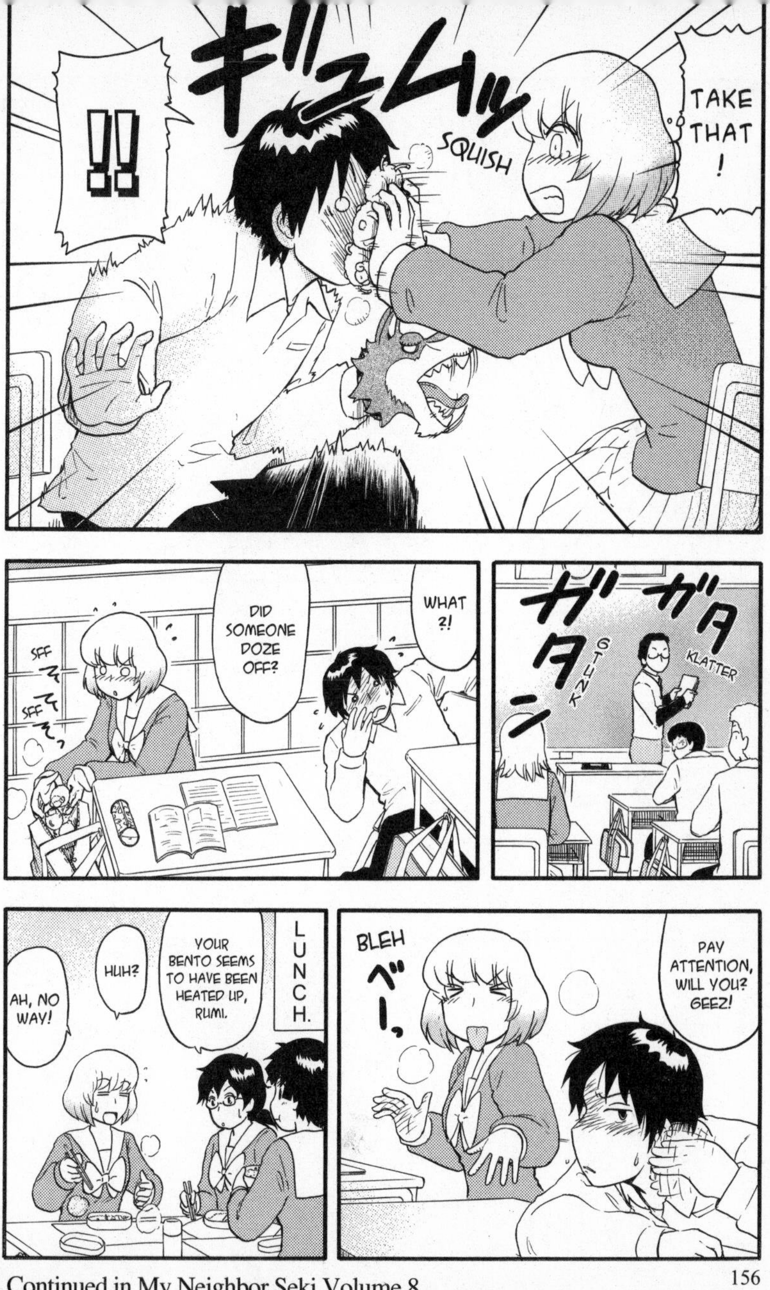
TAKE THAT!
ギュムッ
SQUISH
!!
ガタ
ガタン
KLATTER
GTUNK
WHAT?!
DID SOMEONE DOZE OFF?
SFF
SFF
PAY ATTENTION, WILL YOU? GEEZ!
べー
BLEH
LUNCH.
YOUR BENTO SEEMS TO HAVE BEEN HEATED UP, RUMI.
HUH?
AH, NO WAY!

Continued in My Neighbor Seki Volume 8

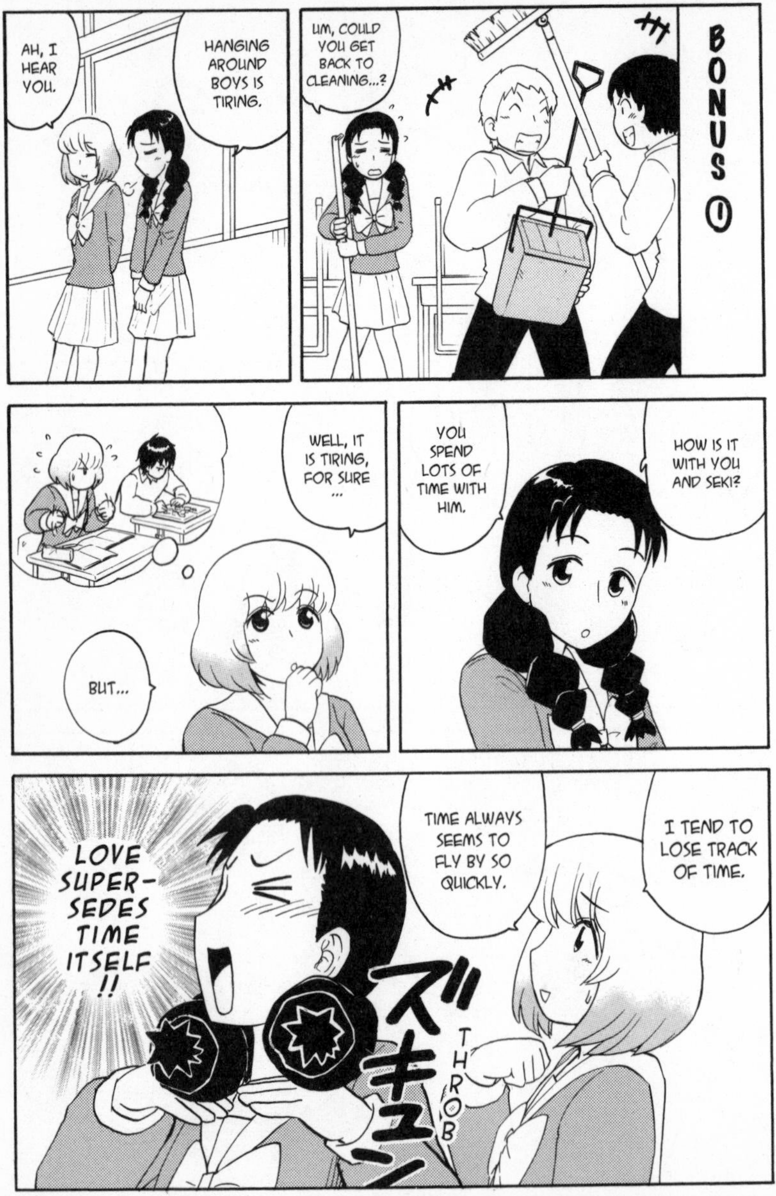
BONUS ①
UM, COULD YOU GET BACK TO CLEANING...?
HANGING AROUND BOYS IS TIRING.
AH, I HEAR YOU.
HOW IS IT WITH YOU AND SEKI?
YOU SPEND LOTS OF TIME WITH HIM.
WELL, IT IS TIRING, FOR SURE ...
BUT...
I TEND TO LOSE TRACK OF TIME.
TIME ALWAYS SEEMS TO FLY BY SO QUICKLY.
LOVE SUPER-SEDES TIME ITSELF !!
ズキューン
THROB

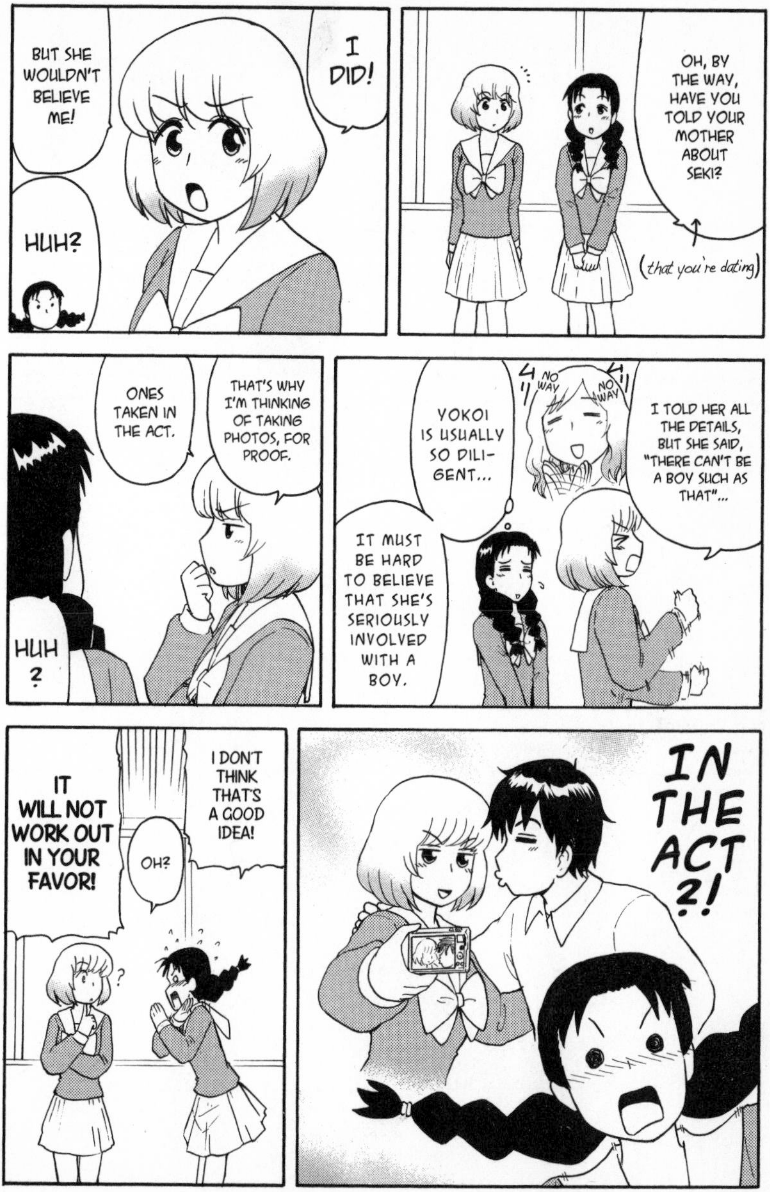
OH, BY THE WAY, HAVE YOU TOLD YOUR MOTHER ABOUT SEKI?
(that you're dating)
I DID!
BUT SHE WOULDN'T BELIEVE ME!
HUH?
I TOLD HER ALL THE DETAILS, BUT SHE SAID, "THERE CAN'T BE A BOY SUCH AS THAT"...
NO WAY
NO WAY
YOKOI IS USUALLY SO DILI-GENT...
IT MUST BE HARD TO BELIEVE THAT SHE'S SERIOUSLY INVOLVED WITH A BOY.
THAT'S WHY I'M THINKING OF TAKING PHOTOS, FOR PROOF.
ONES TAKEN IN THE ACT.
HUH?
IN THE ACT?!
I DON'T THINK THAT'S A GOOD IDEA!
OH?
IT WILL NOT WORK OUT IN YOUR FAVOR!

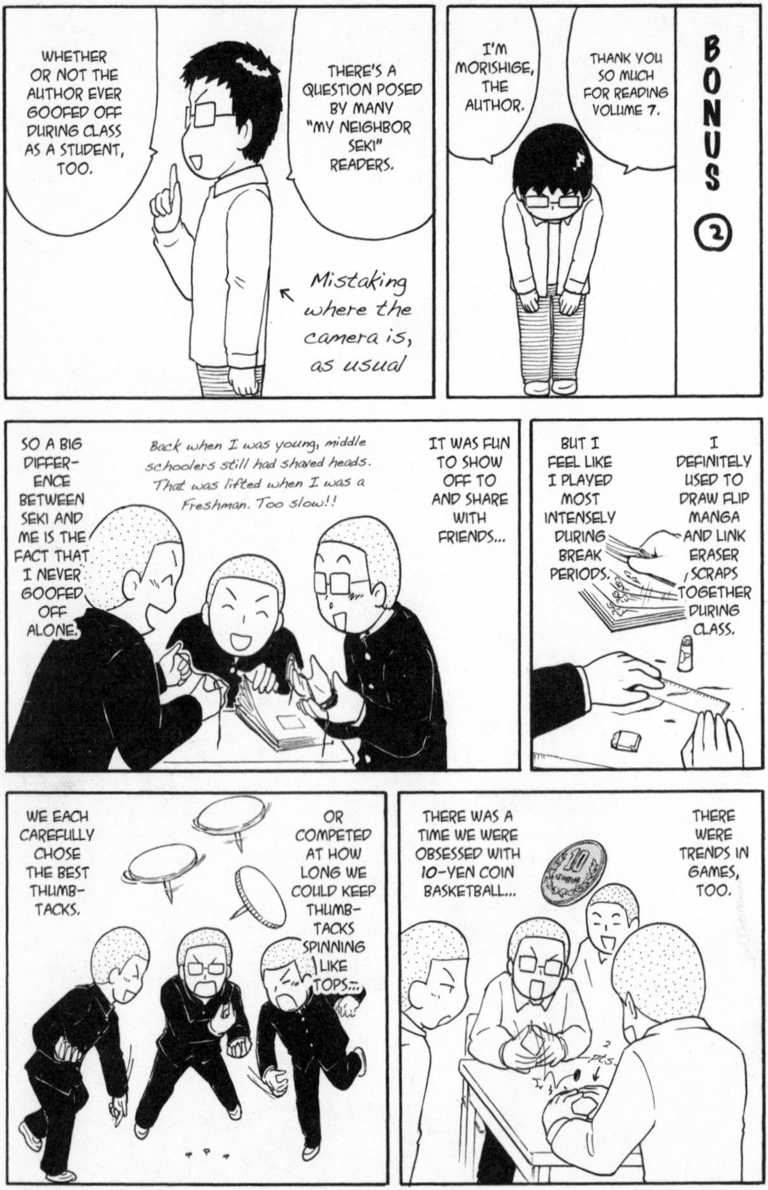
BONUS ②
THANK YOU SO MUCH FOR READING VOLUME 7.
I'M MORISHIGE, THE AUTHOR.
THERE'S A QUESTION POSED BY MANY "MY NEIGHBOR SEKI" READERS.
WHETHER OR NOT THE AUTHOR EVER GOOFED OFF DURING CLASS AS A STUDENT, TOO.
Mistaking where the camera is, as usual
I DEFINITELY USED TO DRAW FLIP MANGA AND LINK ERASER SCRAPS TOGETHER DURING CLASS.
BUT I FEEL LIKE I PLAYED MOST INTENSELY DURING BREAK PERIODS.
IT WAS FUN TO SHOW OFF TO AND SHARE WITH FRIENDS...
Back when I was young, middle schoolers still had shaved heads. That was lifted when I was a Freshman. Too slow!!
SO A BIG DIFFERENCE BETWEEN SEKI AND ME IS THE FACT THAT I NEVER GOOFED OFF ALONE.
THERE WERE TRENDS IN GAMES, TOO.
THERE WAS A TIME WE WERE OBSESSED WITH 10-YEN COIN BASKETBALL...
2 PTS.
OR COMPETED AT HOW LONG WE COULD KEEP THUMBTACKS SPINNING LIKE TOPS...
WE EACH CAREFULLY CHOSE THE BEST THUMBTACKS.

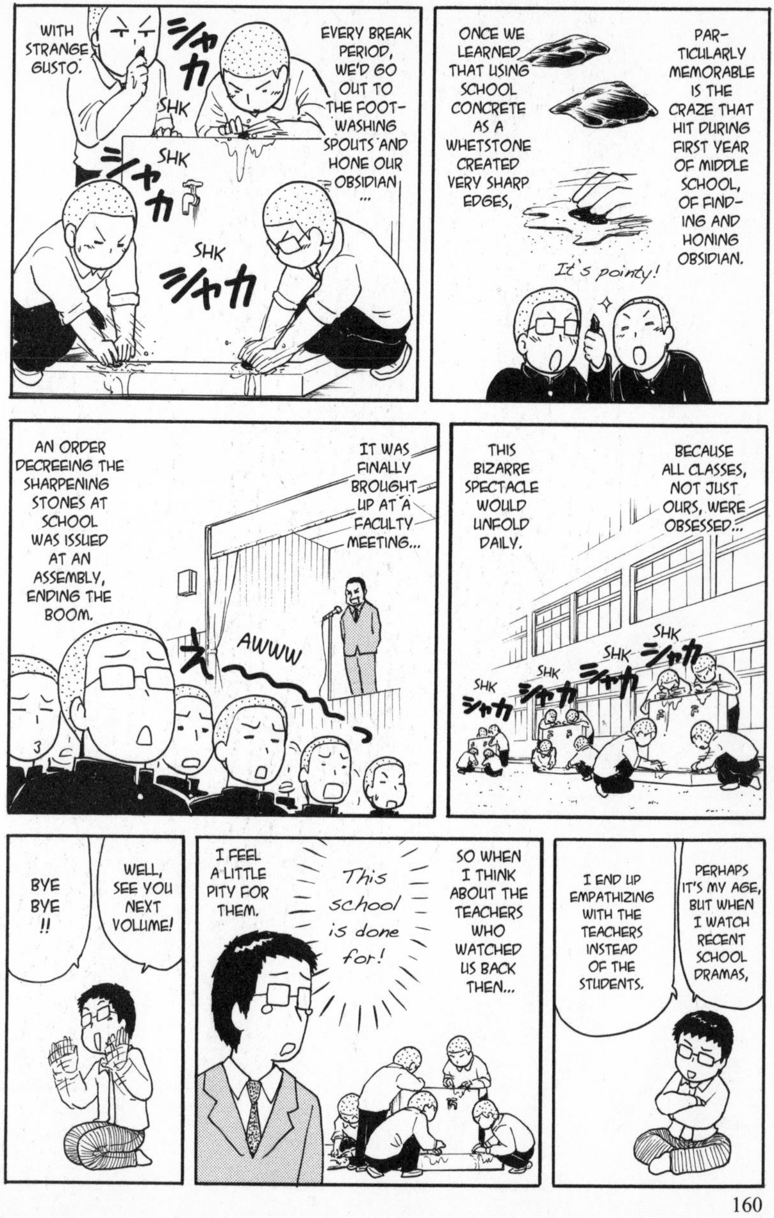

PAR-
TICULARLY
MEMORABLE
IS THE
CRAZE THAT
HIT DURING
FIRST YEAR
OF MIDDLE
SCHOOL,
OF FIND-
ING AND
HONING
OBSIDIAN.
ONCE WE LEARNED THAT USING SCHOOL CONCRETE AS A WHETSTONE CREATED VERY SHARP EDGES,
It's pointy!
EVERY BREAK PERIOD, WE'D GO OUT TO THE FOOT-WASHING SPOUTS AND HONE OUR OBSIDIAN ...
WITH STRANGE GUSTO.
シャカ
SHK
SHK
シャカ
SHK
シャカ
BECAUSE ALL CLASSES, NOT JUST OURS, WERE OBSESSED...
THIS BIZARRE SPECTACLE WOULD UNFOLD DAILY.
SHK シャカ
SHK シャカ
SHK シャカ
SHK シャカ
IT WAS FINALLY BROUGHT UP AT A FACULTY MEETING...
AN ORDER DECREEING THE SHARPENING STONES AT SCHOOL WAS ISSUED AT AN ASSEMBLY, ENDING THE BOOM.
え〜
AWWW
PERHAPS IT'S MY AGE, BUT WHEN I WATCH RECENT SCHOOL DRAMAS,
I END UP EMPATHIZING WITH THE TEACHERS INSTEAD OF THE STUDENTS.
SO WHEN I THINK ABOUT THE TEACHERS WHO WATCHED US BACK THEN...
This school is done for!
I FEEL A LITTLE PITY FOR THEM.
WELL, SEE YOU NEXT VOLUME!
BYE BYE !!

My Neighbor Seki

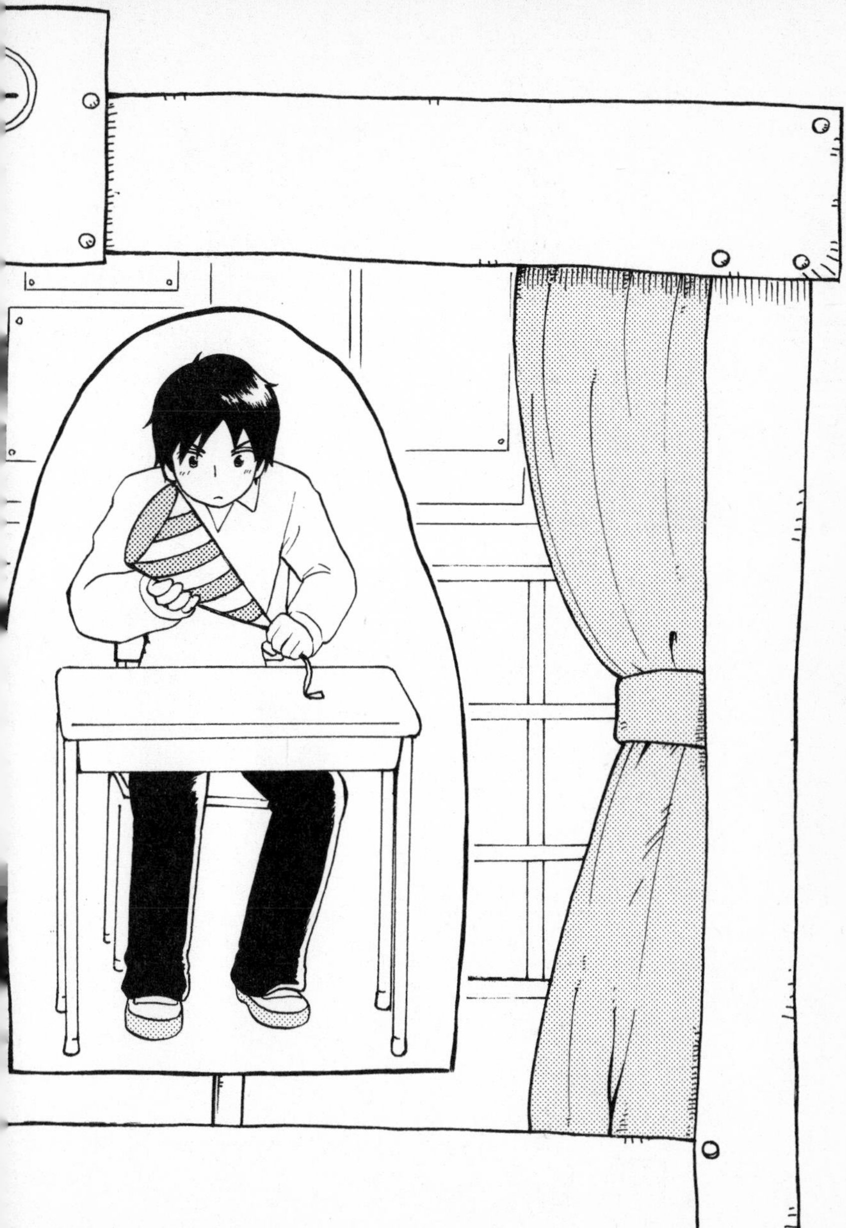

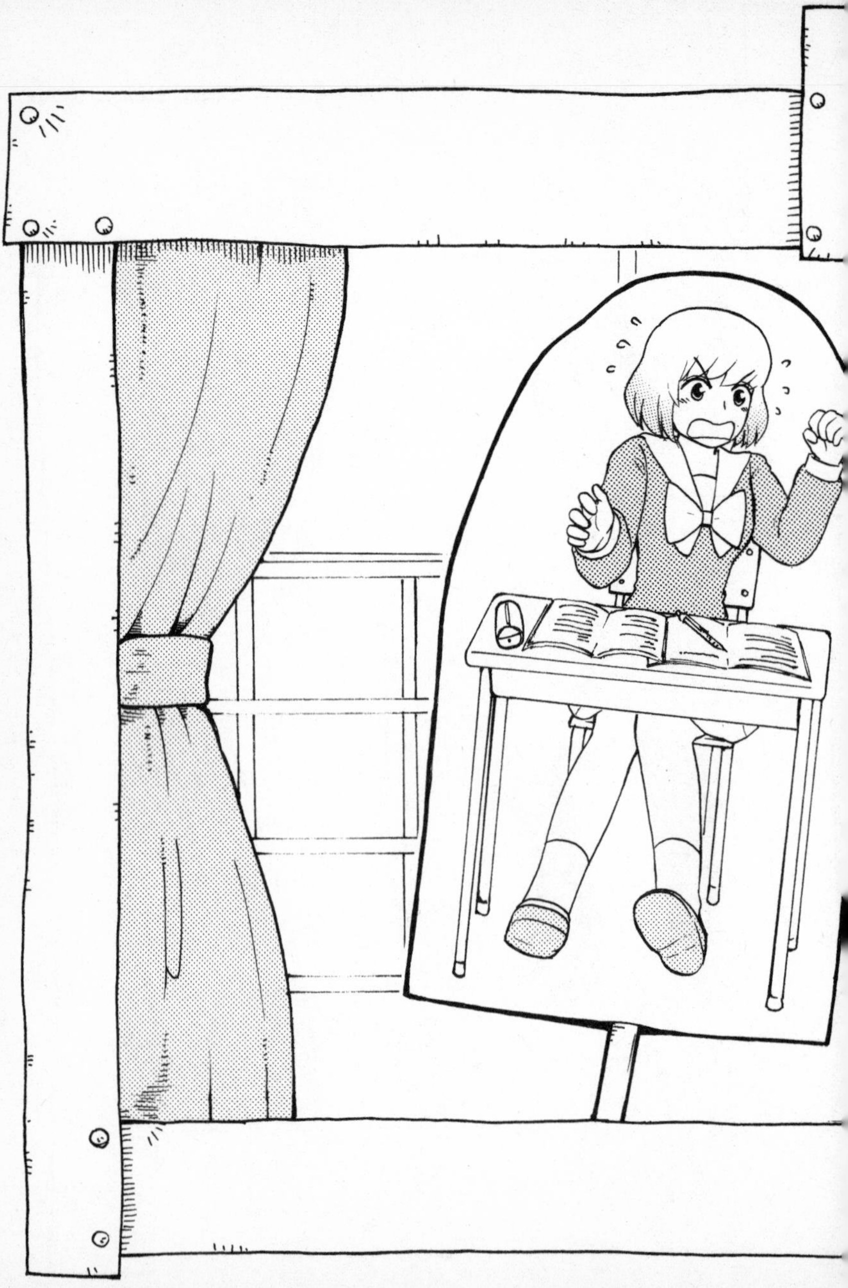

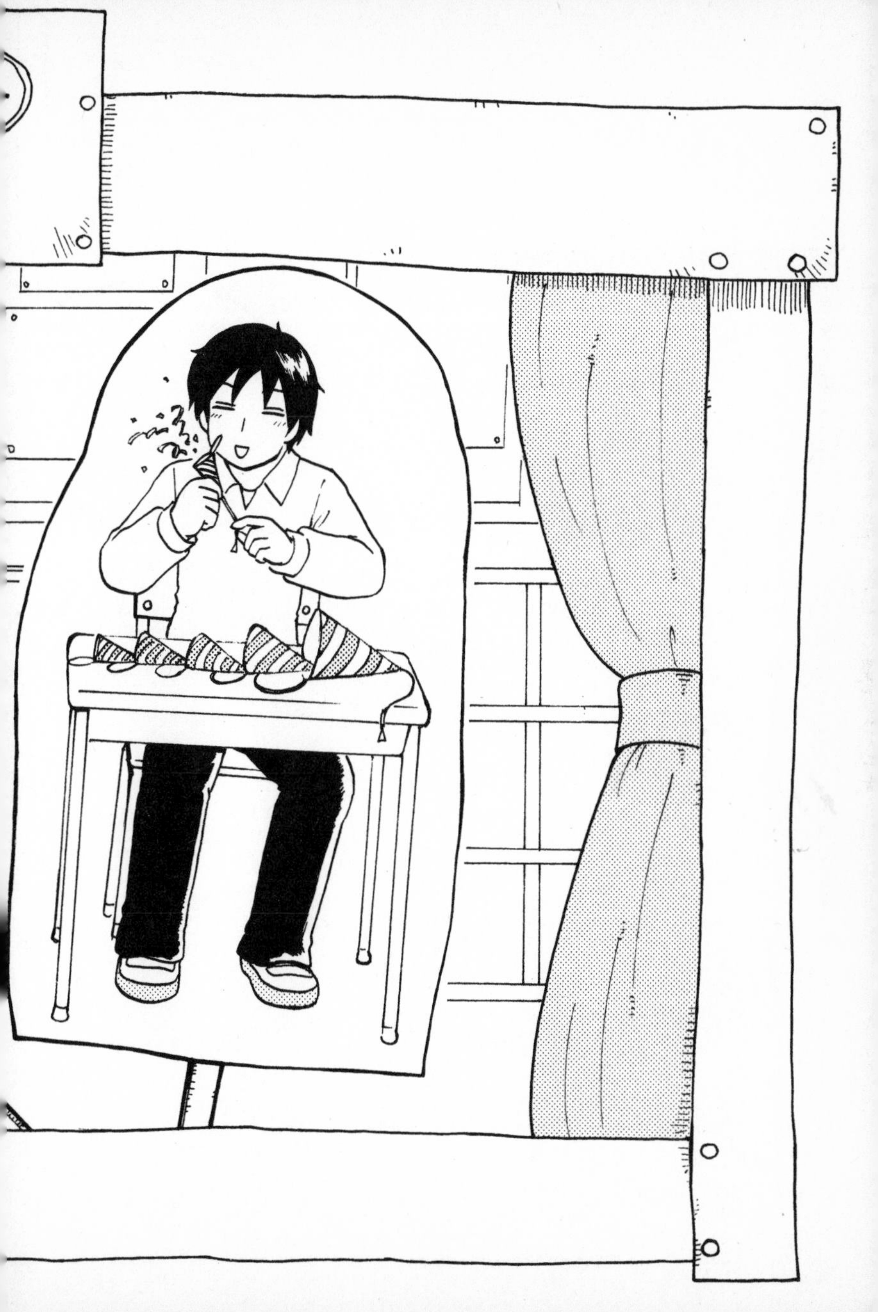

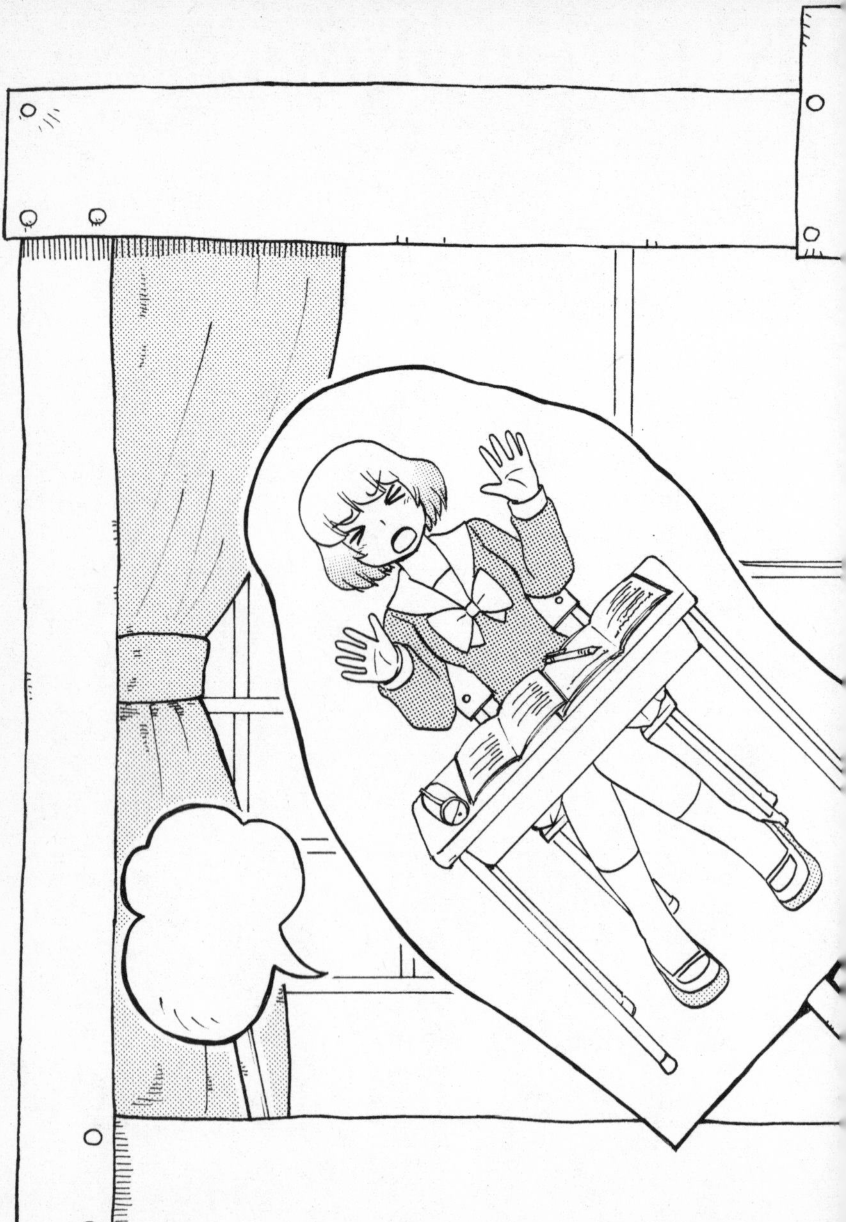

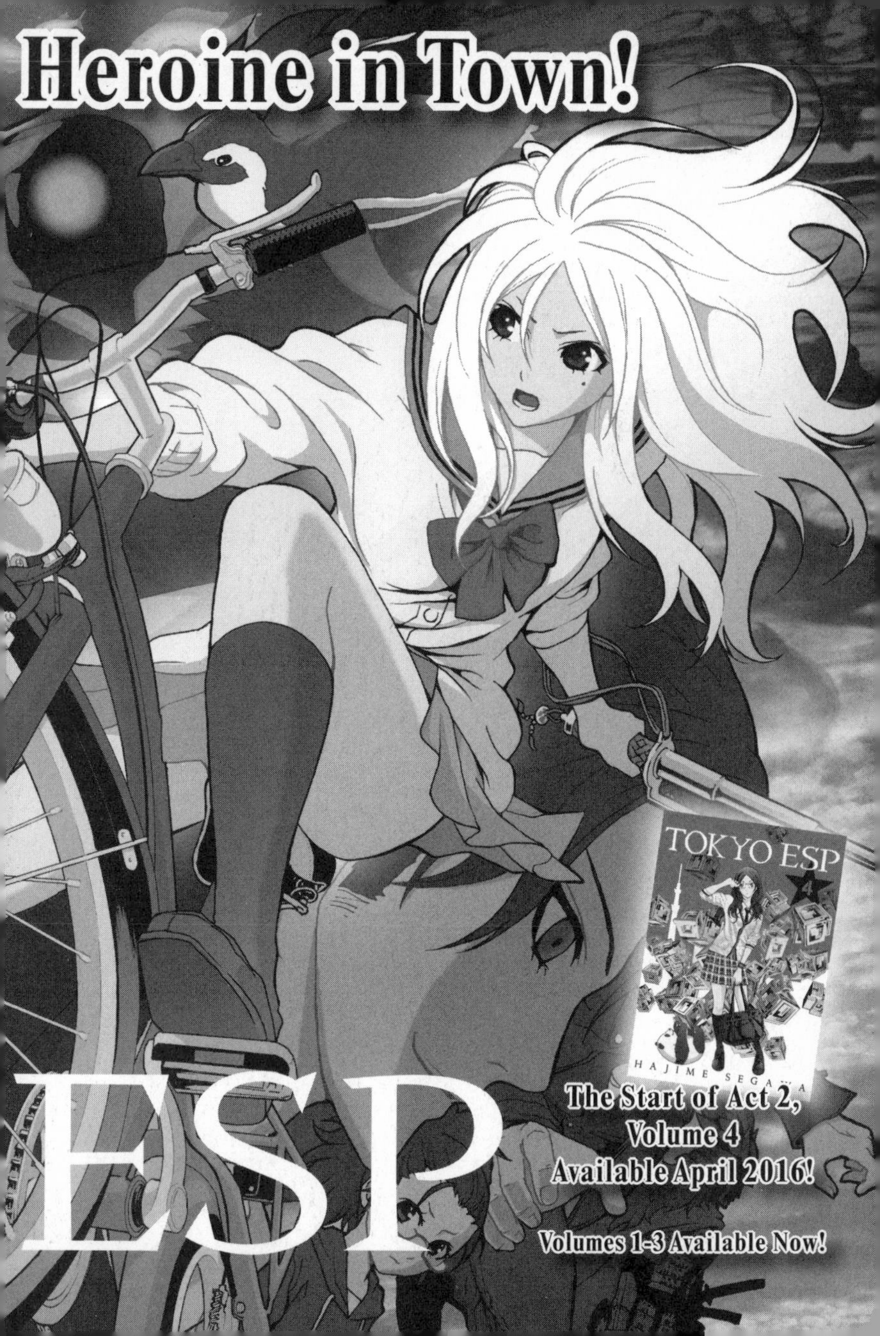
Heroine in Town!
TOKYO ESP
4
HAJIME SEGAWA
ESP
The Start of Act 2,
Volume 4
Available April 2016!
Volumes 1-3 Available Now!

There's a New

Rinka Urushiba's world is turned
upside down when she wakes up
one day–after falling right through
the floor.

Encouraged by another ESPer who
believes that Rinka's destiny is to
become a hero of justice, she soon
learns to use her powers for good.
And not a moment too soon, as those with less-than-
admirable ambitions descend on Tokyo with their
own sets of superpowers. As the mysterious glowing
fish flitting through the city skies gift powers seem-
ingly at random, foes become friends and alliances
are made and broken.

And what about that flying penguin?

HAJIME SEGAWA

TOKYO

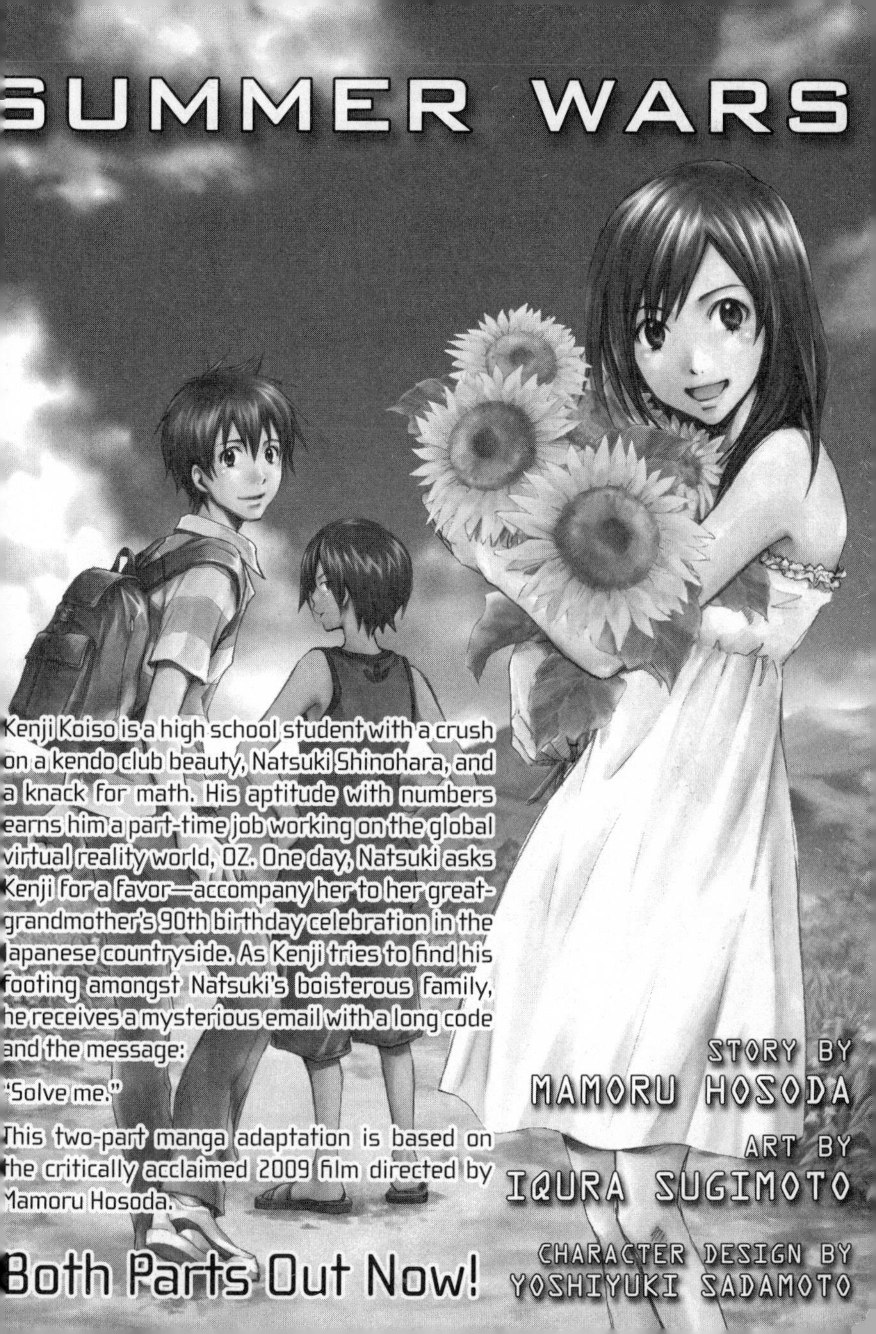

SUMMER WARS

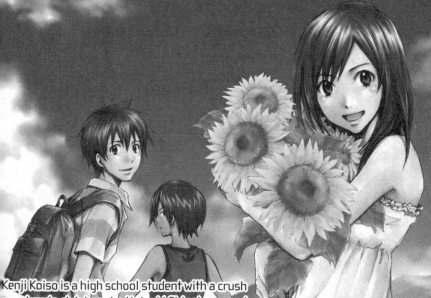

Kenji Koiso is a high school student with a crush on a kendo club beauty, Natsuki Shinohara, and a knack for math. His aptitude with numbers earns him a part-time job working on the global virtual reality world, OZ. One day, Natsuki asks Kenji for a favor—accompany her to her great-grandmother's 90th birthday celebration in the Japanese countryside. As Kenji tries to find his footing amongst Natsuki's boisterous family, he receives a mysterious email with a long code and the message:

"Solve me."

This two-part manga adaptation is based on the critically acclaimed 2009 film directed by Mamoru Hosoda.

Both Parts Out Now!

STORY BY
MAMORU HOSODA

ART BY
IQURA SUGIMOTO

CHARACTER DESIGN BY
YOSHIYUKI SADAMOTO

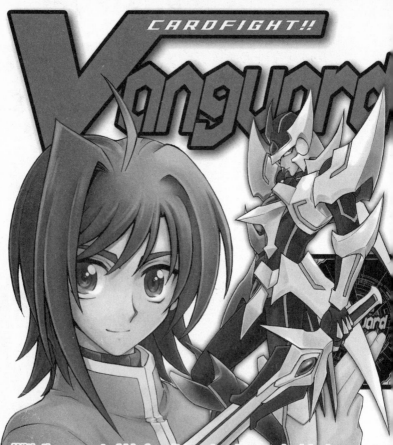

CARDFIGHT!!

Vanguard

With the support of his favorite card and some cherished memories, an unlikely young warrior is ready to stand up for himself and to change his life for the better. Inspired by the hit trading card game and the basis for the beloved anime!

Ready to become a Cardfighter yourself?
First printings include a limited edition PR Card!

VOLUMES 1-6 AVAILABLE NOW!

U.S. $10.95 / CND $11.95 each

My Neighbor Seki, volume 7
Tonari no Seki-kun

A Vertical Comics Edition

Translation: Mari Morimoto
Production: Risa Cho
          Anthony Quintessenza

© Takuma Morishige 2015
Edited by MEDIA FACTORY
First published in Japan in 2015 by KADOKAWA CORPORATION, Tokyo.
English translation rights reserved by Vertical, Inc.
Under the license from KADOKAWA CORPORATION, Tokyo.

Translation provided by Vertical Comics, 2016
Published by Vertical Comics, an imprint of Vertical, Inc., New York

Originally published in Japanese as *Tonari no Seki-kun 7* by MEDIA FACTORY.
Tonari no Seki-kun first serialized in *Gekkan Comic Flapper*, MEDIA FACTORY, 2010-

This is a work of fiction.

ISBN: 978-1-942993-10-0

Manufactured in the United States of America

First Edition

Vertical, Inc.
451 Park Avenue South
7th Floor
New York, NY 10016
www.vertical-comics.com

Vertical books are distributed through Penguin-Random House Publisher Services.